Fitness Facility Management

STEVEN A. TROTTER, MS

Globetrotter Wellness Solutions, LLC

CHRIS STEVENSON, BA, CSCS

The Empower Group

HUMAN KINETICS

Library of Congress Cataloging-in-Publication Data

Names: Trotter, Steven A., 1985- author. | Stevenson, Chris, 1974- author.
Title: Fitness facility management / Steven Trotter, Chris Stevenson.
Description: Champaign, IL : Human Kinetics, 2025. | Includes
  bibliographical references and index.
Identifiers: LCCN 2024019695 (print) | LCCN 2024019696 (ebook) | ISBN
  9781718221253 (paperback) | ISBN 9781718221277 (epub) | ISBN
  9781718221284 (pdf)
Subjects: LCSH: Physical fitness centers--Management. | BISAC: BUSINESS &
  ECONOMICS / Facility Management | SPORTS & RECREATION / Business Aspects
Classification: LCC GV428.5 .T76 2025 (print) | LCC GV428.5 (ebook) | DDC
  796.06/9--dc23/eng/20240509
LC record available at https://lccn.loc.gov/2024019695
LC ebook record available at https://lccn.loc.gov/2024019696

ISBN: 978-1-7182-2125-3 (print)

Senior Acquisitions Editor: Michelle Earle; **Senior Developmental Editor:** Cynthia McEntire; **Managing Editor:** Hannah Werner; **Copyeditor:** E before I Editing; **Proofreader:** Lyric Dodson; **Indexer:** Rebecca L. McCorkle; **Permissions Manager:** Laurel Mitchell; **Senior Graphic Designers:** Joe Buck and Julie L. Denzer; **Layout:** MPS Limited; **Cover Designer:** Keri Evans; **Cover Design Specialist:** Susan Rothermel Allen; **Photograph (cover):** Courtesy of Wade Griffith Photography; **Photographs (interior):** © Human Kinetics, unless otherwise noted; **Photo Asset Manager:** Laura Fitch; **Photo Production Manager:** Jason Allen; **Senior Art Manager:** Kelly Hendren; **Illustrations:** © Human Kinetics; **Printer:** Sheridan Books

Printed in the United States of America   10 9 8 7 6 5 4 3 2 1

The paper in this book is certified under a sustainable forestry program.

Human Kinetics
1607 N. Market Street
Champaign, IL 61820
USA

United States and International
Website: **US.HumanKinetics.com**
Email: info@hkusa.com
Phone: 1-800-747-4457

Canada
Website: **Canada.HumanKinetics.com**
Email: info@hkcanada.com

E9094

Fitness Facility Management

Contents

Preface

If you have opened this book, chances are your goal is to help others reach their own personal fitness and performance goals. Perhaps your mission is to help people achieve athletic milestones that they can't reach on their own. Whether you are a college student taking a health, recreation, or fitness facility management course or a current or aspiring manager, think of this book as your comprehensive guide to managing a world-class fitness facility that can significantly improve the health and well-being of your community or organization.

One of the most critical roles in managing a fitness facility is understanding your fundamental role as a manager. Management and leadership are two very different things; both are important and are needed at different times. Great *managers* have a solid understanding of the individuals who make up their team or organization—what motivates each team member, what they are naturally good at, and what they enjoy. Great managers can then align those individuals, based on their strengths, to achieve team victories and ultimately meet the organization's internal objectives. Great *leaders* have an outward focus as they drive their organization or team forward; it's as if they have an internal compass that can anticipate industry trends and changes and map out a strategic path to success. Great leaders can chart the course for the team. Talented managers and leaders are both needed for a fitness facility or any organization to thrive. Sometimes, it can be the same person. This text will help you hone your managerial skills as you learn or grow in your position.

You may initially think that managing a fitness facility is pretty straightforward. You find a space, buy some equipment, and sell some memberships; how hard could it be? However, as you read this book, you will see that managing a fitness facility goes way beyond that. There are so many different areas of knowledge that a great manager should understand and learn to master. To convey this massive amount of information in a format that you can use in your daily work, we started with a comprehensive outline, in chronological order, of the things you need to know about the business, staff, and facility. We then solicited feedback from industry managers, university instructors, and college students about everything from the first steps in designing an organization through the business strategy of running an operation. This text is written for the post-COVID-19 era and includes more resources and guides than you'll find in any other text on this topic. We called on the expertise of colleagues throughout the fitness industry to contribute to this book with case studies, charts, and checklists. Given the amount and depth of information, specific topics in this book are deeply explored, while others are a high-level view; some subjects could be an entire book on their own! Our 50-plus years of combined hands-on experience in owning, operating, and consulting for fitness facilities, along with diligent and comprehensive research, arms us with the knowledge to create an immersive educational experience for you to learn, retain, and apply knowledge and skills.

This book is divided into four sections. After the introduction briefs you on the history of the fitness industry from its early beginnings to the 2020s, part I covers the organizational profile. Whether you work in a for-profit commercial club or a nonprofit facility such as a university, community center, or military installation, you need to have a solid understanding of business operations. Starting with chapter 1, you will learn about the impacts of the COVID-19 pandemic on fitness facilities and consumer behavior and their short- and long-term effects on physical activity habits. Part I also addresses understanding and creating an organizational mission, vision, and values and helps you understand the importance of identifying your target market. Finally, part I closes by covering the basics of business plans, funding sources, and revenue and expenditures.

Part II covers an essential part of fitness facility management: the team members who make up your organization. A common saying is "If you take care of your people, they will take care of your products." Building a rock star team starts before someone even applies to work for your organization; the recruitment process begins with the brand recognition you have developed. This section covers the entire employee journey, from recruitment to offboarding. Not only will you discover examples of the industry's best hiring and onboarding practices, but you will also understand how to create a robust talent development plan and be well on your way to becoming a strengths-based organization. This book even has an entire chapter dedicated to offboarding, perhaps one of the most neglected steps in the employee journey.

Part III is large, detailing the operational procedures for delivering world-class facilities, programs, and services both in person and virtually. You will learn the basics of facility standards and guidelines, followed by a dive into fitness equipment selection, layout, preventative maintenance, and replacement plans. This section includes a chapter dedicated to a comprehensive program implementation and planning guide for group fitness, small group and large team training, personal training, health coaching, and spa services.

Part IV closes out the text and is dedicated to creating systems for success. You will learn how to attract and engage members throughout the entire member journey, from prospect to offboarding. This section will also cover emergency preparedness and teach you how to apply risk management strategies. The last chapter will cover business strategies and marketing; you will have the opportunity to use the knowledge to formulate goals and objectives.

College instructors using this textbook for a course have access to a comprehensive curriculum and ancillary materials, including an instructor guide and assessment materials. The instructor guide includes a sample course syllabus and course outline as well as suggested in-class activities and paper topics. The assessment materials include chapter quizzes and a test package for quarterly and final exams. For a comprehensive teaching approach, use these materials as reliable teaching aids in conjunction with the accompanying presentation package and image bank.

The fitness industry is one of the most vibrant industries in the world. You rarely find a career where you can have a lot of fun, make a good living, and dramatically and positively affect peoples' lives daily. Too often, well-intended people fail at managing fitness facilities because they don't have the education and tools necessary to succeed. Although we, the authors, have achieved much success in our chosen professions thus far, it would have been a much more effective and less painful experience if we had had a book like this early in our careers! Don't think of this book as the end, but rather the beginning of your journey. By the time you finish this book, you will be armed with the knowledge and confidence to master a fitness facility management role and be ready to take on the world.

Introduction: History of the Fitness Industry

Exercise dates back to well before 500 BCE. Hippocrates, one of the most well-known physicians, is credited with stating that "eating alone will not keep a man well; he must also take exercise. For food and exercise, while possessing opposite qualities, yet work together to produce health."

Birth of the Fitness Club

Throughout history, exercise has been an integral part of daily life. In 1811, German gymnast Friederich Ludwig Jahn opened the first documented fitness club, known as a public Turnplatz, or *turnverein*. Many of these turnvereins began spreading around the globe, including the first American location opening in 1848 in Cincinnati, Ohio. Several milestones and notable events in the fitness industry occurred throughout the 1800s.

- *1847 (Paris, France).* Hippolyte Triat, a famous strongman, opens Gymnase Triat. This was the first club to offer group classes with live music and an observation deck.
- *1850 (Boston, Massachusetts).* First YMCA opens.
- *1860 (San Francisco, California).* The first private athletic club, Olympic Club, opens.
- *1868 (New York, New York).* The New York Athletic Club opens.
- *1894 (New York, New York).* Louis Durlacher, also known as Professor Attila, opens another of the first commercial clubs in New York City. The club stays open until the mid-1970s.

In addition to brick and mortar facilities, the 1800s also had notable achievements in fitness equipment. Dr. Gustav Zander created the first therapeutic exercise machines in the 1850s, and Dudley Allen Sargent developed the first pulley-driven variable resistance machines in the 1880s (Tharrett 2017).

20th-Century Fitness Centers

The 20th century saw notable growth and change in the fitness industry. In 1902, the Milo Barbell Company, founded by Alan Calvert, played a significant role in shaping fitness equipment (Tharrett 2017). The 1940s saw the advent of bodybuilding-style gyms, which helped to make fitness easier to access, offering an annual membership fee of around $60. Vic Tanny's clubs, which were slightly higher end, grew to become the largest chain of their kind in the world, generating an impressive $24 million in collected annual revenue by 1949 (Tharrett 2017).

1950s to 1970s

The midcentury era ushered in a significant evolution in the fitness industry. American Health Studios, founded by Ray Wilson in the 1950s, brought about a new generation of fitness facilities. Game-changing fitness equipment such as the universal gym and Quinton treadmill revolutionized how people worked out. Arthur Jones' Nautilus machines in the early 1970s transformed resistance and strength training. Dr. Keene Dimmick's LifeCycle introduced the first effective stationary cardiorespiratory workout in 1968. Dr. Kenneth Cooper pioneered the benefits of aerobic exercise for maintaining and improving health, reshaping fitness approaches. The American College of Sports Medicine (ACSM) developed and released the first guidelines for exercise testing and prescription in 1975 (Tharrett 2017).

1980s

The 1980s were a transformative period for the fitness industry. The establishment of IHRSA (now called the Health & Fitness Association) in 1981 highlighted the growing interest in the racket sports industry. The number of fitness clubs in the United States skyrocketed to 6,200 by 1982, followed by a second surge to 12,854 clubs serving 21 million Americans by 1990. Smaller "mom-and-pop" fitness clubs became more common. Bally's emerged as an industry icon, while corporate and medical fitness programs gained traction. Personal training and group exercise exploded. Major organizations such as ACE, AFAA, IDEA, and NSCA brought standardization to the field. Equipment offerings diversified when critical players like Eagle Fitness, Body Masters, Paramount, and Universal Gym Equipment entered the market (Tharrett 2017).

1990s

The 1990s saw growth and diversification in the fitness industry. Clubs in the United States grew to 16,000 in number, serving 33 million members (13 percent of the population). Spending on fitness climbed from $6.5 billion to $11.6 billion. The investment world now saw the immense potential of the fitness industry. Larger multiclub operators emerged, and fitness-only clubs gained notoriety. Suburban multipurpose clubs and multimodality studios started to offer diversified options. YMCA and JCC memberships flourished, and fitness centers in apartments and hotels became common. The 1990s brought a surge in creativity and innovation in aerobic dance, Jazzercize, and key organizations such as ACSM. Spinning, yoga, Pilates, weight training, and personal training also saw notable growth. Group fitness took center stage, led by the global brand Les Mills. Products such as Elliptical (EFX) by Precor and advancements in equipment, such as Spinning bikes and plate-loaded machines, transformed how people work out. The 1990s reshaped the fitness industry and set the stage for even more growth in the 21st century (Tharrett 2017).

Year 2000 and Beyond

At the turn of the century, the fitness industry accelerated. By 2019, IHRSA (now named the Health & Fitness Association) estimated the global health club industry to be valued at $96.7 billion, with approximately 20 percent of adults belonging to a health club. There was major market saturation, and many health clubs' member recruitment strategies focused on pulling members from other clubs rather than recruiting people who had never used a health club. Boutiques also began to take residence in shopping centers and live-work-play developments. SoulCycle opened in 2006, followed by Pure Barre in 2008 and Orangetheory in 2010, setting a precedent for a high-end exclusive fitness experience. These changes occurred while small group training was snowballing in the health club space. Fitness facilities attempted to replicate the boutique experience inside a larger box gym facility.

In the early 2000s, the fitness space evolved into a wrap-around industry beyond brick and mortar facilities. The online personal training platform Trainerize came out in 2008, providing clients access to personal training anytime and anywhere. The same year, author and personal trainer Jonathan Goodman created the Personal Training Development Center, an online learning center for personal trainers who train clients virtually. The 2000s changed how people exercise and how exercise professionals work. In 2016, Peloton went public and gained a spotlight that carried it through a pivotal time.

In March 2020, the COVID-19 pandemic spread worldwide and disrupted all parts of life. Federal and state governments in the United States of America began orders for all nonessential businesses and services to close temporarily. Fitness facilities were not considered essential and had to shut their doors, many for good because the economic impact did not allow them to reopen. Individuals found home exercise a way to cope and work on their health and fitness goals. Home fitness equipment prices skyrocketed, and the surge of Peloton had many people on the waiting list. As fitness facilities began to reopen, the changing landscape of the needs and wants of the consumer drove fitness facility owners and operators to reimagine their businesses.

In this book, you will gain the knowledge needed for managing a fitness facility in the post-COVID-19 era. Consumer behavior is rapidly evolving, and a key point to consider is a member's desire for around-the-clock access to a holistically well and physically active lifestyle. Gone are the days when a fitness facility was the only place someone chose to recreate. Individuals now seek the autonomy to decide when, where, and how they exercise. For a fitness facility to thrive, it must be able to anticipate and exceed member expectations. The best starting point is to take a deep dive into the mind of today's exercise consumer.

PART I

Profile: Designing an Organization

1

Current State of the Fitness Industry

Upon completion of this chapter, you will be able to do the following:

- Recognize short- and long-term effects of the COVID-19 pandemic on fitness facilities
- Describe the current physical activity habits of Americans
- Identify barriers to movement and exercise programs
- Analyze the current state of the fitness industry

To effectively manage a fitness facility, you must have a comprehensive understanding of the landscape of the fitness industry. This chapter is an essential starting point to help lay the foundation for that understanding. Understanding issues such as physical activity habits, changes in consumer expectations and behaviors, barriers to exercise, and the short- and long-term effects of the COVID-19 pandemic provides insight into plans such as practical facility layout, program design that meets the expectations of members, adaptations to changes in consumer behavior, and ways to deal with barriers that may keep people from exercising at your facility. Being aware of workforce issues, supply chain challenges, and impacts of the pandemic helps you make more informed and better overall decisions, evolve your business model, and achieve and sustain long-term success. Overall, the foundation this chapter lays allows you to remain relevant, competitive, and adaptable in the ever-changing fitness industry, especially in the face of the ongoing effects of the COVID-19 pandemic.

Effect of the COVID-19 Pandemic on the Fitness Industry

The COVID-19 pandemic changed the world. No one saw it coming and could have ever adequately prepared for its impact. COVID-19 is, hopefully, a once-in-a-lifetime experience that led to some drastic changes. People were in lockdown at home. Businesses were forced to close. The pandemic altered the traditional workplace. Many people started working remotely. Consumer behavior dramatically changed. Some changes were temporary, but others affected how people behave, work, socialize, and address their health and fitness needs.

While all industries were affected, the fitness industry took a massive hit. Facilities of all types had to shut their doors. The length of closure varied depending on location. In some regions, facilities were closed for just a few months, but in certain areas, mandates forced facilities to shut down for over a year. Regardless of how long a closure was, the effect was devastating. Facilities lost a lot of revenue. Organizations had to lay off or furlough staff. Applying for governmental aid was a complicated process. Fitness facilities struggled. The industry's immense frustration was that taking care of health and fitness, the same service that fitness facilities provide, was a key to diminishing the effects of the COVID-19 virus. That important service could not take place because they were closed. It was a real catch-22.

There were a few silver linings to the COVID-19 pandemic. The challenges presented brought our industry together. Competitors sat together to figure out the best practices to create clean and safe environments and worked together to increase advocacy efforts for the industry as a whole. Innovation skyrocketed. Closures forced facilities to provide more virtual and digital programming. While some facilities did this already, the pandemic amplified the practice tenfold. Exercising in the great outdoors also increased. Since facilities could not provide indoor services, many organizations created unique outdoor exercise areas and programming. The final item to note is that COVID-19 brought to the forefront the idea that taking care of health and fitness was essential. A Kaiser Permanente study of people with COVID-19 showed that regular physical activity provided protection from hospitalization, intensive care unit admission, and death. The study also noted that people who exercised consistently decreased their chances of severe outcomes from COVID-19 compared to inactive people (Sinclair and Kanakri 2021). Health, well-being, and fitness matter. Fitness facilities are essential!

As the world reopened, the fitness industry did not necessarily return to normal. The Health & Fitness Association (previously named IHRSA) is a trade association that assists the commercial fitness industry. Their research showed that as of January 1, 2022, 25 percent of all fitness facilities and 30 percent of studios had closed since the start of the COVID-19 pandemic (IHRSA 2022). Most experts agree that even as of this writing, we have not seen the end of COVID-19-related facility closures.

Community and collegiate recreation centers also had closures and setbacks from COVID-19. Many collegiate recreation centers had to furlough employees and were not allowed to refill positions as employees left for other opportunities. In one collegiate recreation center, 50 percent of the positions vacated during the pandemic were cut permanently. Funding for these nonprofit facilities also quickly became a problem. Collegiate recreation centers, which mostly operate as an auxiliary service on a college campus and are primarily funded by student fees, had to quickly decide what to do when college campuses shut down and sent students away. Solutions involved refunding student fees, furloughing employees, and additional drastic but necessary measures. According to a 2023 report on the state of managed recreation facilities, 83 percent of respondents are still taking action on reducing expenditures, such as increasing fees (51.5 percent), improving energy efficiency (35.5 percent),

putting construction projects on hold (34.4 percent), decreasing hours (31.1 percent), or reducing staff (30 percent). In fact, 63.3 percent of collegiate recreation facilities reported reducing operational hours, while 36.4 percent were forced to cut programs, and some (4.6 percent) had to permanently close facilities (Tipping 2023).

Changes in the Industry

Facilities that did survive the pandemic still face long-term challenges, many of which may be permanent. Staffing is one of those challenges. Due to lower membership numbers and decreased revenue, many organizations rely on smaller staff. Team members are wearing more hats and taking on more responsibilities. In many cases, it unfortunately became a do-more-with-less situation. That mindset, rather than a do-less-with-less situation, contributed to the "great resignation," which will be discussed in chapter 7. The other big issues regarding staffing are getting staff back and finding and retaining new team members. The pandemic created a massive change in this area. The great resignation, a shift in work priorities, career changes, remote working options, more employment choices, quiet quitting, and more all contribute to these challenges. Employee engagement and retention are other crucial topics to address. Dealing with rehiring, finding, and retaining talent are not the only issues concerning staffing. There is also a need for enhanced staff training.

As people returned to more activities following the acute phase of the pandemic, there was a need for more comprehensive staff training. This need stems from a few different issues, the first of which is that many organizations have smaller teams. As mentioned earlier, a smaller team means more responsibilities for each team member. This situation requires more training than in the past. More comprehensive training is essential so each team member can do their best work. Increased training takes time and effort. Consistent and enhanced training creates higher productivity, confidence, and morale levels, positively affecting employee engagement and retention. Finally, organizations have many more protocols and programs in the new normal. New requirements create a heavier lift on management and leadership to ensure that team members are trained to execute these changes effectively. These new protocols stem from a change in members' postpandemic needs.

There have been many long-term changes to members' needs and expectations that stemmed from COVID-19. The most obvious are enhanced cleaning protocols. Before the pandemic, it was not shocking to hear a member express delight when a facility was clean. A dirty facility was generally tolerated, and cleanliness was a perk. That is no longer the case. Members expect a facility to be immaculate. When government-regulated standards were required during the pandemic, members came to appreciate this level of cleanliness and now expect it. They want to see, smell, and feel clean when entering a facility.

Related to cleanliness are desired changes in facility design. During the pandemic, there were required changes to spacing. The 30-inch (76 cm) by 48-inch (122 cm) minimum clear space adjacent to fitness equipment required by the Americans with Disabilities Act was no longer sufficient for the new standards. Equipment was moved further apart or removed. Some facilities simply turned off every other piece of cardio so members could not use it. Others capitalized on the technology capability of networked cardio machines and implemented systems that would lock a machine after use until a staff member properly cleaned it, or they activated social distancing mode so the machine wouldn't turn on if someone were using the equipment beside it. Group exercise classes had designated spots and attendance limits to keep a safe social distance between members. Whether members will be comfortable in more crowded environments remains

A clean facility is required to keep members happy and healthy. The COVID-19 pandemic prompted fitness facilities to adopt stricter cleaning protocols, including cleaning equipment thoroughly after each use.

to be seen. There are signs that they enjoy having a little more personal space, which affects facility design moving forward. Changing programming demands, such as virtual and digital options, outdoor offerings, and well-being-related services, also affect facility design moving forward.

Another area where members' needs have changed is in programming expectations. The pandemic exposed the need for virtual and outdoor exercise options. Will members continue to want such programs moving forward? Early signs are that they will not replace the indoor and in-person gym experience, but they support it and probably will be expected by members, to some extent. A desire for this type of programming affects design elements as well. Facilities must consider creating spaces for personal movement experiences, such as filming or streaming virtual programs. They must think about equipping group exercise rooms with the technology needed to stream live classes in a hybrid environment. Considerations for outdoor programming need to be taken into account as well. Where will it take place? How can the outdoor area be designed to create a unique and desirable experience? Will the outdoor experience be an area for people to work out independently with equipment, or will it be guided programming from an instructor or trainer? The most important thing to understand with virtual and outdoor offerings is that they must be crafted as an intentional experience and done well. It is not enough to conduct a class on FaceTime or simply put equipment in a parking lot for people to use. If they

are going to be options for members, these offerings must be well-thought-out and properly executed.

One other area that we have seen an uptick in post-COVID is health and wellness coaching, according to the American College of Sports Medicine (ACSM) (Thompson 2023). This trend demonstrates that members now see value in a holistic approach to health and well-being that involves goal setting and behavioral change. In that regard, facilities are adding more mind–body classes (such as meditation), health-oriented workshops, and mental health resources. Options like this were few and far between before the pandemic. Only time will tell what member demands remain when it comes to programming, but it is safe to say that these new desires will remain a part of fitness facility programming in some way, shape, or form.

These changes have prompted many organizations to rethink and restructure their business models. While specific business models will be explored later in this book, it is worth noting the impact of the pandemic on current models. Before the pandemic, many models focused on maximizing the number of memberships to be successful. With organizations unsure if they will ever reach the same number of people as in the past, many have shifted the focus to maximizing revenue per member. If there are fewer members, they need to spend more to hit revenue targets. Many facilities in the prepandemic era focused heavily on new membership sales. While sales are always a focus, member retention has become more critical

---

ACSM Top Fitness Trends of 2024

1. Wearable technology
2. Worksite health promotion
3. Fitness programs for older adults
4. Exercise for weight loss
5. Reimbursement for qualified exercise professionals
6. Employing certified fitness professionals
7. Mobile exercise apps
8. Exercise for mental health
9. Youth athlete development
10. Personal training

Data from A.M. Newsome, R. Reed, J. Sansone, et al., "ACSM Worldwide Fitness Trends: Future Directions of the Health and Fitness Industry," *ACSM's Health & Fitness Journal* 28, no. 1 (2024): 14-26. https://doi.org/10.1249/FIT.0000000000000933.

than ever. With fewer people joining, keeping current members is now of utmost importance. New business models also include everything we have mentioned: Facilities must consider innovative programming, virtual components, new technology, and outdoor offerings, and they must determine what differentiates them in the marketplace. Size, location, and design will also be reevaluated based on what makes the most sense in this new normal.

The ongoing supply chain issues are one thing that all organizations need to keep in mind when deciding how they deliver their experience. Getting equipment and supplies has been very challenging. *Supply Chain Management Review* attributes this to global political unrest, lack of raw materials, rising fuel and energy costs, and inflation (Waters 2022). It is a time of great change in the fitness industry, and we must wait to learn which changes were temporary and which will last. Operators and managers must do their best to stay on top of economic shifts and industry trends to evolve effectively and remain relevant.

Given that the future is uncertain, operators and managers must attempt to future-proof their facilities. *Future-proofing* refers to creating a strategic plan that allows the organization to continue successfully executing its mission today and into the future. While many components go into future-proofing, it starts with members and employees. Do not guess what your clients and staff want; ask them. Survey members regularly to stay current with their constantly changing wants and needs. The same goes for employees. Employee wants and needs have changed drastically throughout the pandemic. Gathering feedback from key team members creates a superior workplace experience, leading to productive, engaged, and retained employees. Keeping a strong team intact allows consistent delivery of the ever-changing demands of customers.

Outside the human capital component, items that need to be considered for future-proofing an organization are evolving technology, national and domestic economic shifts, local market changes, and building financial stability through cash reserves. Securing financing and capital is easier when an organization is financially sound. Industries change at a breakneck pace. It is essential to stay flexible and agile. Those traits are key to doing the best possible job of future-proofing an organization. The more done to future-proof the health and fitness industry, the better the industry can continue to provide the services people need to regularly stay physically active and take control of their health and well-being.

Exercise Habits and Behavior of Americans

It is not a question of whether Americans understand the value of fitness, exercise, and health. They do. COVID-19 reinforced the importance of being active and healthy, as seen in the Kaiser Permanente study. It is not just adverse outcomes from COVID-19 that are thwarted by physical activity. Physical activity has benefits for many medical issues and chronic diseases. The Centers for Disease Control and Prevention (CDC) reports that regular physical activity helps improve your overall health, fitness, and quality of life (CDC 2023). It also helps reduce the risk of chronic conditions such as type 2 diabetes, heart disease, cancer, depression and anxiety, and dementia. The CDC recommends that the average adult get at least 150 minutes of moderate-intensity aerobic physical activity or 75 minutes of vigorous-intensity physical activity per week.

While people may not know the specific research, few would disagree that regular exercise leads to better health. Does that knowledge increase the number of people who make being physically active a regular part of their lives? The research is not promising. According to the National Center for Health Statistics, nearly 75 percent of Americans consistently fail to meet the CDC's recommendation for physical activity (Elgaddal, Kramarow, and Reuben 2022).

While the benefits of regular physical activity are well known, only a quarter of the adult population is meeting them. Why is this? There are various barriers to exercise and activity that affect Americans.

Barriers to movement and exercise fall into two categories: personal and environmental factors. Personal barriers include health status, socioeconomic status, education, past exercise history, and emotional issues. Environmental factors include access to facilities, lack of time, lack of prioritizing health, and lack of social support. At first glance, it is easy to assume that people are simply choosing not to be physically active or that it is merely a discipline or willpower issue. Barriers are much more complicated than that. Fitness professionals need to understand these barriers to help minimize them. The more barriers that industry leaders and fitness facility managers can remove, the more people will take advantage of the benefits of a physically active lifestyle. Now that we have touched on barriers that keep people from being physically active, let's look at the 25 percent of people who are physically active. Who are they, and what are they doing?

Current Consumer Behavior

According to a 2022 consumer report, 66.5 million Americans had some sort of health club membership, and 76.5 million visited a facility in some capacity (IHRSA and L.E.K. Consulting 2022). Having a membership does not necessarily mean a person is using it. Annual visits to some sort of facility were reported at 4.5 billion. These numbers are improving but are still lower than pre-COVID levels.

Consumers use various types of facilities. Studios are the most visited at 39 percent, followed by fitness-only facilities at 30 percent, other nonprofits at 26 percent, multipurpose at 20 percent, YMCAs/JCCs at 18 percent, and corporate facilities at 6 percent (IHRSA and L.E.K. Consulting 2022). One reason for the lower use of corporate facilities may be more people working remotely. Notice that the percentages total more than 100 percent; that is because around 26 percent of consumers have more than one membership type. These different models have different pricing structures, with studios tending to have the highest price tag and corporate fitness options having the lowest.

Consumers who are using facilities participate in a variety of activities. Regarding equipment usage, the same 2022 consumer report explains that treadmills, resistance machines, and free weights are the most used, while kettlebells, rowing machines, and stair climbers (steppers) are the least used, respectively (IHRSA and L.E.K. Consulting 2022). In addition to simply offering equipment, many facilities offer specialized programming for their members. This includes group exercise classes, small group training, aquatics, racket sports, and more.

According to the 2022 report (IHRSA and L.E.K. Consulting 2022), health club member participation rates in various activities in 2021 revealed distinctive trends in preferred exercise choices. The highest participant rate was observed in yoga, with 23 percent of health club members engaging in this activity. Following closely were high-intensity interval training (HIIT) and swimming, both with a participation rate of 19 percent. Bodyweight exercises and calisthenics captured the attention of 16 percent of participants, showcasing the enduring popularity of fundamental workout routines.

Dance, step, and other choreographed exercises attracted 15 percent of the participants, reflecting the appeal of group-based and dynamic workouts. Tennis and cross-training workouts saw engagement from 13 percent and 10 percent of health club members, respectively. Interestingly, activities such as aquatics exercise and group cycling shared a 9 percent participation rate, highlighting the diversity in workout preferences. Pilates, cardio kickboxing, and boot camp programs attracted 7 percent, 7 percent, and 6 percent of participants, respectively, while activities like badminton, barre, racquetball, tai chi, and squash registered lower participation rates, ranging from 4 percent to 1 percent. This data emphasizes the varied and evolving nature of fitness interests within health club communities, shedding light on the popularity of specific activities and potentially informing health clubs on tailoring their offerings to meet member preferences.

This data and research should paint a pretty good picture of how many people are using facilities, what types of facilities they are using, and what those people are currently doing while visiting facilities. Remember that these numbers do not consider people working out at home or outdoors. Adding those numbers does increase the total number of people who are regularly physically active. However, even with everything added up, the number of people in the United States who are regularly physically active is relatively low. It should be an area that the fitness industry collectively works on to elevate. It is promising to note that more than 62 percent of fitness facility managers expect an increase in facility usage in the coming years (Tipping 2023). The more physically active people are, the more successful fitness facilities will be. Even more important is that more people will take better care of their health and fitness and live longer, higher-quality lives.

Conclusion

Once you deeply understand people's physical activity habits, consumer expectations, the aftermath of the COVID-19 pandemic, and the other factors explored in this chapter, you are much more prepared to manage your fitness facility effectively. This knowledge will empower you to make informed decisions, evolve your business model as necessary, and ultimately achieve and sustain long-term success. Armed with this foundation, you will be able to thrive in the constantly changing landscape of the fitness industry.

THINK IT THROUGH

- How has COVID-19 affected the fitness facilities in your community?
- What short- and long-term effects did the pandemic have on exercise behavior?
- How has health club participation changed over the years?
- What are the top fitness trends as defined by ACSM?
- What are some personal barriers and environmental factors that may influence someone's exercise participation?

KEY TERMS

ACSM
COVID-19
environmental factors
great resignation
Health & Fitness Association (formerly IHRSA)
personal barriers

Organizational Mission, Vision, and Values

Upon completion of this chapter, you will be able to do the following:

- Define mission, vision, and core values
- Formulate organizational values
- Create an organizational mission statement
- Propose a vision statement

Most people who choose fitness facility management as a career are driven by a passion for helping others reach their goals. Some are motivated to inspire others as a mentor once inspired them in the industry years ago. No matter the motivation, serving as a fitness facility manager brings excitement and often the autonomy to make decisions regarding the business, such as creating new programs and initiatives, making improvements to the facility, and hiring personnel. Along with the excitement, a manager will face challenges, such as what offerings to discontinue or sunset as trends change and when to make critical financial decisions.

Whether exciting or challenging, these decisions should have a method to the madness and be grounded in the organization's guiding principles. Enter core values and mission and vision statements. Think of these three things as the DNA makeup of the organization. This chapter teaches you how to understand and craft mission and vision statements and how to make decisions driven by core values.

In fitness facility management, applying the principles of core values and mission and vision statements becomes integral for creating a purpose-driven and successful organization. A fitness-related business should pursue core values that reflect a commitment to health, community, integrity, and member satisfaction. For example, core values may promote a supportive and inclusive environment, foster personal growth, and maintain transparency in business practices. Mission statements in the fitness industry encapsulate the commitment to empowering individuals on their wellness journey, while vision statements project a future where the community embraces a healthy and active lifestyle. The type of fitness facility, whether it's a private for-profit facility, university gym, community recreation center, or nonprofit, can significantly influence the organization's values, mission, and vision. A university gym might emphasize education and student well-being, while a community center may focus on accessibility and inclusivity. Recognizing the unique demands of each setting is crucial in tailoring these guiding principles to align with the organization's purpose and clientele, ensuring a cohesive and effective approach to fitness facility management.

Identify Core Values

Core values are the root fundamental belief system that guides the behaviors of individuals and organizations. Every person and every organization has a set of core values. Core values can be thought of as rules. They are never compromised. No matter what happens, a person or organization stays true to them. They should guide decision-making, differentiate an organization from competitors, inspire team members, and demonstrate what a person or organization stands for.

While very similar, one significant difference between personal and organizational values exists. Personal values may be instilled in us by our upbringing (parents, religious or political views), our journey through life, and ultimately what we hold dearly to our soul. They are internal and are discovered through intentional self-awareness work. On the other hand, organizational values are created intentionally through collaboration among key stakeholders. Generally, there is a crossover between the personal values of the key stakeholders and the organization. Ultimately the development of meaningful core values helps to create the metaphorical DNA and culture of an organization.

A set of well-thought-out core values drives most successful organizations. Generally, organizations create somewhere between 5 and 10 meaningful core values. If there are too few, there are not enough to serve the purpose, and if there are too many, they become watered down and can lose significance. While there isn't a magic number, it is essential to choose what makes the most sense to have the necessary impact on an organization. Some common core values are trust, integrity, innovation, compassion, inclusion, customers first, and loyalty. For example, Nike's athletic apparel brand has the following core values: community, sustainability, diversity, and social responsibility. Accessibility, education, environment, inclusion and diversity, privacy, and supplier responsibility are the core values guiding Apple's tech brand. The iconic Disney brand values are optimism, innovation, decency, quality, community, and storytelling (Cotter 2023). Most of us are familiar with these brands and can probably see these values in our interactions with them. Intentional and meaningful core values can be so powerful. The key is to create them thoughtfully and effectively.

Meaningful core values can be identified in a variety of ways. Many experts have devised exercises and strategies for core value development. There are entire books outlining processes for doing so. It would be impossible to cover all the different approaches in this book, but with any effective method, you see some common themes. All processes have some exploration of the past, such as looking at past high points and observing their present values. Conversely, it may include looking into low points and what values were missing during these down moments. Looking at the past offers insight into what is important to the stakeholders involved in the process.

Team member behavior is another aspect generally examined while creating core values. Looking at the characteristics of the best team members and what is missing with the poorer performing team members can offer a deeper understanding of what matters most.

Finally, most processes encourage you to brainstorm what makes your organization different from competitors. Ask questions like "What behaviors do we exhibit that make us stand out from our competitors?" This particular exercise is crucial to avoid falling into cookie-cutter core values.

Once exercises like these have been completed, organizations must test the results. Ask key stakeholders and staff members questions such as the following: Do the core values inspire you? Do you find them to be authentic? Are they memorable? Would they help guide your behavior and decisions at work? Are you willing to hire and fire based on these? These types of questions help determine if the core values designed are effective and meaningful.

The final step is to wordsmith the core values. While at the surface level, it may seem trivial, using acronyms, alliteration, or catchy sayings helps make the core values easier to remember and resonate more.

Here are a few other resources that offer processes to help you create core values. Nominal group technique is a valuable tool for identifying core values. This approach values both introverted and extroverted personality types in the brainstorming process. Nominal group technique includes the following four-step process led by a facilitator:

1. Individuals generate ideas silently, writing down the perceived values.

2. Ideas are shared among the group. No ideas need to be repeated, and no debate or discussion should occur at this point.

3. Discuss the ideas, with participants asking questions and getting clarification.

4. Rank importance by private voting to identify each person's top three to five choices.

Once the process is complete, the facilitator compiles the results and prepares the final list of core values for validation (CDC 2018).

A method that takes less preparation could be a simple process of elimination. However, just because a value gets crossed off the list doesn't mean it's

What matters most to your team members? Seek insights from the strongest members of your team to develop your core values.

unimportant. For example, an organization may have the following core values: members first, inclusion, team always, respect, and innovation. The management team may be tasked to narrow down, or identify, the top two values. For example, if the team identifies "members first" and "team always," it doesn't mean they don't value inclusion, respect, and innovation; it means that *because* they value "members first" and "team always," they will make decisions that value inclusion, respect, and innovation.

No matter the method to identify core values, one of the most critical questions is posed to determine the validity of the values: Is it true? Often, the individuals participating in the process want to list values they aspire to have or wish were factual rather than reflecting reality. For example, if an organization lists "fun" as a core value but no one can identify the last time an employee smiled or a member expressed their enjoyment, then "fun" is not a core value.

Given the impact of meaningful core values, taking your time in this process is essential. Get team members involved. Seek input and feedback.

Most importantly, have fun. Organizations should reevaluate core values every so often. While core values are often timeless, internal and external shifts make it worthwhile to double-check their efficacy and make revisions if appropriate. Strong core values have a massive positive impact on any organization and are worth the time and effort it takes to create them.

Craft a Strong Mission Statement

A mission statement is a brief description of the higher goals of an organization. Its purpose is to improve the cohesion and coherence of the organization. While core values are the fundamental principles of an organization, they become even more valuable when followed up by a strong mission statement. A mission statement answers the question, "Why do we exist?" Like core values, a mission statement should be authentic, inspirational, and guiding. Don't think of it as filling out a form. Instead, approach it knowing that it is a tool that, when thoughtfully crafted, can be the driving force of your organization. Consumers overwhelmingly prefer to do business with an organization when they identify with the mission. Therefore, one cannot underestimate the power of a strong mission statement.

Generally, a good mission statement is short, catchy (easy to remember), inspiring, ambitious, realistic, and measurable, and it differentiates the organization from the competition. It should be something that resonates with team members and customers. A meaningful mission statement isn't that you sell or provide a service. Instead, it captures the organizational purpose and captivates people. It is what you do, who does it, and why you do it. For example, the mission of the airline Jet Blue is "to inspire humanity—both in the air and on the ground." The American Council on Exercise updated its mission statement to be simply "getting people moving." "To connect the world's professionals to make them more productive and successful" is the mission statement of the widely used business connection platform LinkedIn. The high-end retail store Nordstrom doesn't simply sell you apparel. They strive "to give customers the most compelling shopping experience possible" (Tsang 2020). These mission statements resonate. They engage, inspire, and draw you in. They demonstrate that these brands are more than just products or services. These are brands with a purpose. Employees want to work for organizations with a purpose. Consumers want to do business with an organization with a purpose. Effective mission statements aren't created overnight. They are carefully and strategically crafted.

Just as creating core values takes a strategic process, so does crafting a meaningful mission statement. Many different approaches work well. Regardless of the methodology, certain items must always be present to develop an effective mission statement. When starting, there are a few things to consider. Who are you serving? How are you serving them? How does your method differentiate you from your competition? Why do you do what you do? Answering those fundamental questions is an essential part of the process.

First, brainstorm with your key stakeholders on precisely who you serve. Try to get as specific as possible with your target market. The second item to brainstorm and discuss is how the organization serves that niche market. Finally, clearly identify the value you provide. This item tends to be the easiest part of the process. Once this is crystal clear, it is vital to establish how you deliver your value differently than your competitors do. Think about it this way: What can you say that would encourage someone to do business with you over your competitors? What makes your organization unique? Why should you be the go-to provider? Once these items are crystalized, it becomes all about purpose. Why do you do what you do? As Simon Sinek, the author of *Start With Why*, says, "People don't buy what you do; they buy why you do it" (2009, 49).

On the technical side, keeping mission statements short and memorable is best. Overly complicated and lengthy mission statements tend to lose team members and customers. Instead, craft them shortly and sweetly while ensuring they contain all the required elements. Finally, test them. Have your key stakeholders and staff review them and offer feedback. This involvement not only provides valuable information but also increases team member buy-in.

Organizations should revisit the mission statement more frequently than they do core values. Commonly, a mission statement is evaluated every 15 to 20 years. While it may never change, it is important to reassess and ensure it is still relevant to the organization and marketplace. Even the most thought-out and well-crafted mission statement may need some updating.

Define Your Vision

Core values and a mission statement are two-thirds of the entire identity. The third piece is the organization's vision. When you think about a vision statement, what do you see? First, think of your ideal best self. In a perfect world, what would the organization look like, what would the members be doing, and how would the staff feel? Then, it concentrates on the future. What would it look like if you were wildly successful?

A vision statement charts the course of where the organization is going. Author Jim Collins describes it as a "big, hairy, audacious goal," or BHAG (Collins and Porras 2011). A values-based vision statement should help define the organization's goals, objectives, and plans. Every daily decision should inch the organization closer to that BHAG, no matter how big or small. It shapes the behavior of the team and the organizational culture. A vision statement should be specific, challenging, motivating, and memorable.

The Vision Framework

Developing core values is a crucial component of establishing an organization's culture. The vision framework outlined by Jim Collins (2001) provides a strategic approach to doing this. It examines the organization's fundamental beliefs and principles through thought-provoking questions. Leaders, stakeholders, and key team members should answer questions like "What timeless values should guide our decisions and actions?" and "What principles must remain unwavering, even in the face of challenges?" This initial phase is critical in identifying the bedrock values that serve as the organization's compass.

After that initial reflection, Jim Collins' vision framework suggests a collaborative effort called the Mars Group to refine and validate the proposed core values. The Mars Group is based on the imaginative premise that the organization needs to replicate its values on another planet. In this scenario, only a select few, typically five to seven individuals, can be sent due to limited space on the rocket. These individuals are chosen based on their embodiment of the organization's core values, purpose, credibility, and competence. This group serves as representatives tasked with taking the collective output of all teams into a consolidated draft of the final overall vision for the organization. The Mars Group helps ensure that the core values are as authentic as possible and resonate with all the people involved with the organization.

Here is a look at a few inspiring vision statements:

- *LinkedIn*—Create economic opportunity for every member of the global workforce (LinkedIn 2023)
- *Disney*—To be one of the world's leading producers and providers of entertainment and information (Panmore Institute 2023)
- *Patagonia*—We're in business to save our home planet (McKinsey and Company 2023)
- *Apple*—We believe that we are on the face of the earth to make great products, and that's not changing (Gill 2022)
- *Tesla*—To create the most compelling car company of the 21st century by driving the world's transition to electric vehicles (Business Model Analyst 2023)
- *East Carolina University Campus Recreation & Wellness*—To be an advocate for lifelong wellness and a pioneer for leadership development (East Carolina University, n.d.)
- *The Commons Club at the Brooks*—The Commons Club at the Brooks will be the healthiest community in Southwest Florida (Commons Club, n.d.)
- *Orangetheory Fitness*—To be the trusted global leader of innovative heart-rate-based interval training (Orangetheory Fitness, n.d.)
- *Virgin Active*—We are the world's leading health club (Virgin Active, n.d.)

Share What Guides You

Creating a mission statement, vision statement, and core values are great ways to craft the DNA of a company, but the real value comes about when these items are put into practice. They can't simply be words on paper. These items should guide and inspire an organization. They should never be an organization's best-kept secret. Mission, vision, and core values should be consistently infused into an organization from the top down. The key to the infusion is to share these items internally and externally.

There are many ways to share the mission, vision, and core values internally with team members and key stakeholders. First, market them to your team. Post mission and vision statements and core values in the facility's office, break room, or other areas that team members use. Consider adding a single core value to various staff uniforms for added exposure. Some organizations create collateral such as "core cards" that list the mission, vision, and core values for employees to keep in their pockets while on shift. Training materials, handouts, and email signatures should include mission, vision, and values. The more creative ways of keeping mission, vision, and values in the forefront of your team members' minds, the more they become ingrained.

In addition to consistently promoting mission, vision, and values, managers should incorporate them into the employee journey. This practice starts by including these items in job listings. Doing so makes candidates aware of the importance of these items at the first possible moment. From then on, keep the mission, vision, and values alive throughout all aspects of the employee journey. They should be a part of the interview and hiring process, including new hire onboarding. Evaluations and expressions of appreciation and gratitude should heavily reference mission, vision, and values. Use mission, vision, and values when evaluating whether or not to terminate employment. If a team member isn't living by the organization's values, it may be time to move on from that team member. You will notice a reference to mission, vision, and values and how they are a part of almost all aspects of an organization's operations throughout the remainder of the textbook. As a leader, get creative and find ways to ensure that the mission, vision, and values are always visible internally in an organization.

Internal sharing of mission, vision, and values isn't where the sharing ends. There are real benefits to sharing externally with customers. Customers generally prefer to do business with an organization that doesn't simply provide a product or service but does something with a higher purpose. Now is a great time to recall the Simon Sinek quote from earlier in this chapter: "People don't buy what you do; they buy why you do it" (2009, 49). External sharing is how an organization tells the world why it does what it does. There are many ways to share mission, vision, and values externally with customers. Adding them to the website, newsletter, and email signatures are all examples of sharing externally. Many facilities also incorporate mission, vision, and values into marketing and social media. Some organizations go so far as to integrate them into the physical design through wall imagery and signage. Note that there is a secondary benefit internally from sharing externally. When team members see that their organization shares the mission, vision, and values with customers, it reflects how seriously the organization takes these items. Similar to leaders finding ways to share the mission, vision, and values internally effectively, the same should be done to communicate it externally effectively.

Conclusion

Mission, vision, and values cannot simply be words on paper. The thoughtful creation of a mission, vision, and values, combined with a strategic effort to infuse those items internally and externally, differentiates an organization in a marketplace. They offer a road map to success for an organization to follow. Ultimately, mission, vision, and values are not what's written on walls but what happens in the halls. Mission, vision, and values truly lived are among the most powerful tools an organization can have.

THINK IT THROUGH

- How does having a well-defined mission help make progress toward your organizational goals?
- What are examples of a well-crafted vision statement?
- How are personal values and organizational values similar?
- How often should you update your mission statement, vision statement, and core values?

KEY TERMS

core values
mission statement
stakeholders
vision statement

3

Identifying Your Target Market

Upon completion of this chapter, you will be able to do the following:

- Conduct a market analysis
- Identify your target market and audience
- Conduct a manager and organizational SWOT analysis
- Illustrate buyer personas

Once an organization has established its mission, vision, and values, the next step is to strategize how to serve customers uniquely. The U.S. Small Business Administration explains this clearly (2023). Market research helps you find customers for your business. Competitive analysis helps you make your business unique. Combine them to find a competitive advantage.

Organizations must ensure people are available to purchase services and that their offers are compelling enough to encourage people to buy from them. Successful organizations spend the same time and energy crafting an effective mission statement, vision statement, and core values as they do when identifying a target market. Dedicating energy and time to performing these tasks dramatically increases an organization's chances of creating and sustaining success.

Performing a Market Analysis

The first step in identifying a target market is performing a market analysis, which will help you find customers for your business. A market analysis provides insight into the type and availability of potential customers that could use an organization's services. Simply put, an organization needs customers for it to succeed.

A market analysis begins with understanding the demographics of the area where an organization plans to operate. Depending on location, the studied area can vary. For example, a suburban area may base its target market area on mileage. Those conducting the analysis may look at a 5- and 10-mile radius to study. Consumers in these areas are more willing to drive a little further because there is less traffic, and there may be fewer choices. Conversely, commute time may be a better predictor than mileage in a metropolitan area. For example, an organization downtown may look at a 5-minute and 10-minute commute time in places where most consumers walk. The market may also be saturated with options.

It is essential to recognize that many providers now offer fitness classes and training online, eliminating geographic constraints and expanding the potential target market. Beyond geography, defining a target market area involves considering characteristics such as demographic profiles, psychographics, and behavioral traits. Understanding potential customers' preferences, interests, and behaviors becomes crucial in tailoring services to meet their specific needs. Factors such as age, fitness goals, preferred workout styles, and technological proficiency play a significant role in identifying and reaching the right audience. Conducting a comprehensive market analysis that incorporates these diverse factors enables organizations to strategically position themselves and effectively attract a broader and more diverse customer base in the competitive landscape of online fitness services.

Once the geographic area of study is decided, it is time to investigate several other factors inside that area. An organization should examine the total population, gender, age, race, employment status, median income, and the like. This information gives you an idea of who lives in the area and who might use the organization's services. It is a predictor of consumer demand.

Economic factors play a part in this initial research as well. Questions related to domestic, state, and local economic trends must be examined to present an accurate market analysis. Understanding economic trends is a great way to predict the future behavior of customers. Promising economic trends are a good sign that the consumers in the area are willing to spend. On the contrary, an impending recession should raise red flags and promote a shift to a more conservative approach to business planning. Therefore, economic trend research is crucial for a thorough market analysis.

The third piece of the market analysis puzzle looks outward at what is currently happening in the fitness space in the area. There is an overlap between a market and a competitive analysis, and this puzzle piece falls into that overlap. Competitive analysis will be explored more in a moment. Several questions need answering to understand the saturation of the market:

- Who are the competitors in the area in which the organization intends to operate?
- What services do those competitors offer?
- What do they charge for those services?
- Who are the typical customers of those competitors?

Answers to questions like these provide tremendous insight into the competitive landscape of the area and what an organization may need to do to differentiate from competitors to be successful.

Table 3.1 provides a comprehensive overview of sample fitness centers in an area, each catering to distinct audiences with diverse offerings. From the upscale Gym of Champions targeting serious fitness enthusiasts to the family-friendly Body Shop with child care services, the comparison covers aspects such as equipment, amenities, pricing, and strengths and weaknesses of each competitor, assisting potential members in making an informed choice based on their unique preferences and priorities.

A base-level understanding of economic trends, demographic research, and a look at what is currently happening in the local fitness space paint a powerful picture that significantly affects the initial stages of business planning positively and insightfully.

A properly executed market analysis must be considered for effectively identifying the target market. Proper execution involves collecting the information discussed earlier and ensuring it is accurate. The good news is that precise information is prolific if you look in the right places. There are several ways to gather the information crucial for a complete market analysis.

You can find a great starting point for compiling information in resources provided by small business associations (SBAs). These resources are free, reflect the current marketplace, and are tools designed to help organizations accurately understand the market.

Table 3.2 shares some specific examples of helpful resources (U.S. Small Business Administration 2023). While these resources are specific to the United States, other countries have their equivalents that entrepreneurs can explore. Many countries, for instance, have government agencies or business development organizations that provide similar resources and support for start-ups and small businesses. Look for online platforms and industry-specific associations that provide global insights and resources for business planning and market analysis.

An analysis of this data and these trends will paint an overarching picture of what is happening at a high level in the marketplace.

Small Business Development Centers (SBDC) provide many complimentary resources for small businesses operating in the United States. SBDC regional locations all over the country are accessible and regionally focused. SBDCs provide resources that assist in conducting market analysis and ongoing support for organizations as they operate and grow.

Focus groups bring people together to supply thoughts, ideas, and feedback about a product or service. Participants usually represent the typical customer who would use the product or service. This concept is referred to as a *buyer persona*. The buyer

TABLE 3.1   Sample Competitive Analysis

Competitor name	Location	Equipment and amenities	Price	Targeted audience	Strengths	Weaknesses
The Gym of Champions	Midtown	Cardio machines, weight machines, group fitness classes, personal training, swimming pool, basketball court	$120 per month	Adults who are serious about fitness and want a luxurious experience	Large selection of equipment, experienced staff, state-of-the-art facilities, luxury amenities	High prices, not as convenient as some other gyms
The Fitness Factory	Uptown	Cardio machines, weight machines, group fitness classes, tanning beds, massage therapy, cryotherapy chamber	$30 per month	Everyone who wants a variety of amenities	Variety of amenities, convenient hours, affordable prices	Not as many experienced trainers as in other gyms
The Fit Republic	South side	Cardio machines, weight machines, group fitness classes, virtual reality fitness classes	$20 per month	People who are looking for a unique fitness experience	Virtual reality fitness classes, affordable prices	Limited selection of equipment, not open 24/7
The Athlete's Edge	South side	Cardio machines, weight machines, group fitness classes, personal training, massage therapy	$35 per month	Adults who are serious about fitness	Large selection of equipment, experienced staff, and state-of-the-art facilities	High prices, not as convenient as some other gyms
The Body Shop	North side	Cardio machines, weight machines, group fitness classes, child care	$25 per month	Families, women, and people who are new to fitness	Low prices, convenient hours, child care available	Limited selection of equipment, not as many amenities as other gyms
The Yoga Studio	Downtown	Yoga studio, Pilates studio, meditation room	$150 per month	People who are interested in yoga or Pilates	Variety of yoga and Pilates classes, experienced instructors	Not as many amenities as other gyms, not open 24/7

persona will be discussed shortly. Once the right participants are in the room, a facilitator leads an interactive discussion to reveal the possible insights from the participants. A practical focus group encourages everyone to participate in gathering the best and most diverse feedback possible. In an article published by the online commerce platform Shopify (2022), the following types of questions are recommended to get the best possible information from the participants:

- *Engagement questions* are simple questions designed to connect participants, put them at ease, and acquaint them with the discussion topic.

- *Exploration questions* are deeper and more probing questions created to gather more powerful feelings and opinions toward the subject.

- *Exit questions* are used after valuable information is attained to ensure everything is noted.

Focus groups are inexpensive, efficient, and effective ways to gather valuable market information.

In addition to focus groups, organizations can do surveys, phone calls, and interviews as supplementary ways to collect more information. Generally, the more information an organization can acquire, the better, with the caveat that the data should be relevant and accurate.

TABLE 3.2 Free Small Business Data and Trends

Focus	Goal	Reference
General business statistics	Find statistics on industries and business conditions.	NAICS USA.gov statistics U.S. Census Business Builder
Consumer statistics	Gain information on potential customers and consumer markets.	Consumer credit data Consumer product safety
Demographics	Segment the population for targeting customers.	U.S. Census Bureau Bureau of Labor Statistics
Economic indicators	Know unemployment rates, loans granted, and more.	Consumer price index U.S. Bureau of Economic Analysis
Employment statistics	Dig deeper into employment trends for your market.	Employment and unemployment statistics
Income statistics	Pay your employees fair rates based on earnings data.	Earnings by occupation and education Income statistics
Money and interest rates	Keep money by mastering exchange and interest rates.	Daily interest rates Money statistics via the Federal Reserve
Production and sales statistics	Understand demand, costs, and consumer spending.	Consumer spending Gross domestic product (GDP)
Trade statistics	Track indicators of sales and market performance.	Balance of payments USA Trade Online
Statistics of specific industries	Use a wealth of federal agency data on industries.	Statistics of U.S. businesses

Reprinted from "Market Research and Competitive Analysis," U.S. Small Business Administration, last modified February 1, 2024, www.sba.gov/business-guide/plan-your-business/market-research-competitive-analysis.

Performing a Competitive Analysis

The next step for identifying a target market is to supplement an effective market analysis with a thorough competitive analysis to craft a complete competitive advantage. Competitive analysis helps paint a clear picture of what potential competitors are doing to attract customers to an organization. It should also provide insight into an organization's value proposition. While elements of a competitive analysis take place during the market analysis phase, much more needs to happen to maximize its effectiveness.

The first piece of a competitive analysis is understanding market share. This understanding comes from answering specific questions about the competition. For example, who are the other players in the market who wish to serve the same customers? What specific services do they offer? What amenities do they have? What do they charge? What is their primary service delivery model? What is their marketing strategy? What is their online presence and reputation? Questions like these help organizations understand who they are competing against, which in turn can help lead to differentiation strategies. The answers also aid in creating a strengths, weaknesses, opportunities, and threats analysis (SWOT), another component of competitive analysis.

A SWOT analysis is precisely what the acronym indicates. It is a strategic tool designed to bring an organization's strengths, weaknesses, opportunities, and threats to light. Strengths are things an organization does well, attributes that differentiate it from competitors, and other unique resources. Weaknesses are a combination of items such as organizational deficiencies, insufficient resources, or competitive disadvantages that may exist. Opportunities are the possibilities that arise from things such as competitors' deficiencies, underserved customers, innovative products or services, and favorable market trends. Finally, threats can be anything from emerging competition, changing demographic or economic trends, and shifting consumer behavior or expectations. SWOT is used at different points in an organization's journey and for many purposes. A SWOT analysis can be used for overall business review and strategy, to evaluate new

Strengths	Weaknesses
Customer service, fitness equipment quality, size of facility	High cost of membership for younger members, lack of specialty fitness classes, difficult access due to limited parking
Opportunities	**Threats**
Social engagement groups, renovation of racquetball courts to specialty fitness, longer hours on weekends	Specialty gyms (boxing, Pilates), gyms with child care service, low-cost memberships for younger members

FIGURE 3.1   Organizational SWOT chart.

product or service launches, and for many other reasons. A SWOT analysis can be viewed as internal and external. Internal SWOT items are things generally under an organization's control, while external factors affect an organization but are not in its control. The strengths and weaknesses are often internal to the organization, while opportunities and threats are external. For an organization to leverage the potential power of a SWOT analysis, it is essential to take a strategic approach to executing it.

Conducting a SWOT analysis (figure 3.1) is fairly straightforward. It begins by bringing together the key stakeholders necessary to be part of the process. Involving the right team members creates a complete analysis. Which team members are included depends on the preference of the organization. On a large flip chart, sticky note, or whiteboard, draw and label four quadrants (strengths, weaknesses, opportunities, and threats). Next, as a team, brainstorm the items that fall into each category. After thoroughly brainstorming, discuss the listed items, delete what may not be relevant, and add others that arise. After completing the session, organize the findings into a simple document to distribute to the participants for further reflection and edits. Finally, set up a follow-up meeting to further discuss and create necessary action items.

If executed correctly, a SWOT analysis allows an organization to understand where it sits in a competitive marketplace and what direction it should take. It is also a good practice to run SWOT analyses on competitors. While there will be unknown details, spending time doing this can create a higher understanding of competition and offer more insight into an organization's SWOT analysis. Note that doing a SWOT of a competitor will never be as thorough as the SWOT analysis an organization does for itself. Still, it is worth doing if you have available time and resources.

To complete the competitive analysis, an organization must also consider barriers to entry, which are hurdles or roadblocks preventing start-up organizations from entering a market. Examples of barriers include high start-up costs, regulatory burdens, or other issues that prevent new competitors from easily entering a business sector (Hayes 2023).

While some barriers to entry are out of an organization's control, others provide challenges that can be planned for and dealt with effectively. New organizations must carefully analyze the barriers to entry and make educated decisions to minimize risk and increase the chance of creating and sustaining success.

Creating Buyer Personas

A final component an organization must examine when identifying its target market is the buyer persona. A buyer persona is a semifictional character that mirrors an organization's ideal customer. Customer insights, market analysis, competitive analysis, and other relevant data are used to create this "avatar" (Qualtrics XM 2023).

Some organizations are so niche they have only one primary buyer persona, but most use a few different buyer personas. The variations of personas reflect the distinct needs of the various customers that an organization wishes to serve. Creating buyer personas helps organizations visualize the interactions and experiences they desire to create for potential customers, leading to better strategy and execution. They aim to create a more thorough understanding of customers. Personas take ideas and strategies from paper to theoretical practice.

Buyer personas typically include demographic info such as age, gender, income, location, family situation, annual income, and education; personal background, including hobbies and interests; and

---

SWOT Analysis Example

Greg Corack

A SWOT (strengths, weaknesses, opportunities, threats) analysis is an industry-standard assessment to determine product value in a particular market. *Strengths* and *weaknesses* typically refer to inputs controlled by your company, while *opportunities* and *threats* refer to external factors. The process entails asking employees, and often customers, to provide a subjective reflection on a product's standing. The data from a SWOT analysis allows company leaders to accentuate strengths, sunset weaknesses, seize opportunities, and address threats whenever possible.

Process

Super Recreation Center owners noticed a drop in new members and renewals over six months. Staff members recruited current and former members to attend a one-hour SWOT session focused on improving recruiting efforts at the facility. During the session, participants were prompted to provide specific examples of recreation center strengths and weaknesses and opportunities for growth. Similarly, participants were asked to provide threats to their continued membership focused on other recreational offerings in the community. A discussion ensued after a 30-minute ideation process to clarify comments and achieve consensus. A similar process was offered via an online survey to engage other members.

Results

- *Strengths*—customer service, fitness equipment quality, and size of facility
- *Weaknesses*—high cost of membership for younger members, lack of specialty fitness classes, no ease of access due to limited parking
- *Opportunities*—social engagement groups, renovation of racquetball courts for specialty fitness classes, longer hours on weekends
- *Threats*—specialty gyms (boxing, Pilates), gyms with child care service, low-cost memberships for younger members

Changes

The owners of the Super Recreation Center took data from the SWOT analysis process and made essential changes to their operational philosophy. They offered a new promotion for members under 25, reducing the costs and eliminating an initiation fee. They worked with an adjacent business owner to lease parking options after five o'clock in the evening on weekdays and contracted with a local fitness vendor to redesign an underused racquetball court. Although they could not address everything they learned from the process, they made significant and immediate changes to show their members they mattered.

---

professional information, such as industry, job title, and company size. Through buyer personas, organizations can look at the values and goals of customers, evaluate how their products and services fit into customers' lives, and develop ways to address customers' specific pain points. This data can be acquired through discovery techniques similar to those used in the market analysis and competitive analysis that identify the target market. It is helpful to use methodologies such as surveys, focus groups, and interviews to gain even more details and insight. Creating the buyer persona involves taking all this information and using it to build the avatar of the imagined person an organization identifies as its ideal customer. The sidebar Sample Buyer Personas provides a few examples of buyer personas.

As buyer personas are created, an organization must reflect on its vision, mission statement, and core values. The main question in this reflection exercise is, "Can this buyer relate to the vision,

Sample Buyer Personas

Buyer Persona 1: Fitness Enthusiast Felicia

Felicia is a 26-year-old working professional interested in maintaining a healthy lifestyle. She's committed to her fitness routine and likes strength training and cardio workouts, but her real passion is group exercise classes. Felicia values a variety of classes and a well-designed group exercise studio. She's also looking for a facility with knowledgeable group exercise instructors who can provide guidance and motivation. Felicia is willing to invest in her health and is open to exploring additional services, such as nutritional counseling and personal training. Convenience and accessibility are essential for her because she often works long hours and prefers a facility with flexible hours and a flexible class schedule.

Buyer Persona 2: New Mom Natalie

Natalie is a 35-year-old mom who recently gave birth to her first child. She's looking to regain her overall fitness levels postpartum. Natalie is interested in a facility that offers postnatal programming options and has a supportive community of mothers. She values a clean and safe environment, and amenities such as child care services or a designated family area are necessary. Natalie also looks for flexible programming schedules to accommodate her baby's needs. She's budget-conscious but is willing to spend more if a facility offers options that meet the needs of her well-being and the well-being of her child.

Buyer Persona 3: Active Ager Steve

Steve is a 65-year-old retiree who believes in staying active and maintaining mobility as he ages. Steve intends to spend significant time at a facility, given his free time. He's looking for a fitness facility that caters to seniors and offers specialized programs for older adults. Steve is interested in low-impact exercises, gentle yoga, and flexibility training. He values a supportive and inclusive environment where he can exercise at his own pace. Access to experienced trainers who understand the unique needs of older adults is crucial for him. Steve also appreciates facilities that offer amenities such as accessible locker rooms and comfortable seating areas.

mission, and values of our organization?" If yes, the odds are the organization created effective buyer personas. If the answer is no, the personas need more revisions to be practical tools. Customers' alignment with an organization's culture helps identify the target market.

Another way to verify whether a buyer persona is compelling is to cross-check it against an organization's elevator speech or elevator pitch, which is a brief talk or pitch intended to sell or win approval for something, such as a product, service, or business proposal. The term *elevator speech* refers to creating a message that one can effectively communicate during a short ride on an elevator. It typically includes the organization's name, its primary product or service, the customer problem it solves, and its foremost competitive differentiator and unique selling proposition. When examined, does the elevator speech compel the buyer personas to

do business with the organization? Like the vision statement, mission statement, and core value test, an organization is on the right track if the answer is yes. If the answer is no, revisions to the buyer personas are necessary.

Conclusion

Creating a meaningful vision statement, mission statement, and core values is the first step an organization must take to be successful. The second step is carefully and diligently identifying its target market. Finally, an organization must recognize the importance of operating in the right market. Organizations with incredible visions, missions, and values may not have desirable products and services in viable markets. Despite top-notch DNA, they still can't overcome a lousy market. Thus, they fail.

On the other hand, there are cases of average organizations that stumble on great markets and succeed despite a subpar culture and product or service. Taking the steps discussed in this chapter to ensure an organization identifies its target market and is genuinely viable is crucial to long-term organizational success. Once an organization is confident they have identified the target market, it is time to explore the world of business operations, which we will cover in the next chapter.

THINK IT THROUGH

- How can performing a thorough market analysis contribute to your facility's success?
- What effective resources can you use to gather information when conducting a complete marketing analysis?
- How do economic trends influence your facility's target market identification and overall business strategy?
- What items, both internal and external, fall into the strengths, weaknesses, opportunities, and threats categories of a SWOT analysis of your facility?
- Why is creating various buyer personas an effective tool for uncovering the target market for your organization?

KEY TERMS

buyer persona
competitive advantage
competitive analysis
demographics
elevator speech
market analysis
SWOT analysis
target market

4

Business Operations

Upon completion of this chapter, you will be able to do the following:

- Explain the purpose and components of a business plan
- Discover current fitness business models
- Identify characteristics of various business structures
- Differentiate various funding sources
- Demonstrate an understanding of basic finances and budget forecasting
- Interpret a profit and loss statement
- Identify potential revenue opportunities
- Describe typical operational expenses

The next step in the process of creating a viable fitness facility is the creation of a business plan. The work performed previously in creating the vision statement, mission statement, and core values provides the organization's identity. This DNA answers why the organization exists and what it stands for. Identifying the target market helps define where the organization will operate and who it will serve. The next step, the business plan, is the foundation of the business. A complete business plan leads you through each stage of starting and running an organization. The plan can be considered a road map for creating, executing, and expanding the organization. It's a complete method to think through all the key elements of the organization. Think of the business plan as a way to make everything tangible and bring the organization to life.

Even within established businesses, a deep understanding of business plan concepts is paramount. Whether navigating expansions, diversifications, or strategic shifts, familiarity with these principles equips professionals to contribute meaningfully to the organization's growth, adaptability, and sustained success.

Business Plans

In addition to the high-level reasons mentioned earlier, there are many other reasons to invest time and effort into carefully crafting a complete business plan. First, a strong business plan helps to reinforce that your concept works. A business plan helps assess the likelihood of success. Part of a business plan includes financial planning and competitive analysis, similar to identifying the target market in the last chapter, which is essential to understanding how long it takes to break even and when and what profit will look like. This ties into the activity of goal setting. Short-, mid-, and long-term business goals are essential to a business plan; they demonstrate a time line for benchmarks as the organization matures. A well-done business plan can significantly reduce risks. According to Chase (2023), the following are the reasons organizations fail:

- Lack of capital
- Lack of market impact or need
- Unresearched pricing (too high or low)

- Explosive growth that drains capital
- Saturation of competition

The research must support a business plan to mitigate these issues. The business plan provides guidance on avoiding these issues and an approach to dealing with them if they arise. Business plans help an organization identify the infrastructure it needs to operate, the team members needed to execute the plan, the marketing tactics and strategies that should be used, and everything in between. The business plan is where the rubber meets the road and demonstrates the concept's viability, how it will be executed, and the results of that execution.

Another important purpose of a business plan is to help secure funding. Funding will be discussed in detail later in this chapter. Whether an organization is applying for a loan, using investors, seeking a grant, or acquiring it through other means, the business plan shows how the funds will be used to accomplish the organization's goals. For example, if a privately owned commercial facility is raising capital from a private investment group, the business plan would show the investment group how much capital is desired, what it will be used for, the return the investment group would receive, and when they would receive it. In addition to those tangible items, the plan is also an opportunity to convey the organization's vision to the potential funding sources. Most funding entities want to align with an organization's culture that they support. Think of the business plan as a marketing tool for raising the capital needed to launch, operate, achieve, and sustain success (Chase 2023).

As you can see, a business plan serves many purposes. For a business plan to effectively serve all intentions, it must be carefully crafted and include several key components. While there isn't necessarily one standard way a business plan must be created, they all should contain most or all of the following seven components (Small Business Administration 2023).

1. *Executive summary.* The executive summary is a high-level summary of the organization and its goals. Generally it includes the business concept, a description, the service provided by the business, the market for that service, and why this particular business holds a competitive advantage. It also includes, to some extent, financial information, such as start-up costs, the source of capital, and the potential for sales revenue, profits, and return on investment (ROI). The executive summary is a place to share the organization's current business position, including information about the owners, experience, and specific legal structure. It is also good practice to share major achievements in the executive summary, such as awards received, specific protocols of the business, notable clients, or local or national celebrities who agree to be used in marketing materials or endorsements. This section may be the only part someone may read, so it has to be something that gives a solid summary and creates interest.

2. *Company description.* While the executive summary gives a high-level overview of the plan, the company description goes into more detail. Think of this section as what you do, why, and how you do it uniquely. In this section, the operating model and its unique selling point (USP) are explained in detail. This is an appropriate place to share information from the market and competitive analysis, such as the current state of the fitness industry specific to the local market, the present financial situation, and the outlook for future growth. Details should be provided, such as the number and location of competitors, how many employees they have, and the number of clients to whom they provide services. This section is capped off by sharing high-level details of the management team members, highlighting their knowledge, skills, and experience.

3. *Products and services.* This is the component of a business plan where it is made known what services and products your organization will offer, why there is a need for those services and products, and how the delivery of those services and products will be unique, thus differentiating the organization from its competitors.

4. *Market analysis.* This component offers a complete analysis of the area where an organization wishes to operate. Much of this information has been covered previously when identifying the target market. This section should summarize that information, indicating why the market is ripe for the organization. After reading this section, a reader should understand the area demographics, service and product demand, and the organization's USP. This component answers why this organization will succeed in this market.

5. *Strategy and implementation.* This component is where the rubber meets the road. This is the action plan. It brings all the ideas to life. It is the go-to-market strategy. This section should explain, in detail, the operations of the organization. The strategy and implementation component

answers the following questions: How will the service and product be delivered? What is the customer journey? What is the marketing plan? This component should create a clear understanding of how the organization will do business, grow, and hit goals. This section is all about organizational operations.

6. *Organization and management team.* This component details the organization's structure and who will do what by when to implement the strategy. The organizational piece of this section dives into the hierarchy of the organization. Often this is best visualized through an organizational chart ("org chart"). The org chart names the different roles, identifies which people report to whom, and shows where everyone sits in the chain of command. Understanding the chain of command provides insight into who makes decisions and the process. The management piece specifies who is in the roles described for the organization. While mentioned at a high level earlier in the plan, this section goes into more specific detail as to who the key team members are and why they are qualified to guide the organization to success. In addition to the team members involved in day-to-day operations, this includes ownership, board members, and other key stakeholders.

7. *Financial plan and projections.* The final component of a business plan is the financial analysis. This section simply explains what it costs to run the organization and what revenue it can generate. This section also includes time lines for certain financial benchmarks, such as break-even and specific growth points that will be achieved. This particular topic will be examined more in depth throughout this chapter, but it could be a book in itself. Regarding expenses at a basic level, the plan lists all the costs of starting up an organization and the ongoing costs associated with operating. When doing financial planning, keep in mind that operating costs will increase over time due to growth-related increases, general inflation, and more.

Revenue is the flip side of expenses. This is where the sale of services and products is projected. Revenue considers primary sources and ancillary, also called secondary, sources of revenue. Just like expenses, these will change over time. When projecting revenue, account for adding new products or services and raising prices to remain on par with or exceed expenses.

In addition to these basic projections, financial plans and projections include benchmarks and goals. When does an organization expect to break even? When does it expect to be profitable? What can be expected in year-over-year growth? The rest of the plan should support the financial plan and projection component of a business plan, especially the strategy and implementation section. It is one thing to create projections but another to create projections fully supported by the rest of the business plan. The latter is what an organization needs to be successful.

These seven components make for a well-rounded business plan. There is no right or wrong to writing a business plan as long as it is practical and useful to the organization creating it. It should keep an organization inspired and on track. A well-crafted business plan is one of the most powerful tools an organization can use as a road map to create and sustain success.

Business Models

When constructing a business plan, you need to consider the type of business model you plan to use. Various business models can work effectively for a fitness facility; ultimately, they fall into one of two macro-level categories, for-profit or nonprofit.

Table 4.1 provides a comprehensive breakdown of business models for fitness facilities, categorizing them into for-profit and nonprofit entities. This table not only distinguishes various types of fitness establishments but also offers insights into their pricing structures, typical amenities, and target audiences, aiding entrepreneurs in aligning their business plans with the specific characteristics of their chosen model.

For-Profit Facilities

The for-profit category of fitness facilities has several subcategories, divided by different variables such as size, price, amenities, service levels, and more. These various models give consumers different options based on the experience they desire when caring for their health and fitness. Whatever the specific for-profit model is, it generally falls into one of the following categories.

Budget Clubs

Budget clubs are a relatively newer type of for-profit business model. These facilities meet an exerciser's basic need of having a place to go and exercise. These clubs generally have a smaller footprint than traditional fitness facilities, limited amenities, minimal service levels, flexible membership options, and a significantly lower price point. They may or may

TABLE 4.1   Fitness Facility Pricing and Amenities Model

Model	Category	Price range	Typical amenities
FOR-PROFIT FACILITIES			
Budget clubs	Low cost	$10 to $30 per month	Basic fitness equipment, limited classes
Midmarket clubs	Moderate cost	$30 to $80 per month	Wide range of equipment, group classes
Premium clubs	High cost	$80+ per month	State-of-the-art equipment, spa, sauna, premium classes
Boutique studios	Specialized studios	$15 to $40 per class	Specialized classes (e.g., yoga, spin, Pilates)
FOR-PROFIT OR NONPROFIT, DEPENDING ON FACILITY			
Golf and resort facilities	Luxury resorts, country clubs	$200 to $500 per month	Golf courses, pool, spa, fitness center
Corporate wellness centers	Workplace	Generally included in benefits	On-site fitness center, wellness programs
Medical fitness facilities	Health care facilities	Varies	Rehabilitation services, specialized equipment
NONPROFIT FACILITIES			
YMCAs and JCCs	Nonprofit organizations	$20 to $80 per month	Gym, pool, classes, community programs
Colleges and universities	Educational institutions	Included in student fees paid with tuition	Athletic facilities, fitness classes, student discounts
Federal government and military facilities	Government institutions	Included in benefits	Gym, classes, specialized training programs
Community centers	Local community	$10 to $50 per month	Gym, classes, community events

not have group fitness studios or specialized programming; if they do, it tends to be on a small scale. Planet Fitness, YouFit, and Fitness 19 are brands that fall into this category of for-profit health clubs.

Membership pricing for these clubs can be as low as $9.99 monthly. Note that this is often known as a "hook" price. It is designed to get people interested but is followed up with an upsell to a slightly higher membership price that includes more perks, such as 24-hour access, infrared saunas, massage chairs, or multiple-club access.

A trend that is occurring in the budget club space is a shift to what is known as a high-value, low-price model (HVLP). These budget clubs are finding ways to keep the membership price down while providing a higher level of customer service. The HVLP model often uses the hook price and upsell strategy. Blink Fitness and énergie Fitness are brands that have excelled at this. Blink Fitness and énergie Fitness excel in the HVLP model by combining affordable membership costs with enhanced customer experiences. Blink emphasizes a welcoming atmosphere, free fitness classes, and personalized training, while énergie offers a tiered membership approach, providing affordable options with

opportunities for premium upgrades. These brands showcase the effectiveness of the HVLP model in the budget club space through a strategic focus on customer satisfaction.

Budget clubs tend to appeal to people who are newer to exercise, are looking for convenience, and are price conscious. Budget clubs have seen significant growth in recent years.

Midmarket Clubs

Midmarket clubs are aptly named because they sit in the middle of the for-profit fitness facility market, and midmarket is one of the oldest existing models. This club category includes brands such as Gold's Gym, Onelife Fitness, O2 Fitness, LA Fitness, and 24 Hour Fitness. This specific type of club has a higher price point than a budget club but isn't as expensive as some clubs at the higher end of the market. The typical membership price for these clubs can range from $29.99 to $59.99 per month.

Midmarket clubs usually have more amenities than budget clubs, such as larger and more complete locker rooms, pools, basketball courts, group fitness classes, child care services, and specialized programming. While they have more amenities,

Ownership Models

For-profit fitness facilities have a variety of ownership structures:

- *Independently owned facilities* are privately owned by an individual or small group of people. While this ownership structure gives full control over all decision-making and operations, it may have limited resources and lack brand recognition.
- In *corporate-owned facilities*, a larger company or organization owns the brand. Given the scale, they generally have more access to resources and stronger marketing and branding opportunities but often lack the flexibility to adapt to local market conditions.
- In the *franchise model*, an individual purchases the rights to use a franchisor's business model and branding. They receive training, systems, and support but must strictly adhere to the franchisor's regulations, guidelines, and standards. A franchise can be a great structure to combine the independence of owning a business with the support of a larger company.

they aren't generally noted as having significantly higher levels of customer service.

Midmarket clubs generally attract a more savvy exerciser than a budget club. The typical client generally understands exercise and is looking for this model's extra amenities. The consumer is typically willing to spend a little more but is still budget conscious.

This model has seen some challenges in recent history. Two main issues causing some struggle are that they don't have the same low-cost price advantage as the budget club model and can't offer some of the higher-end customer experience that the premium clubs and studios can offer. To some extent, they are stuck in the middle.

Premium Clubs

Knowledgeable exercise aficionados with higher incomes are the ideal consumers for the premium model of health clubs. These consumers seek a high-end customer experience, which a premium club aims to deliver. Brands such as Life Time, Equinox, the Houstonian, the Oxford Athletic Club, VIDA Fitness, and Bay Club service this market.

A premium price accompanies this premium experience, with some of the most expensive memberships in the industry. Clubs in this category may start around $79.99 monthly and can be as high as several hundred dollars monthly.

Premium clubs commonly offer top-of-the-line equipment, multiple group fitness studios, luxurious locker rooms with best-in-class amenities, steam rooms, saunas, world-class personal training, and more. These types of facilities can offer services that people may not typically associate with big box

gyms, such as spa services, cafés, high-end retail shopping, social areas, and even bars!

In addition to the physical features described, these facilities tout the highest possible level of customer service. This model of the for-profit club will likely remain strong in the market due to its ideal customer and the importance placed on a high-end fitness experience as part of their ongoing lifestyle.

Boutique Studios

The boutique studio is a concept that has been trending for several years. Boutique studios are typically small-footprint facilities that focus on delivering a hyperpersonalized fitness experience built on one or two niche fitness modalities. When thinking of boutique studios, brands like Orangetheory Fitness, CorePower Yoga, Barry's, and CycleBar come to mind, featuring yoga, indoor cycling, HIIT training, and other formats. This more specific focus allows for a personalized, tailored fitness experience that appeals to the customer base. The typical boutique studio customer might dislike a large gym environment and, seeking a specific service the facility offers, is willing to pay a premium price for that tailored experience. Studio prices are often in line with those of premium clubs. Members can expect to pay up to $300 per month, depending on the number of classes they take.

In the early days of fitness, size and amenities drove value. The onset of the studio market flipped that notion on its head, and the success of boutique studios stems from doing the opposite and offering one or two services in a small space. Consumers simply love an experience that feels personalized to them. While studios don't have nearly the amenities of premium clubs, you might see a hip retail shopping area, a smoothie and snack bar, and an elevated customer experience. Due to the success of boutique studios, premium and midmarket health clubs have begun trying to add studio-style experiences to their models. Studios have provided an excellent alternative to typical gyms. The studio market should continue to evolve and grow because of the smaller footprint, changing trends, and the desire for a personalized fitness experience.

Budget clubs, midmarket clubs, premium clubs, and boutique studios encompass most fitness facilities in the for-profit space. They present a good overall view of the for-profit market. Remember that everything is fluid and is not set in stone. The pricing examples provided vary based on location, demographics, and competition. While some models fit solidly in one category, some will overlap. Case in point: Facilities connected to brands such as Crunch Fitness and Fitness Connection may be more like budget clubs or more like midmarket clubs based on where they are located and how they are managed. There are boutique studio models that compete by offering lower-than-market prices. A for-profit model can fall into one or multiple categories, which is great because it offers endless exercise options to fit the needs of providers and consumers.

For-Profit or Nonprofit Facilities

In the dynamic fitness world, some fitness facilities can operate under either for-profit or non-profit models. These facilities are designed to adapt their operational structures to align with changing business goals, community needs, and funding opportunities. Strategic choices related to the financial and organizational framework enable the flexibility of the following categories to lean toward a profit-drive approach or adopt a non-profit mission.

Golf and Resort Facilities

Fitness facilities can also be found as part of golf courses, resorts, and hotels. These tend to provide a luxury experience catering to a higher-end clientele of guests and members. These facilities often have higher-end equipment; personal training; wellness services such as steam rooms, saunas, and group fitness classes; and outdoor activities such as hiking or biking. These facilities are more expensive than community centers or parks and recreation centers but offer a premium experience in a resort-style setting.

Corporate Wellness Centers

Corporate wellness centers (figure 4.1) are near the fence between for-profit and nonprofit fitness facilities. Corporate wellness centers are fitness

FIGURE 4.1 Corporate centers often display modern design and maximize natural light to create an environment where employees desire to maintain a healthy lifestyle.

onurdongel/E+/Getty Images

facilities dedicated to a specific company's employees or dedicated to a commercial office building and all the companies and their employees within. These facilities may range in size from a smaller 1,000-square-foot facility to the 73,000-square-foot fitness center in the Skyview 6 hotel complex on the American Airlines training campus at Dallas Fort Worth International Airport. Amenities typically include cardiorespiratory equipment, at least one strength-based selectorized circuit, free weights, and locker rooms and showers. Some of the larger facilities include amenities similar to those of premium clubs. Corporate wellness centers can be managed either by an in-house team as part of the company's structure or may be contracted out to one or more corporate wellness companies.

Medical Fitness Facilities

Medical fitness facilities (figure 4.2) are integrated facilities focusing on whole-person health through lifestyle medicine. Most medical fitness facilities are attached to a hospital campus (Medical Fitness Association 2023). Amenities include cardiorespiratory and strength equipment, medical fitness-specific equipment, and aquatic areas. Medical fitness facilities offer exercise programs such as personal training and group fitness, nutrition education and health coaching, chronic disease

management, and health education and promotion. Like corporate wellness centers, medical fitness facilities can operate either as for-profit or nonprofit, depending on affiliate organizations or ownership. The organizational structure and makeup determine whether the facility operates as a for-profit or nonprofit facility.

Nonprofit Facilities

Nonprofit fitness facilities, distinct from their for-profit counterparts, are another important category within the realm of fitness facilities. Various models of nonprofit fitness facilities cater to different preferences, emphasizing aspects such as size, amenities, price, and service levels. This section explores the unique characteristics that define nonprofit models committed to fostering health and well-being.

YMCAs and JCCs

YMCAs and Jewish Community Centers (JCCs) are some of the most common and well-known nonprofit fitness, recreation, family, and community centers around the globe. The YMCA was founded in 1844 in industrial London by George Williams and friends; in 1851, Thomas Valentine Sullivan formed the first YMCA in the United States in Boston. Today there are over 12,000 YMCA locations in more than 120 countries worldwide

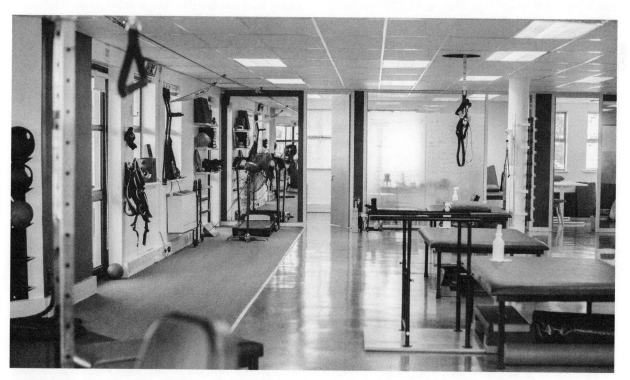

FIGURE 4.2   An example of a therapeutic treatment room within a medical fitness facility.
NickyLloyd/E+/Getty Images

(YMCA Canada, n.d.), with 2,650 located in the United States (YMCA of the USA, n.d.). The JCC movement began in Baltimore in 1954 (JCC Association of North America 2023). There are more than 1,000 JCCs worldwide and more than 350 in the United States and Canada.

YMCAs and JCCs play an important role in the community and members' lives. These large, comprehensive community centers serve many purposes in their members' lives. Amenities include equipment similar to what one would see in a midmarket health club; however, they usually include more and a larger variety. Some facilities even include features of a premium club but typically at a lower cost. Programs also include adult and youth recreational sports leagues and camps. Many centers have large aquatic facilities and play a key role in safety education and training for youth and the communities. YMCAs and JCCs operate primarily from single and household memberships and on philanthropic efforts to raise money. These nonprofit centers have a C-suite organizational structure, similar to a corporate company with a chief executive officer reporting to a board of directors.

Colleges and Universities

Some of the largest recreation and fitness centers can be found on college campuses (figure 4.3). These comprehensive recreation and fitness centers are built to meet the growing needs of a college's population. They can take up more than 240,000 square feet, such as the facilities at Auburn University, Texas A&M University, University of Wisconsin–Madison, University of Alberta, and the University of Auckland. Offering fitness programs, recreational sports programs, outdoor recreation, aquatic facilities, and integrated health and well-being programming, these facilities are meant to serve the students, faculty, and staff—and sometimes the community.

College and university fitness centers are often funded through student fees in addition to self-generated revenue collected from membership fees from faculty and staff, household members, community members and affiliates, and guest fees. Some colleges and universities subsidize faculty and staff memberships by providing money to the organization in exchange for faculty and staff complimentary access.

These fitness facilities normally have a director or executive director reporting to an associate vice president or vice president of the university. College and university facilities are most often managed within the university. However, they may occasionally be contracted out to a third-party management company.

Federal Government and Military Facilities

In the United States, federal and military installation fitness facilities operate similarly to corporate fitness centers. Federal fitness facilities are operated by in-house teams or contracted to third-party management companies that specialize in federal facilities. These facilities exist primarily for federal government employees and are a part of their employee benefits packages. The branches' morale, wellness, and recreation (MWR) divisions often manage fitness facilities operating on military installations. These facilities are primarily used by active duty or retired military members and their families. Think of MWR as the YMCAs of military installations. Access can be included in a benefits or housing package with add-on options for families.

Community Centers

A few other types of fitness facilities are worth mentioning. Often, parks and recreation districts and community centers offer some fitness programming and facilities to the local community. This model generally has a low membership fee and offers programs and activities for fitness levels of all ages. While these facilities can be less advanced and savvy than others, they provide affordable, accessible health and fitness solutions for various people.

Financial Management 101

Understanding basic financial management is crucial for a fitness facility manager. The size, organizational makeup and structure, and type of facility influence how much involvement a fitness facility manager has with financial planning.

Even for fitness facility managers who have backgrounds in financially related positions, a foundational understanding of financial management is crucial. This knowledge empowers managers to make informed decisions, align operational strategies with fiscal goals, and contribute effectively to the overall financial health of the facility, ensuring its sustainability and success in the competitive fitness industry.

FIGURE 4.3 Texas A&M University Rec Center. University recreation and wellness centers are creating spaces that mimic the varsity athletic environment.

Courtesy of Wade Griffith Photography

Funding Sources

Depending on the type of facility, there are various methods of funding. The following list outlines funding sources that may be used:

- *Membership dues.* Members pay dues to use a fitness facility and its programs and services.
- *Student fees.* Besides tuition, college and university students often pay student fees. These fees support auxiliary services and programs such as campus recreation and well-being center access.
- *Taxes.* Residents of towns, cities, and communities pay taxes that support community and parks and recreation facilities.
- *Grants and sponsorships.* External grants from federal and state sources can be used for recreational facilities and programs. Corporate sponsorships can also be used to support the funding for a facility.
- *Government loans.* Government loans may be available for funding, but unlike grants, loans must be repaid.
- *Personal equity, friends, or family.* Personal investing is essential so for-profit facilities can show banks and investors that the owner is serious about the business. You can also solicit equity and investments from friends and family; it's always best practice to involve an attorney to draw up terms and conditions.
- *Angel investors.* These are business people outside your inner circle who invest in your facility. Investments are often less than $50,000. Angel investors do not look for control but do expect 10 times the return on their investment.
- *Venture capital.* This money comes from investments from institutions looking for a high return on investment.
- *Private equity.* These are investments made by high-net-worth individuals and managed by a third-party firm. This is one of the more popular investment methods in the health club industry.
- *Bank debt.* An owner can apply for bank loans to fund their fitness facility.
- *Crowdfunding.* This is a commonly used nontraditional method of developing capital by owners recruiting donors to participate in the process.

Cash and Accrual Accounting

The two primary types of accounting are cash and accrual. Cash accounting records revenue and expenses as items are *paid*, while accrual accounting records revenue and expenses as items are billed and *earned*. Cash accounting is a simpler accounting practice and good for businesses bringing in less than $25 million in annual revenue. It also is easier to understand and track revenue and expenses. Accrual accounting is more complex and follows guidelines set forth in the generally accepted accounting principles (GAAP).

Any business bringing in more than $25 million in annual revenue or that is publicly traded is required by U.S. law to use accrual accounting. According to QuickBooks (2022), accrual accounting is the most-often used accounting method and gives a better picture of the company's financial health; however, cash accounting is the "easier to understand" method. If a fitness facility isn't bringing in large amounts of revenue, a manager may inaccurately estimate spending and make purchases without an adequate amount of money in the bank. Cash accounting can also be helpful for smaller businesses when it comes to tax season since this method doesn't require paying taxes on income that hasn't yet been received or reconciled (QuickBooks 2022).

Profit and Loss Statements

A crucial financial statement used to guide decisions while operating a fitness facility, or any business for that matter, is a profit and loss statement (P&L). This valuable tool encapsulates a business's revenue, costs, and expenses over a specific period. Typically, P&L statements are viewed monthly, quarterly, and annually. A P&L statement demonstrates whether or not the business made a profit by showing the difference between total revenues and expenses.

A P&L statement provides insight into the overall financial health of a business. An in-depth analysis of a P&L statement allows operators to understand various sources of revenue, all expenses, and whether or not they are profitable. In an effectively run fitness facility, the P&L is reviewed and analyzed regularly. The information in the P&L statement guides business strategy and decision-making. It allows an operator to track the business, find areas for improvement, adjust pricing, regulate spending, update marketing, and decide on investments. Without a P&L, an operator lacks a clear understanding of the current financial situation, which dramatically hampers an organization's chance of success.

Revenue Sources

Understanding revenue sources on a P&L statement is essential because revenue is the backbone of an organization. If there is no revenue, there is no ability to cover the expenses. Thus, an organization will cease to exist. By understanding and analyzing revenue sources, you know which revenue sources are doing well and which are not. This guides what sources should be reinvested in and marketed more and which should be discontinued. This information can also provide insight into what new sources of revenue could be added. There are numerous revenue sources seen in fitness facilities.

Membership   Membership is generally the primary source of revenue for a fitness facility. Since dues are usually paid monthly or annually, they can be counted as a consistent source of revenue. This predictable and relatively stable source of revenue allows for more effective business planning and growth projections.

Specialized Programming   Another revenue source for fitness facilities comes from specialized programming. These programs include personal training, small group training, and sometimes even group fitness classes. Personal and small group training are often some of the larger revenue streams for facilities. Group fitness classes are often included with a membership but can be unbundled

and fee-based, which adds another revenue source. Beyond those common programs, facilities sometimes offer health coaching, nutritional services, and weight loss programs. Larger full-service facilities may offer programs such as tennis, golf, or swim lessons. The sky's the limit with specialized programs, provided a facility has the space, resources, and talent to execute them effectively. Specialized programming is a great opportunity to create multiple sources of revenue.

Spa Services   Some facilities, often premium and luxury clubs, resort and hotel facilities, and even some university and community centers, offer spa services. These spa services can include massage, facials, manicures and pedicures, body treatments, and even hair styling. Although not directly related to fitness, they are complementary and often appealing, especially to a higher-end clientele. If the fitness facility model is conducive, spa services can be an excellent source of revenue.

Food and Beverage   Food and beverage services are another revenue source for many fitness facilities. On a smaller scale, this could take the form of vending machines or selling snacks, supplements, and drinks from behind the front desk. This grab-and-go setup can be convenient for members and creates extra revenue for the facility. On a larger scale, facilities can allocate space for an on-site café or restaurant. This can be a great source of revenue, and it creates a convenient place for members to relax, grab a bite to eat, and socialize after workouts. It can also be a place to attract nonmembers who are looking for healthy food options. Using this service to bring nonmembers to the facility is a great way to generate membership leads. While not effective for all models, food and beverage services can add to the bottom line.

Retail   A retail shop, often called a *pro shop*, is a space in the facility that sells products and merchandise. Sometimes this space is owned by the facility, but it can also be leased to a third party. Products sold in a pro shop include workout apparel, branded apparel, fitness accessories, workout equipment, and supplements. The products sold depend on the facility model. Premium and luxury clubs may carry high-end brands such as Lululemon or Vuori. A yoga boutique may carry items such as yoga mats, blocks, and straps. An independently owned facility may focus on branded workout gear. What a retail space sells depends on the facility model and the demographic it serves.

A retail shop provides members with a convenient place to purchase fitness-related gear and products, brings like-minded fitness enthusiasts together, and provides another source of revenue for the facility.

Youth Programming   Youth programming is another potential source of revenue for fitness facilities. Youth programs are specifically designed to address the health and fitness of younger populations. Youth programming includes youth fitness classes, martial arts, dance, gymnastics, swim lessons, camps, health education classes, and child care. Depending on the size and model of the facility, youth programming can be a huge component of the revenue stream. Another benefit of youth programming is that it allows facilities to service the entire family and promote the health and well-being of younger populations.

Rentals   Many facilities have rental services. Rental opportunities can include equipment, towels, lockers, and more. Some facilities rent out designated areas to members for events. Studio space could be rented out for private fitness events or birthday parties. If a facility has the space, it may be able to rent it out for corporate events or weddings. Couple this rental with a café or restaurant, and the facility could generate a significant source of revenue. What can be rented depends on a facility's model and resources. Rental services can be a great way to add value for members while generating more ancillary revenue.

Successful facilities understand and use various sources of revenue. By diversifying revenue sources, a facility can mitigate some vulnerability to changes in the market and consumer behavior. More simply stated, if one revenue stream falls apart for any reason, there are others to fall back on. Relying solely on one revenue stream is risky and not ideal. While understanding sources of revenue is essential for success, it is critical to examine the other side of the coin—expenses.

Expenditures

As the saying goes, you have to spend money to make money. That statement also applies to running a successful fitness facility because there will be expenses associated with it. Most expenditures can be categorized into either departmental expenses or undistributed expenses.

Departmental Expenses   Departmental expenses are directly related to revenue generation for the fitness facility. Total payroll, which includes salary and benefits for personnel, is the largest portion of expenses in the departmental expenditure category. Payroll alone accounts for 15 to 50 percent of total operating expenses and could be 75 to 80 percent of the total departmental expenses. Benefits include Social Security, retirement, medical insurance, unemployment insurance, and other costs associated with hiring employees. Benefits vary based on part-time versus full-time employees, accounting for 15 to 30 percent of total payroll expenses. Larger organizations, such as commercial facility groups and government facilities, have a specific formula for calculating benefits.

An additional expense to consider that will be covered more in chapter 6 is the education and training of employees. Considered to be an integral part of the employee life cycle, education and training costs do not follow a set industry standard. Still, it is recommended to spend annually a minimum of 1 to 3 percent of the total payroll cost toward the education and training of team members.

Additional departmental expenses can be categorized into supplies, current services, property plant equipment, purchased contractual services, and other expenses and adjustments. General supplies include office supplies, janitorial cleaning supplies,

---

Increasing Revenue

While considering different methods to increase revenue generation, you might be thinking about raising prices. First, look for two important factors: a favorable competitive market and a favorable supply and demand ratio. Another, perhaps more viable, option is to increase the revenue volume. This can be done by upskilling sales team members, increasing internal marketing efforts, and implementing new sales models, products, or programs. A popular method is to transition personal training into a subscription model rather than the traditional method of selling packages; this provides longer-term revenue planning and increases the likelihood of client behavior adherence.

Controlling Expenses

Controlling expenses is always at the top of mind for a fitness facility manager. Monitoring and avoiding overtime is vital for controlling payroll expenses. Assess the facility's traffic to limit staffing during off-peak hours and make programming decisions based on key performance indicators (KPIs), such as group fitness cost per head. Supply costs can be optimized by using a purchase order system, keeping track of inventory, and negotiating preferred pricing with vendors. Implement cost-saving practices to maximize energy efficiency to limit utility costs. If leasing a facility, negotiating property owner investment into structural upgrades can decrease energy costs.

food products, clothing and uniforms, educational supplies and books, and other miscellaneous supplies. You can expect to spend approximately 2 percent of total revenue on general supplies.

Current services expenses include advertising, promotion, and marketing of the facility. (External marketing is considered an undistributed expense.) Other current services expenses include printing, software subscriptions, and general maintenance and repair to maintain the facility's operation.

Property plant equipment includes computer-related expenses and some small equipment purchases; however, larger equipment purchases are considered an undistributed expense.

Purchased contractual services include contracted services and labor, rental fees for events, service agreements such as food and beverage service, parking and transportation, and food expenses for team members.

Finally, other expenses and adjustments account for membership dues for team members, subscriptions to magazines, publications, and programming such as Les Mills licensing fees.

Costs of goods sold must also be factored into fitness facilities that offer a pro shop. Spending at most 60 to 80 percent of the price you plan to sell an item for is recommended.

Undistributed Expenses Undistributed expenses are expenditures related to the overall operation of the fitness facility and are not necessarily tied to revenue or a specific department. External sales and marketing will cost approximately 2 to 5 percent of the total fitness facility revenue. Utilities are another operating expense and can vary significantly based on location, services, hours of operation, and more. Member services expenses such as focus groups, rewards and perks, and appreciation events will also be classified as undistributed expenses.

Fitness facility managers must remember to plan for general and administrative expenses, referred to as *G&A costs*. These average about 7.8 percent of your total revenue and account for credit card transaction fees, electronic fund transfer charges, bad debt and chargeback expenses, and postage.

New fitness equipment is one of the most exciting purchases you make as a manager. You should allocate approximately 2 to 5 percent of your total annual revenue toward replacement and roughly 15 percent of revenue every five to seven years. You

EBITDA

EBITDA is an acronym that stands for earnings before interest, taxes, depreciation, and amortization. This financial metric is a key indicator of operational performance, allowing managers to assess the facility's core profitability by excluding nonoperational expenses.

Understanding the concept of EBITDA is essential for fitness facility managers. This knowledge enables informed decision-making, strategic planning, and effective financial management, ultimately contributing to the long-term success and financial health of the fitness facility.

You can calculate your EBITDA by taking your total revenues and subtracting the departmental expenses, undistributed expenses, and fixed expenses. To calculate your EBIT, or earnings before interest and taxes, take your EBITDA and subtract expenses associated with capital replacement, depreciation, interest on loans, and amortization.

FOAPAL

In college and university recreation centers, the Banner chart of accounts system is commonly used to understand financial statements. The acronym FOAPAL stands for fund, organization, account, program, activity, and location.

- *Fund*—source of funds (e.g., fitness center operations, group fitness programs, personal training, membership, sports programs)
- *Organization*—the department (e.g., Well-Being and Recreation)
- *Account*—transaction type (e.g., revenue, salary and benefits, supplies, fitness equipment)
- *Program*—how the expense or revenue benefits the mission, goals, or objectives for the organization (e.g., public service, transformational change, community involvement, member appreciation)
- *Activity*—further definition of expenses, including associating revenue and expenses to a specific activity or event (e.g., triathlon, powerlifting meet, small group training)
- *Location*—larger purchases associated with a specific location (e.g., fitness equipment in a multisite location)

Understanding the FOAPAL structure equips managers with the tools to effectively navigate and analyze financial data, facilitating informed decision-making and strategic financial management within the context of educational recreation centers.

will learn more about capital replacement plans in chapter 9.

Finally, every fitness facility has fixed expenses that are relatively consistent each year and are not necessarily affected by the fitness facility's operation. These expenses include insurance, rent and lease or commercial mortgage, real estate and property taxes, management fees, depreciation, and principal and interest. You should consult your tax professional, chief financial officer, or business manager to understand fixed expenses.

Figure 4.4 is an example of a profit and loss statement for a health club, and table 4.2 is a sample balance sheet for a university-based recreation center.

Budgeting and Forecasting

Once you understand the basics of fitness facility financial management, you should be able to budget and forecast accordingly. Four common budgeting methods include incremental, activity-based, value proposition, and zero-based budgeting.

Incremental Budgeting

In incremental budgeting, a management team takes the existing budget and slightly adjusts it to develop a new budget. According to the Corporate Finance Institute (Schmidt 2023a), incremental budgeting is the most financially conservative approach but isn't the most effective method. One of the most significant disadvantages of using incremental budgeting in a fitness facility is that it doesn't promote innovation and can encourage excessive spending in the wrong categories. A fitness facility manager needs to be able to make changes in budgeting based on the market needs and trends.

Activity-Based Budgeting

Activity-based budgeting is a formula-based approach where costs are associated with each activity, and the anticipated activity level determines estimated expenditures (Accounting Tools 2023). This method can provide the most transparency of all methods; however, it can be tedious for a fitness facility management team due to the level of detail that needs to be put into the budget tracking. It is also a great way to shift fund allocations based on meeting the needs of the fitness facility's goals and objectives.

Value Proposition Budgeting

Value proposition budgeting is more of a mindset and operational philosophy than it is specifically a budgeting formula. The primary goal of the value proposition is to ensure that expenditures match the values of the organization, the management

Fitness Center
Profit and Loss Statement

Description	Actual Jan 23	Actual Feb 23	Actual %	Budget Feb 23	Budget %	Budget F(NF)	Actual YTD Current Year	YTD Actual %	Budget YTD Current Year	YTD Budget %	Budget YTD Variance F(NF)
New Joins	0	0	0.0%	0	0.0%		0	0.0%	0	0.0%	0
Attrition	0	0	0.0%	0	0.0%		0	0.0%	0	0.0%	0
Ending Membership	**0**	**0**		**0**			**0**		**0**		**0**
Registration Fees:	-	-	0.0%	-	0.0%	-	-	0.0%	-	0.0%	-
Individual Dues	-	-	0.0%	-	0.0%	-	-	0.0%	-	0.0%	-
Add-on Dues	-	-	0.0%	-	0.0%	-	-	0.0%	-	0.0%	-
Providence Employee Subsidy	-	-	0.0%	-	0.0%	-	-	0.0%	-	0.0%	-
Dues Adjustments	-	-	0.0%	-	0.0%	-	-	0.0%	-	0.0%	-
Total Dues	-	-	0.0%	-	0.0%	-	-	0.0%	-	0.0%	-
Day Pass Usage Fees	-	-	0.0%	-	0.0%	-	-	0.0%	-	0.0%	-
Program Revenue:											
Program Revenue	-	-	0.0%	-	0.0%	-	-	0.0%	-	0.0%	-
Other Program Revenue	-	-	0.0%	-	0.0%	-	-	0.0%	-	0.0%	-
Sports & Rec Leagues	-	-	0.0%	-	0.0%	-	-	0.0%	-	0.0%	-
Total Program Revenue	-	-	0.0%	-	0.0%	-	-	0.0%	-	0.0%	-
Spa Services:											
Spa Services Revenue	-	-	0.0%	-	0.0%	-	-	0.0%	-	0.0%	-
Total Spa Services	-	-	0.0%	-	0.0%	-	-	0.0%	-	0.0%	-
F&B and Retail:											
Food and Beverage Revenue	-	-	0.0%	-	0.0%	-	-	0.0%	-	0.0%	-
Pro Shop Revenue	-	-	0.0%	-	0.0%	-	-	0.0%	-	0.0%	-
Total F&B and Retail	-	-	0.0%	-	0.0%	-	-	0.0%	-	0.0%	-
Other Revenue:											
Other Revenue	-	-	0.0%	-	0.0%	-	-	0.0%	-	0.0%	-
Child Care Revenue	-	-	0.0%	-	0.0%	-	-	0.0%	-	0.0%	-
Total Other Revenue	-	-	0.0%	-	0.0%	-	-	0.0%	-	0.0%	-
Bad Debt Expense	-	-	0.0%	-	0.0%	-	-	0.0%	-	0.0%	-
GROSS REVENUE	-	-		-		-	-		-		-
Program Cost of Sales:											
COGS Labor - Programs	-	-	0.0%	-	0.0%	-	-	0.0%	-	0.0%	-
COGS Labor - Aquatics	-	-	0.0%	-	0.0%	-	-	0.0%	-	0.0%	-
Total Program Cost of Sales	-	-	0.0%	-	0.0%	-	-	0.0%	-	0.0%	-
COGS - Retail	-	-	0.0%	-	0.0%	-	-	0.0%	-	0.0%	-
COGS - Food & Beverage	-	-	0.0%	-	0.0%	-	-	0.0%	-	0.0%	-
Total Cost of F&B and Retail	-	-	0.0%	-	0.0%	-	-	0.0%	-	0.0%	-
Total Cost of Sales	-	-	0.0%	-	0.0%	-	-	0.0%	-	0.0%	-
NET REVENUE	-	-		-		-	-		-		-
Labor:											
Manager Salaries	-	-	0.0%	-	0.0%	-	-	0.0%	-	0.0%	-
Staff Wages	-	-	0.0%	-	0.0%	-	-	0.0%	-	0.0%	-
Commissions	-	-	0.0%	-	0.0%	-	-	0.0%	-	0.0%	-
Bonus Expense	-	-	0.0%	-	0.0%	-	-	0.0%	-	0.0%	-
Total Labor	-	-	0.0%	-	0.0%	-	-	0.0%	-	0.0%	-
Benefits:											
PTO Expense	-	-	0.0%	-	0.0%	-	-	0.0%	-	0.0%	-
PTO Accrue Expense	-	-	0.0%	-	0.0%	-	-	0.0%	-	0.0%	-
Payroll Taxes	-	-	0.0%	-	0.0%	-	-	0.0%	-	0.0%	-
Medical, Dental, & Life Insurance	-	-	0.0%	-	0.0%	-	-	0.0%	-	0.0%	-
Workers Comp Insurance	-	-	0.0%	-	0.0%	-	-	0.0%	-	0.0%	-
Total Benefits	-	-	0.0%	-	0.0%	-	-	0.0%	-	0.0%	-
Rent:											
Base Rent	-	-	0.0%	-	0.0%	-	-	0.0%	-	0.0%	-
Deferred Rent Expense Adjmt	-	-	0.0%	-	0.0%	-	-	0.0%	-	0.0%	-
CAM Charges	-	-	0.0%	-	0.0%	-	-	0.0%	-	0.0%	-
Total Rent	-	-	0.0%	-	0.0%	-	-	0.0%	-	0.0%	-
Recruiting Expense	-	-	0.0%	-	0.0%	-	-	0.0%	-	0.0%	-
Marketing Expense	-	-	0.0%	-	0.0%	-	-	0.0%	-	0.0%	-
Computer Support	-	-	0.0%	-	0.0%	-	-	0.0%	-	0.0%	-
Marketing:											
Payroll Burden	-	-	0.0%	-	0.0%	-	-	0.0%	-	0.0%	-
Office Expense	-	-	0.0%	-	0.0%	-	-	0.0%	-	0.0%	-
Travel Expenses	-	-	0.0%	-	0.0%	-	-	0.0%	-	0.0%	-
Liability Insurance	-	-	0.0%	-	0.0%	-	-	0.0%	-	0.0%	-
Management Services	-	-	0.0%	-	0.0%	-	-	0.0%	-	0.0%	-
Total Operating Costs	-	-	0.0%	-	0.0%	-	-	0.0%	-	0.0%	-
EBITDA	-	-	0.0%	-	0.0%	-	-	0.0%	-	0.0%	-
NET EARNINGS	-	-	0.0%	-	0.0%	-	-	0.0%	-	0.0%	-

FIGURE 4.4 Fitness center profit and loss statement.

TABLE 4.2   Sample University Recreation Center Balance Sheet

	Budget	Actual + encumbrances	Budget balance available	Percent earned/ spent
Activity fee	$16,000,000	$16,750,000	−$750,000	104.69%
Memberships	$2,500,000	$2,900,000	−$400,000	116.00%
Fitness	$1,750,000	$1,900,000	−$150,000	108.57%
Food and beverage/vending	$300,000	$250,000	$50,000	83.33%
Youth programs/camps	$1,000,000	$1,200,000	−$200,000	120.00%
Outdoor programs/ experiential education	$700,000	$850,000	−$150,000	121.43%
Rentals	$1,500,000	$1,675,000	−$175,000	111.67%
Sponsorships	$150,000	$200,000	−$50,000	133.33%
Oper revenue	**$23,900,000**	**$25,725,000**	**−$1,825,000**	**107.64%**
Salaries and benefits	$11,233,000	$12,090,750	−$857,750	107.64%
Education and training	$336,990	$362,723	−$25,733	107.64%
Contract labor	$100,000	$110,000	−$10,000	110.00%
Supplies	$717,000	$771,750	−$54,750	107.64%
Marketing and promotion	$300,000	$325,000	−$25,000	108.33%
Printing	$150,000	$125,000	$25,000	83.33%
Dues and subscriptions	$75,000	$74,650	$350	99.53%
Maintenance and repair	$350,000	$300,000	$50,000	85.71%
Sales and marketing	$478,000	$475,000	$3,000	99.37%
Utilities	$1,195,000	$1,200,000	−$5,000	100.42%
Member services	$169,810	$300,000	−$130,190	176.67%
General administration and accounting	$1,864,200	$1,865,000	−$800	100.04%
Capital replacement and repair	$717,000	$750,000	−$33,000	104.60%
Fixed expenses	$6,214,000	$6,214,000	$0	100.00%
Oper expenditures	**$23,900,000**	**$24,963,873**	**−$1,063,873**	**104.45%**
TOTAL PROFIT/LOSS	**$0**	**$761,128**	**−$761,128**	

team, the team members, and the members. According to the Corporate Finance Institute (Schmidt 2023b), when using the value proposition method, the management team should ask themselves the following questions:

- Why is this amount included in the budget?
- Does the item create value for customers, staff, or other stakeholders?
- Does the value of the item outweigh its cost? If not, then is there another reason the cost is justified?

Zero-Based Budgeting

Zero-based budgeting relies on the principle of starting fresh each fiscal year. It allows the management team and department heads to return to the drawing board and view the operations with a refreshed view. It is excellent for redefining priorities, goals, and objectives and allocating resources to support reaching them. Although zero-based budgeting can be helpful, Deloitte, one of the four largest global consulting firms, reports that this method is drastically declining, specifically in the United States (Aguilar and Shaikh 2023).

Zero-based budgeting is very time consuming and is an intensive annual process, which is why most organizations choose not to use this method.

Conclusion

Each type of budgeting method has advantages and disadvantages, and ultimately, the selected method should match the values of the organization and help the organization progress toward goals and objectives despite any challenges that may arise. No matter the method, accurately tracking expenses and revenues is critical when analyzing the financial health of the fitness facility.

You should review budgets on a monthly and quarterly schedule. This will help you plan and redirect funds as needed and help you and your team meet financial landmarks along the way. You and your team's collective effort can help drive business operation success. A rock star team is vital for any fitness facility manager, and the next section will address how to build one.

THINK IT THROUGH

- Why is a well-structured business plan crucial for the success of your fitness facility?
- What are the roles of the executive summary and the company description sections of a business plan?
- Why is it important to have a good understanding of P&L statements?
- What business models, for-profit and nonprofit, exist in the marketplace?
- What are some of the different sources of revenue and different types of expenses that exist in fitness facilities?

KEY TERMS

budgeting
business models
business plan
EBITDA
expenditures
FOAPAL
forecasting
profit and loss (P&L) statement
revenue sources

People: Building Rock Star Teams

5

Recruiting, Hiring, and Onboarding Top Talent

Upon completion of this chapter, you will be able to do the following:

- Explain the employee journey and life cycle
- Compare and contrast employees and independent contractors
- Identify various positions, qualifications needed, and pay structures
- Draft a talent-based job description
- Formulate an organizational chart
- Recognize various recruitment channels
- Describe best practices in hiring
- Write appropriate interview questions
- Examine the process for making an offer
- Create a new employee checklist
- Conduct an effective onboarding process

The people who make up your organization are the most important part of your organization. A general rule of thumb is that if you take care of your people, they will take care of everything else. According to Gallup's book *Wellbeing: The Five Essential Elements*, career well-being is the most important element (Rath and Harter 2010). The Gallup World Poll estimates that the average full-time worker will spend 81,396 hours working (Clifton 2022). With that many hours invested by an employee, an organization and a manager must invest substantial effort in creating a positive employee experience.

The employee experience can be broken into three phases that parallel the service journey you will learn about later in the discussion of the member experience, chapter 11. The first phase includes the first steps of the seven-step employee life cycle as defined by Gallup. The steps include recruiting

talent, hiring the right people, and onboarding your newly hired employees.

Fitness Facility Positions

Recruiting top talent is challenging and essential for a fitness facility management team. First, you need to determine the types of positions you need and their purpose within the organization.

One of the critical parts of talent management is understanding the key differences between an employee and an independent contractor. An employee can be full-time or part-time, has a job description written by the employer, and is provided with documentation that sets clear expectations and key performance indicators (KPIs), defining how and when the employee will be evaluated. The employer is responsible for providing the employee with the tools and resources to perform the job duties safely, effectively, and successfully. It is also the employer's responsibility to provide training, development, and continuing education for employees; many employers see advantages to providing financial support to employees for maintaining required certifications. Salary, wages, and bonus structure may be negotiated but are ultimately determined by the employer. The fitness facility employee is traditionally provided with a uniform and work schedule set by management and paid in an ongoing manner, such as bi-weekly or monthly. Social Security, federal income tax, and other mandatory taxes are deducted from an employee's paycheck. Many U.S. states also withhold state income taxes. Employers should cover their employees under the organization's liability and umbrella insurance policies. Although not always mandatory, some employers provide employees with benefits such as health insurance, complimentary fitness center membership, and retirement contributions. A classic example of a fitness facility employee is a membership sales associate who works a set schedule with an hourly wage and receives a commission based on sales.

In comparison, an independent contractor typically provides temporary or short-term skilled services. The independent contractor is responsible for the tools and resources to perform the services safely, effectively, and successfully. An independent contractor is responsible for maintaining any certifications or licenses and is solely responsible for their own training, development, and continuing education. One of the most significant differences between an employee and an independent contractor is the pay. Independent contractors determine their own compensation and work schedule and do not wear a fitness facility's uniform. The independent contractor is typically only paid once services

are rendered. It is also the responsibility of the independent contractor to carry their own insurance policies. They should consult a tax advisor familiar with local, state, and federal law regarding financial planning.

Although the independent contractor makes most decisions, an engagement letter should be developed, outlining the details of the arrangement, including the responsibilities of both parties, and signed by both the independent contractor and a representative of the fitness facility. A classic example of an independent contractor is a certified personal trainer who pays a fitness facility a rental fee in exchange for selling and providing training services to clients and members.

The number and types of positions available at a fitness facility vary depending on the facility size, membership base, services provided, hours of operation, budget, and any local or state requirements. Pay structure and job type often vary based on whether a fitness facility is private, commercial, corporate, community-based, university, or state or federal government. Table 5.1 illustrates specific positions you may find in a fitness facility.

Organizational Charts

Organizational charts depict the framework of positions within an organization. Although organizational charts may change based on evolving roles and responsibilities, keeping the reporting structure updated is critical. An organizational chart includes each position, the associated position number, the supervising position, and any positions that are direct reports. You should also indicate if any jobs are funded from external sources or have mandatory reporting requirements.

Figures 5.1, 5.2, and 5.3 show examples of organizational charts in various fitness facility settings.

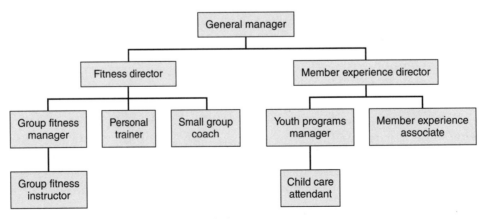

FIGURE 5.1 Health club organizational chart.

TABLE 5.1 Typical Fitness Center Staffing Roles and Requirements

Job title	Job type	Purpose	Qualifications needed	Pay structure
General manager	Full-time	Serves as the executive leader of the facility; responsible for the overall safe, effective, and successful operation	Two- or four-year degree from an accredited college or university	Salary plus commission
Fitness director	Full-time	Responsible for a financially prosperous small group and personal training program, including hiring and evaluating certified personal trainers and small group coaches	Two- or four-year degree from an accredited college or university; personal trainer certification accredited by the National Commission for Certifying Agencies; CPR/AED and first aid certification	Salary plus commission
Group fitness manager	Full-time or part-time	Responsible for developing and delivering a world-class group fitness experience, including the hiring, scheduling, and evaluation of group fitness instructors	Group fitness instructor certification accredited by the National Commission for Certifying Agencies; CPR/AED and first aid certification	Salary or hourly
Member experience director	Full-time	Responsible for developing and delivering a first-class experience to all members and guests, including the hiring, training, and scheduling of member experience associates; responsible for revenue generation concerning membership sales, food and beverage, and pro shop	Two- or four-year degree from an accredited college or university	Salary plus commission
Youth programs manager	Full-time or part-time	Responsible for a safe and positive experience for youth members and guests that may include drop-in child care or instruction	Two- or four-year degree from an accredited college or university; CPR/AED and first aid certification	Salary or hourly
Personal trainer	Full-time or part-time	Designing and delivering safe and effective individualized exercise programs	Personal trainer certification accredited by the National Commission for Certifying Agencies; CPR/AED and first aid certification	Salary or hourly plus commission
Small group coach	Part-time	Designing and delivering safe and effective exercise programs to groups of 3 to 12 members at one time	Personal trainer certification accredited by the National Commission for Certifying Agencies; CPR/AED and first aid certification	Hourly plus commission
Group fitness instructor	Part-time	Designing and delivering safe and effective exercise programs for presumably healthy adults in a drop-in format	Group fitness instructor certification accredited by the National Commission for Certifying Agencies; CPR/AED and first aid certification	Hourly or per class pay
Member experience associate	Part-time	Responsible for delivering a positive first impression to members and guests as they enter the facility; also responsible for selling memberships and food, beverage, or pro shop items	CPR/AED and first aid certification	Hourly plus commission
Fitness specialist	Part-time	Responsible for the oversight and safety of members and guests as they engage in self-directed exercise programs	CPR/AED and first aid certification	Hourly

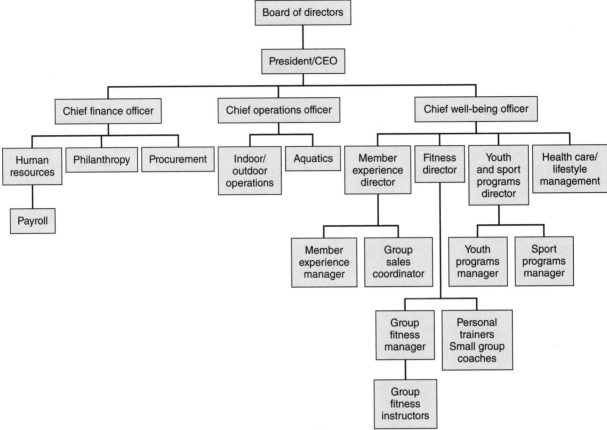

FIGURE 5.2 Community recreational facility organizational chart.

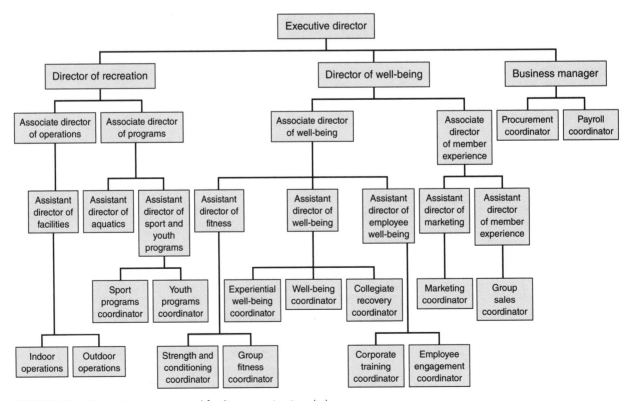

FIGURE 5.3 University recreational facility organizational chart.

Figure 5.1 illustrates an example of an organizational chart you might find in a commercial health club setting. Figure 5.2 illustrates an example of an organizational chart you might find in a community recreation facility. Figure 5.3 illustrates an example of an organizational chart you might find in a college or university recreation facility.

Job Descriptions

Once a fitness facility manager has established the types and number of positions needed to operate a facility, it is time to construct the job descriptions. A well-written and talent-based job description can help present a positive first impression of the organization to a potential employee. A manager can teach knowledge and skills, while talent is almost impossible to teach. Therefore, you should hire for talent.

Let's compare talent versus knowledge and skills by looking at a world-class group fitness instructor. Music is a crucial component of a group fitness experience and is often applied to a group fitness class in one of two ways: to drive movement or to create motivation. A group fitness instructor who teaches a class in which music drives movement needs to understand music structure and a 32-count beat; this is knowledge. The group fitness instructor also needs to be able to teach movement to the beat of music using the principles of musical phrasing; this is skill. Technically, you could teach anyone the knowledge and skills to be a group fitness instructor. So what sets a world-class group fitness instructor apart from an average instructor? Talent. A world-class group fitness instructor has a knack for selecting the perfect playlist and matching the music to the moves to inspire participants to keep

---

Sample Talent-Based Job Description

Group Fitness Manager

As a talented group fitness manager, you will provide frontline management for an innovative, dynamic, and collaborative effort to promote a culture of well-being that celebrates movement and exercise and creates an environment where all members and guests can thrive. You, specifically, will be responsible for the day-to-day operations of a multifaceted group fitness program that offers more than 100 land- and water-based movement experiences each week. You will work closely with colleagues to market, evaluate, and grow these world-class movement experiences and programs. You will be directly responsible for recruiting, onboarding, and developing group fitness talent. The group fitness manager reports to the fitness director.

You will join a team that engages members and guests in diverse well-being and movement experiences and values impact, inclusivity, and excellence. We are cultivating a workplace that celebrates the contributions of all team members and strives to deliver a world-class experience every time, every day.

This is the perfect opportunity for you if you meet the following criteria:

- Enjoy creating an environment where everyone feels like they belong
- Feel a sense of purpose in coaching and mentoring others
- Possess a keen eye for detail
- Find satisfaction in getting things done
- Strive to set trends, rather than follow them

To be eligible for this role, you will need to have the following:

- Group fitness instructor certification accredited by the National Commission for Certifying Agencies
- CPR/AED and first aid certification
- At least one year of experience working in a health and fitness setting

This is a hybrid role with the expectation to spend approximately 40 percent of your time and energy on-site and in-club each week. Expected salary range: $65,000 to $75,000 USD.

going through challenges and can elicit emotion through the use of music.

A talent-based job description enables potential employees to see themselves working within the organization and thriving as engaged team members. Here are a few tips to keep in mind when writing a talent-based job description:

- Include the organization's mission, vision, and values in the position summary.

- Capture the potential employee's attention by allowing them to imagine the impact they would have in the role.

- Highlight where and how the potential employee will dedicate most of their energy.

- Define outcomes by using phrases that start with "This is the perfect opportunity for you if you _____".

- Always include salary and whether the role is fully on-site, hybrid, or remote.

Recruiting

Having a well-written job description is essential; however, knowing where to look for your future talent is another milestone to be met. Cast a wide net to capture a wide range of talent in a diverse candidate pool. Perhaps one of the best ways to recruit is within your organization. Having meaningful conversations with your team members and understanding their strengths and goals may present an opportunity to promote from within or encourage someone to gain additional responsibilities by changing roles or departments.

Internet job boards such as Indeed are a great way to advertise your openings outside your organization. That well-written job description will pay off because many people looking for a job set up job alerts using keywords with Internet job boards so they are notified when new positions open. In addition to posting on general job boards, it's also a good idea to advertise on niche job websites. Many Internet job boards are dedicated to fitness, recreation, and well-being-specific jobs; some allow you to manage your application process within the platform.

Apprentice or internship programs are also great options for finding potential employees. Connect with your local college or university to inquire about becoming a host site for interns. Create a pipeline for graduates to connect directly to your facility for potential job opportunities. Opting into internship programs is a great way to build your workforce and prioritize the onboarding and training process without feeling rushed to get a body in a shift. Many colleges and universities also host job fairs for part-time and full-time work; signing up as an employer to have a booth at one of the fairs affords face time with prospects before the application process.

Word of mouth is one of the most effective recruitment methods. Word of mouth can be accomplished through many different channels. First, ask your existing team members to share with their networks about job openings. Ask them to include a personal testimonial about what it's like to work for the organization. Personal invitations to a candidate help them feel more connected to the organization before applying. Don't forget about your members when asking people to share word-of-mouth experiences. The fitness facility members are a word-of-mouth marketing resource for new members and future employees. Share job descriptions and positions with members so they may share them with their networks; perhaps a member may become an employee. Consider offering referral bonuses to current employees and members if they refer a successful candidate to a position.

Social media is another avenue to recruit candidates. Create attention-grabbing posts, stories, and infographics that allow potential employees to envision themself working in your facility. Ask your followers and networks to share the posts on their channels. Some social media platforms even allow you to create and post a job through the platform itself. If at any point you feel that the social media strategy needs an extra boost, consider using paid advertisements on the various platforms.

Recruiting Tip

Volunteering to guest lecture for a health and fitness faculty member's class at your local college or university allows you to build relationships with the staff and students. If the college teaches a course in fitness facility management, offer your location as a site tour.

Recruiters and search firms are other recruitment methods for open positions. Not only will recruiters and search firms reach out to candidate pools, they also personally invite people to apply to the positions and even conduct the initial screening to narrow down the top candidates. This method also allows the fitness facility management team to focus on recruiting and engaging members while outsourcing talent acquisition to a third party.

No matter which recruiting method is used, be transparent in the advertising by including anticipated salary ranges, any relocation assistance provided, and available sign-on or performance bonuses.

Once you advertise your open positions, it's time to get interested parties to apply. Ensure that the application process is seamless and doesn't create additional barriers. Anyone who makes the decision to apply for a job should be able to do so in one sitting. If possible, allow candidates to directly upload their résumé or connect their LinkedIn profile to the application so they won't have to reenter any information already provided. Be sure to include when the application will close, when a hiring manager will review applications, and when candidates should expect to hear back from someone at the organization.

Hiring

Just as the application process should be smooth, the screening process should be free from bias and include the hiring manager and key stakeholders who may be working closely alongside the candidate. The screening process should separate those who do and don't meet the minimum qualifications for the position so the hiring committee can determine a short list of candidates to be interviewed. If possible, communicate with candidates who do not meet the requirements or don't make the short list to inform them they are no longer being considered for the position.

Depending on the number of applicants and the position level, plan to conduct one or two interviews. Typically, part-time positions can be filled after one interview; however, full-time or managerial positions may require additional screening. Some positions, such as personal trainers and group fitness instructors, require a practical skills application portion during the interview process; this could also be accomplished by asking candidates to submit a prerecorded short video of themselves instructing or coaching a movement experience.

When scheduling a first-round interview with a candidate, set clear expectations of the interview process, including the number of interviews expected and the anticipated hiring and start date. If there will be two rounds of interviews for a position, the first round is typically conducted via telephone or a video interview platform. First-round interview questions should be focused on clarifying any information gathered from the application and clarifying for the candidates any specific job requirements, such as hours, work locations, work environment and hazards, and any conditions of employment eligibility. Additional questions should include opportunities for the candidate to showcase how they will add value to the organization, demonstrate their commitment to cultivating a welcoming environment, and share how they have had an impact in previous roles. After the first-round interview, thank the candidate for their time and effort and inform them of the next steps.

Following first-round interviews, candidates usually can be classified into one of three categories: finalist, nonfinalist but still under consideration, and no longer considered. If appropriate and possible, the hiring manager should communicate the status with each candidate to maintain integrity in the hiring process. Once the finalists have been selected, the hiring manager must contact the candidates to schedule their final-round interviews.

Since each fitness facility's working environment and manager preferences are different, inform the candidate what attire to wear during the interview and if any practical application skills need to be demonstrated. If you call the candidate to set up the interview, be sure to follow up with an email to the candidate outlining the details of the interview, including the time, location, duration, who will be in attendance, and any logistical instructions such as parking, arrival information, and how to check in for the interview. Make sure to collect any pertinent information from candidates who are not local so appropriate travel arrangements can be made.

A final-round interview isn't only an opportunity for the organization to see if a candidate is the best choice for the organization but also an opportunity for the candidate to see if the organization is the best choice for them. Interviews are a two-way street; it is an opportunity for the organization

Employee Engagement Starts With Recruitment

Marisa Hoff

Consider this scenario. Your fitness facility has seen a recent increase in employee turnover. There are several vacant positions across various departments; you need to find out why. You recently returned from a conference where you learned about the Employee Net Promoter Score (eNPS) survey (Qualtrics 2023). The eNPS measures how satisfied, happy, or loyal employees are, so you decide to implement the survey for all employees. You are disappointed to learn that the score for your facility is in the low 30s. (The lowest possible score is −100 and the highest is +100.) You understand the importance of overall employee engagement; however, you choose to begin by focusing on recruitment for employee engagement because this also helps you hire your new employees. You need to revamp your entire hiring process. Once that is set, you can focus on other areas of employee engagement. Create a new hiring plan for your organization using the scenario and guiding questions.

Guiding Questions

- How can you engage current employees in the hiring process?
- Which traditional methods will you use for recruiting?
- What other outside-the-box methods can you use to find potential new employees?
- How can you use your website and social media channels to best highlight the employment opportunities?
- What should you include in a talent-based job description?
- How will you display your organizational culture—your company, mission, vision, and core values?
- What will the time line be for hiring?
- What will the process and time line be for communication with potential candidates?
- How many steps or rounds will potential candidates go through?
- How will you assess the fitness of candidates? Specifically, what types of questions and practical skills scenarios will you ask?
- How will you assess the experience of the potential new employees?
- Will you be doing any reference or background checks?

Based on your outline, you are ready to hire new employees for your organization. A strategic recruitment plan is in place, and you have assembled a hiring team that is excited and ready to hire new employees. Your organization has used various outlets and mediums to recruit new employees. The new job descriptions are written to appeal to candidates and highlight your organizational culture. You capture the potential employee's attention by allowing them to imagine the impact they will have in their new role. You are set to bring on new, engaged employees and are prepared to start the next process of enhancing employee engagement.

As you implement your new hiring process, you realize that each department manager has their own method of interviewing and communicating with recruits. Although you have established guidelines and strategies for the hiring process, your spot checks and candidate feedback reveal that there still needs to be more consistency between departments in the process. You discover that a few qualified candidates were never allowed to interview. You also determine that candidates are being asked vastly different questions and scenarios and that the communication could be more consistent.

Things to Consider

- How can you ensure that the screening process is free from bias?
- Using consistent interview questions is extremely important for a variety of reasons. How can you ensure that managers are consistent with their interview questions while allowing them latitude to make interviews more conversational?
- Are there reliable tools to evaluate potential employee performance within interviews?

Consistency in recruiting ensures that organizations use the same selection criteria and reference points for making decisions. It also provides efficiency and makes it easier to justify hiring decisions. By working through the details in this case study, you should feel confident that your recruitment process will bring the best candidates to your organization, and you will begin elevating your eNPS and overall employee engagement.

to showcase why a candidate should work there. Components of a final interview might include the following:

- Tours of the facility; candidates should be able to envision themselves working there
- Tours of the area; candidates should be able to envision themselves living in the area and being a part of the community
- Any practical demonstrations or case studies
- Informal meet and greets with various employees and, potentially, members
- One-on-one time with the hiring manager
- One-on-one time with any direct reports of the position being interviewed

Questions asked in the final interview should focus on behaviors and communication styles and showcase strengths and talent. Situational-based questions and open-ended questions allow the candidate to give in-depth answers and showcase their personality. Interviews should encourage the candidate to show who they are just as much as what they know. See the sidebar Sample Interview Questions for a sample list of interview questions.

It is important to note that there are interview questions that should be avoided. Questions about certain personal characteristics, such as age, marital status, family plans, religion, disability, national origin, gender, race, and sexual orientation are typically considered illegal or inappropriate during job interviews in many jurisdictions. These inquiries can lead to discriminatory hiring practices. It is advisable for employers to focus on questions related to the candidate's qualifications, skills, and ability to perform the job duties in compliance with local employment laws and regulations.

Once you have completed the final candidates' interview process, it is time to make the selection. The hiring manager should collect feedback from staff or members who interacted with the finalists during the interview process; this feedback could be helpful in the decision-making process. Depending on the organization's structure, the hiring manager, owner or operator, executive-level team member, board, or key stakeholder could make the final decision. If possible, the hiring manager should discuss salary ranges and start dates with candidates in the final interview to limit any delays during the hiring process. Before making any offers, be sure to conduct appropriate reference and background checks. Ideally, you should plan to check references on all the finalists; this will help keep the process quick if the number one candidate either declines an offer or accepts a position elsewhere.

Reference checks should be used to validate your candidate selection for the position. It is best to keep the questions for a reference check at a minimum. A simple reference check will verify how long the reference has known the candidate, in what capacity, if they would recommend the candidate for a potential hire, and if the candidate would be eligible for rehire if the reference was a previous supervisor or manager. Some organizations only verify dates of employment for a reference check. To promote a positive experience for all parties involved, the hiring manager should notify candidates that references will be checked and confirm if there are any off-list references that the candidate does not want to be used. Follow organizational, local, state or provincial, or federal guidelines when conducting background checks.

The final step of the hiring process is to make a job offer. The job offer includes an informal verbal

Sample Interview Questions

Personal Preferences and Background Information

- Given what you know about the organization and the surrounding community, how do you see yourself acclimating and adding value?
- What qualities are most important to you when looking for a mentor?
- What are three qualities of a workplace that you look for when applying for a job?
- What is your personal mission statement? Why do you exist?
- What makes you thrive?
- How do you like to celebrate success?
- What questions do you have for us?

Performance or Situation-Based

- What has made you successful in your current or previous job?
- What experience or training have you participated in that left the most significant impact on your professional development, and how or why?
- Describe a time you have had a conflict with an employee, colleague, or supervisor. How did you handle the conflict? Looking back, would you do anything differently?
- Describe a time that you had to make a difficult decision. How did you decide what action to take? Looking back, would you change anything about your decision?
- Describe a partnership you established, individually or as part of a team, that helped you reach a goal.
- How have you recently used your strengths?

Belonging and Well-Being

- What strategies or initiatives do you believe can help foster a sense of belonging within a team or organization?
- Tell us a time that you overcame adversity or a challenge. What did you learn from the challenge?
- How can technology or digital platforms be used to enhance a sense of belonging, especially in remote or virtual work environments?
- Please describe how you work to create a welcoming and inclusive environment.
- Can you provide examples of specific practices or policies that organizations can implement to cultivate a culture of belonging?
- How do you maintain a positive work environment and foster a sense of psychological safety for your colleagues, contributing to their overall well-being?

Management

- Describe your leadership style, and explain how you used it while mentoring or managing others.
- Describe when you felt proud as a mentor or manager. What made it so special?
- Tell us about a time you had to provide a coaching conversation related to an employee's performance. Based on your conversation, how did the employee's performance change? Looking back, would you do anything differently?
- What are two or three ideas you would implement to recruit world-class employees? (Use specific positions that would be reporting to this candidate.)
- Tell us about a time you successfully improved employee engagement in the team.

offer of employment, a negotiation period, and a formal offer and acceptance. When calling the selected candidate, speak clearly when going over the offer and ask the candidate for any questions they may have. While on the phone, agree on a date when the candidate will have a decision made. Follow up the phone call with an email to the candidate summarizing the call, including the information regarding the offer and when the negotiation period is to end. Once all terms have been agreed on, a formal offer letter should be issued to the candidate of choice and signed by the candidate and the hiring manager or other representative.

The interview process can create added stress and anxiety for candidates. To minimize stress, notify the candidates who were interviewed but were not selected as quickly as possible. Provide feedback to the candidates not selected if they ask and the organization allows; however, it's best to schedule a feedback call at a later date and not at the time of notification. All applicants should be kept informed throughout the process and notified when they are no longer being considered for the position, regardless of whether they are selected for an interview.

The timing of the notification to the employees is as important as the notification to the candidates. Until a formal offer letter is signed and all candidates not selected are notified, the decision should be kept confidential and only be known by the hiring manager and any human resources team members. Keep the announcement to employees focused on the positive attributes the candidate will bring and when to expect the individual to start employment. If the candidate approves, share contact information with the employees so they may reach out and welcome the new staff member. At no point should a new employee discover that they were perhaps the second or third choice and were offered the position because the first candidate declined.

Onboarding

Work with the new employee to complete as much of the human resources, payroll, and administrative paperwork as possible before the official start date. If the employee receives benefits, indicate when the selection has to be completed. Gather employee information such as uniform size, preferred name on the name badge, contact information, and emergency contact information to expedite ordering or purchasing processes. Consider having the employee complete a personal preferences questionnaire with favorite snacks, podcasts, colors, or television shows. Assign a current employee outside the new employee's department to act as a liaison or mentor throughout onboarding.

Gather items such as uniforms, name tags, company merchandise, and other welcome gifts for the new employee's first day. Prepare any tools, materials, and resources needed for the individual to perform their job successfully. This may include a laptop, keys, business cards, parking permits, and access to required technology systems. Host a welcome meeting with the liaison or hiring manager on the employee's first day and provide a tour of the facilities. If appropriate, allow the employee to settle into the workspace and minimize stressors throughout the first day. Consider organizing a lunch on the first day to welcome the individual to the team.

Once settled in to the office space, the supervisor should meet with the employee to review job expectations, how and when the individual will be evaluated, and with what criteria and key performance indicators. Establishing a relationship built on trust and respect early on and expressing interest in an individual's overall well-being is vital. The supervisor should also explain the onboarding process to the employee, allow time for the employee to review the onboarding information, and ask any clarifying questions.

Onboarding can be overwhelming, so categorize or batch the items into easily digestible content and tasks. Most onboarding items can be organized by administrative or transactional functions, which may or may not need much collaboration; training and development tasks that typically can be done asynchronously and on one's own; or relationship building, which requires much collaboration and has to be completed over time. Rank the items in order of importance, such as primary, secondary, and tertiary; include any deadlines or due dates within the tasks. See the sample onboarding checklist in the sidebar New Employee Onboarding Checklist.

Welcoming a New Employee

Showcase new employees to members through the use of email, social media, and digital signage platforms. Include a photo, name, and title, and highlight some of the team members' successes and interests and any personal information they would like to share.

New Employee Onboarding Checklist

Primary Onboarding

Administrative

- Obtain laptop, keys, access cards, business cards, parking, and the like.
- Obtain uniform and name tag.
- Obtain access to the required technology.
- Obtain headshots.
- Obtain organizational credit cards (if applicable).
- Submit copies of transcripts, certifications, and licenses.

Training and Development

- Complete finance training and purchasing procedures.
- Complete timekeeping training.
- Complete human resources paperwork, benefits enrollment, and job-specific training.
- Complete technology systems training.

Relationship Building

- Review organizational charts.
- Set up 30- to 45-minute chats with direct reports.

Secondary Onboarding

Administrative

- Set up communication systems.
- Set up technology systems.

Training and Development

- Complete level 2 training for any technology systems.
- Complete any organizational culture–specific training.

Relationship Building

- Set up 30-minute chats with indirect reports.
- Set up 30-minute chats with same-level colleagues and key internal stakeholders.

Tertiary Onboarding

Training and Development

- Complete CliftonStrengths, Myers-Briggs, or other employee or team training.
- Review any strategic plans or organizational goals.
- Read any annual reports and review past departmental KPIs.
- Review job-specific standard operating procedures (SOPs).

Relationship Building

- Set up 30-minute chats with key external stakeholders.
- Set up 15- to 20-minute chats with internal colleagues.
- Set up 15- to 20-minute charts with external tier 2 stakeholders.

Investing in a thorough onboarding process sets up the new employee and the organization for success. Continue to evaluate the onboarding process, including asking for feedback from new employees. This survey can include items such as the clarity of job responsibilities, effectiveness of training programs, adequacy of support received, and overall satisfaction with the onboarding process. It is advisable to administer the survey shortly after the completion of the onboarding period, allowing employees to provide timely feedback.

Conclusion

Any organization is made of people. If you take care of your people, they will take care of everything else. Positive employee experiences don't happen by accident. The diligent fitness facility manager invests substantial effort to make each employee feel like a key part of the organization. This means focusing on the crucial steps of recruiting talent, hiring the right people, and onboarding employees.

THINK IT THROUGH

- How many and what types of positions do you need for your fitness facility?
- How can you craft your job descriptions to be talent-based?
- What are effective interview questions appropriate for each type of position?
- What are the best recruitment channels to use in your location?
- What makes a world-class onboarding experience?

KEY TERMS

employee life cycle
employee versus independent contractor
Gallup
interview
job description
offer letter
onboarding process
organizational chart
reference check

6

Engaging and Retaining Top Talent

Upon completion of this chapter, you will be able to do the following:

- Define management and leadership
- Explain strengths-based organizations
- Develop an employee communication plan
- Assess levels of employee engagement
- Create a system for gathering employee feedback
- Design a strategy for rewards and recognition
- Conduct effective employee evaluations

Now that you understand how to recruit, hire, and onboard new employees, it is time to move into the next stage of the employee life cycle—retention and engagement. Employee retention is the fourth stage of the employee life cycle and goes hand in hand with engagement.

According to Gallup's *State of the Global Workplace* report (Gallup 2023a), highly engaged employees are likelier to remain with their organization. High levels of employee engagement save time and money, lead to higher morale and productivity, and provide a better member experience. Although member experience will be covered in detail later in the book, it is essential to note that organizations with high employee turnover tend to diminish member experience. The Medallia Institute recently performed a study looking at 800 locations in a transaction-based business (Tran 2016). The study measured average monthly turnover versus Net Promoter Score (NPS), a method of measuring customer satisfaction. They found that the organizations with the lowest average monthly turnover had the highest NPS, and thus the highest customer satisfaction. They surmised that this was because

longer-tenured employees are more in line with the organizational culture, are more technically skilled, have better relationships with customers, and better understand customers' needs. In other words, successful organizations take a strategic approach to employee retention by ensuring employees are highly engaged.

Management Versus Leadership

Where does engagement start? It starts at the top with solid management and leadership. As you recall from the preface, management and leadership are very different. However, one person may serve as an organization's leader and manager. Think of it this way—leaders look outward, while managers look inward. Another way to look at it is leaders help drive the organization forward, while managers ensure that everything functions internally so that it can move forward.

Management is defined as the activity required to run and control a business or organization. While managers are involved in budgeting, marketing, and other activities, most of their work revolves around creating and engaging team members. Managers spend their time finding candidates, conducting interviews, running new hire onboarding programs, providing development opportunities, delivering coaching, and administering evaluations. What all of those responsibilities boil down to is a proficient manager who puts team members in a position to succeed. When team members flourish, organizations thrive.

The goal of a manager is to create what Gallup has defined as a strengths-based organization (Gallup 2023b). A strengths-based organization is precisely what it sounds like, an organization where team members can best use their strengths to make the most significant impact in helping achieve a vision. Having a strengths-based organization can distinguish your organization from others by helping you attract the best candidates to maximize your team members' performance. Gallup research (Gallup 2023c) shows that when employees know and use their strengths, they are almost six times more engaged, perform at a much higher level, and are far more likely to stay with the organization. An integral approach to creating this type of organization is to shift from a boss to a coach.

A boss mentality centers around giving orders and assignments. Bosses tend to be rigid and reactive. They tend to follow the letter of the law with a "blinders on" mentality. They see team members as people who serve them. A coaching mentality is the opposite and is far more effective in creating a strengths-based organization. Great coaches bring out the best in team members by nurturing and developing them. Coaches are flexible and proactive.

Contrary to bosses, coaches see themselves as people who serve team members. For example, let's examine the following scenario from the boss's and coach's points of view. A team member falls short with a new customer experience best practice that has been added to your minimum service standards. A boss will likely ask them to improve by a specific date, or there will be inevitable consequences.

A coach, however, takes a much different approach. A coach expresses empathy, exploring with the team member why they are falling short, and then providing training, coaching, and support to improve performance. A coach's mentality is the best way to create a strengths-based organization and healthy culture.

When maximizing your or your team's strengths, think of it as a strengths star. Each team member is a star, and each one of the points on the star represents a particular strength or talent. Most of us tend to think of performance as a circle. We believe if we spend time and energy on improving our team members' weaknesses, they become more well-rounded, making them more effective team members. While there is some truth to this, there are also some significant downfalls. All people have things that they are inherently good at and also things they don't do so well. Investing time and energy into improving weaknesses generally only produces minimal improvements. In addition, it takes resources away from working on maximizing strengths. So, instead of making employees well-rounded, help them become a star. Each point on the star represents their strengths. Work with them to develop their strengths, and don't waste much time on their weaknesses. This approach not only allows employees to perform at the highest level possible but it also improves morale and happiness in the workplace. Question 3 of the Gallup Q^{12+} (Gallup 2023c) employee engagement survey is "At work, I have the opportunity to do what I do best every day." You effectively address this crucial component of employee engagement when you coach employees to become strength stars. While this is a highly effective approach to employee satisfaction, high engagement levels, and improved retention, it presents one question. If there isn't a focus on improving employees' weaknesses, won't there be overall performance gaps in the organization? The answer is no, as long as the metaphorical bus is full and everyone is in the right seat.

Great Managers

Using the guidance of Buckingham and Coffman in their book *First, Break All the Rules* (2016), a great fitness facility manager is consistently able to identify and select team members based on talent, is able to articulate a vision, and encourages team members to spend more time on things they naturally do well. A great fitness facility manager is able to plant people in roles where they will grow instead of simply expecting someone to grow where planted.

Great Teams

In his book *Good to Great*, Jim Collins (2001) writes about his concept of having the right people on the bus, the wrong people off the bus, and the right people in the right seats. In essence, this is the key to assembling effective teams. The *right people* refers to those who are excellent additions to the facility culture. They believe in the mission, vision, and values of the organization. They are great team members who are engaged, add value, and lift other team members. This type of positive attitude and work ethic elevates other team members' buy-in. These are the team members who are crucial for success. Make sure they are on the bus.

The *wrong people* are the polar opposite, obviously. Often, they were just bad hires. Likely, they are doing the bare minimum to get by, actively or passively looking for another job, adding little value, and bringing down other team members. These employees need to be removed from the bus as soon as possible.

The final piece is to ensure the right people are in the right seat. The *right seat* refers to the proper role. The right role is a role that, you guessed it, provides the opportunity to do what they do best every day. It is a position where they can use the points of their strength star. When the right people are in the right roles, their strengths are maximized, and they fill the gaps of other team members' weaknesses to create a cohesive and effective team. A highly engaged and productive team helps an organization maximize its potential. The more effective the team, the more involved team members are, and the more likely they remain with the organization for a long time.

Good fitness facilities have the right people in the right positions.
Hirurg/E+/Getty Images

Communication Plans

One last component essential for engagement and productivity is creating and executing strategic communication plans. Communication plans are necessary for organizations to be effective and efficient. All team members must be aware of all information that they need to know. There are different types and methods of communication.

One-on-One Communication

One-on-one communication is effective for a variety of reasons. Whether in-person or virtual, one-on-one communication allows for a high level of focus and personalized communication. It also creates an opportunity for solid two-way dialogue. When it comes to critical conversations—ones that carry a lot of weight—one-on-one (in-person or virtual) conversations are often the best options. These are crucial parts of an overall communication plan that must be a part of every manager's repertoire.

One-on-one conversations assist with role and relationship management, meaning they help build strong relationships between managers and team members. *Quick connects* are frequent interactions to touch base quickly. These can be as simple as saying good morning and asking how someone is doing. *Check-ins* are a weekly form of one-on-one communication that is more in-depth than a quick connect. These may involve discussing project updates, key performance indicators (KPIs), and sales goals. The overarching purpose of these methods of one-on-one communication is to build solid personal relationships between managers and team members and ensure that all critical information is shared.

Daily coaching is another valuable one-on-one communication tactic. Effective coaching is a vital skill for leaders, and coaching positively through clear communication is essential for success (Stevenson 2020). It ensures you get the most out of team members, leading to an outstanding member experience. Successful coaching increases team member engagement, improves performance, and enhances employee retention. Bad coaching, on the other hand, disengages team members, lowers morale, and leads to high turnover.

There is a six-step approach to effective coaching:

1. Coach in the moment without embarrassing the team member.
2. Explain, in detail, the desired behavior. Explanations of desired behaviors must be crystal clear. Clarity ensures that team members know precisely what is expected and how to deliver it, leaving nothing to interpretation.
3. Clarify the why. Team members are more apt to perform a task well when they know the reasoning and agree with its necessity.
4. Model the desired behavior. Always lead by example. Modeling is an essential trait of leadership. One of the worst things a leader can do is ask team members to do one thing while they do the opposite.
5. Role-play. Once you have corrected the behavior, explained the logic behind it, and modeled it, make sure to practice it. Take time to role-play. Role-playing allows the skill to build without pressure, leading to increased confidence.
6. Observe and coach more, if needed. Once the skill or task has been appropriately trained, watch team members in action. Praise successes and positively tweak as needed.

One final method of one-on-one communication is the progress check. *Progress checks* can also be called casual conversations. In a nutshell, these are informal, one-on-one meetings to give brief overarching feedback and answer questions. Think of one-on-one communication, in person or virtual, as the most personal way for managers to connect with team members and the most appropriate for important information.

Additional Communication Avenues

Other forms of communication besides one-on-one are appropriate for different reasons. Text and short messaging systems (SMS) are effective ways to share information with individuals or groups. As described, these are short messages with few characters that are sent to smartphones and cellular devices. Text and SMS have high open rates. There is a good chance that team members will receive the information. One drawback is that it is hard to add emotion and context when using this medium. Use this medium for data that needs to get out quickly and that is easily understood, such as when and where a meeting might occur. It is also effective when a quick and immediate response is needed. Avoid delivering negative information via this method.

Voice messaging systems are a crucial part of a comprehensive communication plan. Voice messaging technology allows people to send pre-recorded messages to groups of team members without contacting each individually. It is convenient and efficient. While this method is similar to text and SMS, voice messaging allows one to use tone and emotion to communicate, which better illustrates context. Voice messaging should be used when text and SMS cannot adequately convey a message. Since the message has to be listened to, it generally holds attention and focus.

Another component of communication plans is phone and video calls. Phone calls allow for audio communication, while video calls do the same but add a visual component. Phone and video calls are a step up from voice messaging because they allow for real-time, two-way interaction. They demonstrate a level of care for a team member and build trust. You are not talking "at" someone; you are talking *with* someone. As a manager, you need to assess the seriousness of a particular communication and decide if it requires the level of connection that a phone or video call provides. If a situation involves emotion, negativity, discipline, or the like, this is the best medium for communicating, other than an in-person one-on-one meeting.

There is a place for meetings in a communication plan. Meetings are an effective communication tool when done strategically. While you lose the intimacy of one-on-one communication, you add the benefit of group discussion and team bonding. Every meeting should inform, educate, and inspire the team members attending. Meetings require strategic planning to be effective. Meetings will be covered in-depth in this section shortly.

Email is one of the most prolific ways people in organizations communicate in today's world. It plays a part in an organization's communication plan. Email comes with its pros and cons. Some of the benefits of email are that it is easy, accessible, trackable, and generally cost-effective. It can reach a team member regardless of where they are located. It also creates a written record of communication. There are cons, however. People are often inundated with email, personally and professionally, so there is the risk of an email being missed. Furthermore, email can be impersonal, similar to text and SMS, leading to a lack of clarity. All those positive and negative factors must be considered when deciding what and when to communicate using email.

Additional complementary technology tools can be implemented to facilitate effective communication with teams. Technology tools include Slack, Google Meet, Basecamp, Facebook groups, and Microsoft Teams. These tools provide one-on-one communication, focused group communication, project planning, and more. Using one of these tools is an excellent complement to a robust communication plan.

Overcommunication is key to a successful communication plan in an organization. Using various methods helps achieve this because different team members have different preferred ways of receiving information. That said, use the appropriate medium for the message and information that needs to be communicated. Use simple methods such as text and SMS, voice messaging, and emails for information that needs to be disseminated rapidly, needs a quick response, and is logistically oriented. Use face-to-face, phone or video calls, or meetings to communicate when conversations require more tone, discussion, and interaction and are more serious. Well-structured communication plans are crucial to employee engagement and retention as well as the overall success of the organization.

Meetings

While meetings are crucial to a communication plan, they warrant a deeper dive. Meetings bring team members together, promoting the exchange of information and ideas, building relationships, and developing teamwork. Meetings are also a great way to ensure team members are on the same page because they hear the messaging simultaneously.

In a fitness facility environment, scheduling meetings poses distinctive challenges due to the diverse and dynamic nature of team members' roles. The presence of various shifts and schedules, including for part-time staff, makes it difficult to find common time slots for meetings. Team members might be occupied with training clients, teaching classes, or conducting sessions at different locations, leading to a lack of cohesive availability. Additionally, the unpredictable nature of client appointments further complicates scheduling efforts. To address these challenges, a comprehensive digital scheduling platform can be implemented to allow team members to input their availability and streamline the process of finding suitable meeting times. Using virtual meetings or communication tools can also facilitate discussions, enabling team members to participate regardless of their physical location. Moreover, implementing a culture of flexibility and open communication can foster understanding among team members, encouraging collaboration and adaptability in this dynamic fitness environment.

Meetings as a whole should be as long as necessary and to the point. Several components should be present to maximize the effectiveness of meetings. All meetings should begin by having a defined purpose. Never have a meeting just to have a meeting. That is a waste of everyone's time and can disengage employees. A defined purpose is the "why" behind the meeting. Once you have the defined purpose, the next step is determining logistics such as time, place, and length. Those are the types of details that must be decided and communicated to the attendees before the meeting takes place. Once the purpose is defined and the logistics have been agreed on, it is time to set an agenda. Creating a well-thought-out agenda is key to making sure that the attendees value the meeting and that it accomplishes the defined purpose. A sample agenda is provided here:

- Introduction
- Ice breaker
- Explanation of the purpose of the meeting
- Topics for discussion
- Action items
- Questions and answers

The introduction is designed to welcome and inspire the attendees. One team member should be responsible for taking notes. In lieu of taking notes, recording meetings can serve as a valuable resource, especially for team members with conflicting schedules or those unable to attend live sessions. However, it's essential to exercise discretion and respect privacy concerns, avoiding the recording of sensitive discussions or client-related meetings that require confidentiality.

Whether the notes are handwritten or the meeting is recorded, it is crucial to accurately document meetings to have a record and something to refer back to if necessary. The notes will also be included in a follow-up, a topic explored shortly.

An icebreaker is a good idea to create engagement right from the start and lay the foundation for encouraging participation. After the first two steps, remind everyone why they are attending, thereby explaining the desired purpose of the meeting. Next, all subtopics related to the desired purpose should be presented and discussed. The

interactive and constructive discussions are then used to create action items. A simple way to think about action items comes from the book *Who Will Do What by When?* (Hanson and Zacher 2007). For example, suppose we tackle the issue of synchronizing class schedules among part-time group exercise instructors with varied availability in our fitness facility team meeting. Through collaborative discussion, we pinpoint actionable steps, such as introducing a shared digital calendar and exploring staggered shift options. Each team member is then assigned specific tasks to ensure the seamless resolution of scheduling conflicts, demonstrating a practical application of our strategies for efficient coordination.

Attendees should always leave a meeting knowing what to do and when to do it. They should also know what the other team members need to do as well. That collective knowledge lends itself to increased engagement and better teamwork.

Finally, after the meeting, it is essential to follow up. Follow-up should happen within 24 hours of the meeting. A great way to follow up is by email, thanking everyone for their attendance and participation. The email should recap the events of the meeting, including the notes and action items. Following up helps team members remember the purpose and details of a meeting, which is vital since team members have other responsibilities and can easily forget.

How do you know if your meeting is effective? One way is by seeing results. Then, as the results from the different action items come to fruition, you know the meeting was good. Another method is by using meeting effectiveness surveys. A meeting effectiveness survey is a tool that can be sent to team members after a meeting to gather feedback. Meeting effectiveness surveys can include statements rated with a 5-point Likert scale:

- The meeting was the right length.
- I learned something new at the meeting.
- I could participate in the meeting.
- The content of the meeting will help me do my job better.

Meeting effectiveness surveys are a great way to ensure that meetings are a good use of team members' busy time and that they are better at their job by attending. In addition to a survey, many virtual meeting platforms have features that provide feedback and effectiveness based on artificial intelligence and augmented reality (AI/AR).

Communication Tools

Effective communication is crucial to success in the fast-paced and interconnected world of fitness facility management. Organizations must use communication tools to ensure that operations run smoothly and that team members are on the same page. A multifaceted approach allows team members to communicate efficiently, share information and ideas, coordinate tasks and projects, and drive creativity and innovation. Such an approach assists in building relationships and keeping everyone focused on the same goal. Here are some examples of methods organizations often use to execute their communication plan.

- Microsoft Teams is used for communication and collaboration, with minimum task assigning. Each morning the team has a quick "coffee chat" in the team chat. "Hello, this is what I'm up to today; this is where you can find me." Be casual; be fun. Each Monday morning, our coffee chat is a little longer. Let us know what went great the week before, anything that frustrated you or for which you need team support, what your upcoming week may look like, and how we can assist. Remember, team chat is for quick chatting only. You should not assign tasks and have long conversations about a topic or project.

- Voxer is for voice communication and collaboration when talking is easier than texting, but a phone call is unnecessary. Voxer is an app you can download on your phone and send voice messages. It's a quick, easy, and effective means to communicate.

- Phone calls are for communication and collaboration when a more extended discussion should take place.

- Trello is used to assign and communicate tasks. Trello serves as the team's main project management board. It's a one-stop shop, and you should log in to Trello first thing every morning.

- Team meetings are in person or virtual communication with a purpose. Both the management team and the executive management team meet monthly. Direct report check-ins should happen weekly (ideally multiple times per week or even a day!). Any meetings that occur should have an agenda set prior to the meeting, celebrate some success, and end with action items and a follow-up date.

- Email is a last resort means to communicate because of its inherent limitations. Unlike messaging and phone calls, there is no ability for real-time interaction. This can lead to misinterpretations and misunderstandings because it solely relies on one-way communication via text. In addition, using email to communicate internally can clog up a colleague's inbox when their energy should be focused elsewhere, such as engaging members or coaching team members.

Evaluating Employee Engagement

You should now understand what it takes to create high employee engagement. Implementing the items discussed takes significant time and energy; therefore, assessing employee engagement is vital for verifying if efforts are effective. Both positive and not-so-positive results provide valuable insight. All feedback, positive or negative, is an opportunity. Positive feedback demonstrates what is being done well. Negative feedback sheds light on where improvements can be made. Let's look at a few methods of assessing levels of employee engagement.

One great tool for assessing levels of employee engagement is the Gallup Q^{12+} (Gallup 2023c). Building on the success of the original Gallup Q^{12} survey (the foremost survey to assess levels of employee engagement), Gallup has continued its observation and study of millions of people's workplace behavior and engagement over the years, leading to the development of Gallup Q^{12+} as the most accurate predictor of employee engagement. The Q^{12+} survey identifies the 12 most crucial needs that employees have, covering basic, individual, teamwork, and development needs, with four additional questions to provide deeper insight into levels of employee engagement and reflect postpandemic work environments.

The original questions combined with the additional questions in the Gallup Q^{12+} help organizations gain a comprehensive understanding of employee engagement, identifying areas where they excel and areas that need improvement. By addressing these needs and taking appropriate actions, companies can foster a more engaged and productive workforce, leading to increased satisfaction and better overall performance.

Employees rate how they feel each need is being met using a 5-point Likert scale. The higher the rating, the more they feel the need is being met. All the points are totaled and then divided by the number of survey participants. The ultimate result is a percentage. In general, 50 percent is considered a good score. The Gallup Q^{12+} is one of the most popular methods of assessing employee engagement and is highly effective.

Another excellent tool for assessing employee engagement is the Employee Net Promoter Score or eNPS. eNPS is a derivative of the Net Promoter Score (NPS), a measure of customer loyalty created by Fred Reichheld, a partner at Bain & Company, in 2003 (Bain & Company, n.d.). The Bain NPS survey asks consumers one question: "How likely are you to recommend (your product or service) to a friend or colleague?" The response is indicated on a scale of 0 (not at all likely) to 10 (extremely likely). The score is then calculated by adding responses and subtracting the percentage of detractors (people who score from 0 to 6) from the percentage of promoters (people who score 9 or 10). This score is a benchmark for customer loyalty. The higher the score (the highest possible being 100), the higher the level of loyalty. Global benchmarking data indicates the median NPS is +44. The creators of NPS suggest a score above 20 is favorable, above 50 is excellent, and above 80 is world-class.

This effective system for measuring customer loyalty was then adapted to measure employee loyalty. For eNPS, the question is modified to read, "How likely are you to recommend our company as a workplace to a friend or colleague?" The results are calculated in the same manner that NPS is. The higher the score, the more likely your employees will be engaged and retained.

Both the Gallup Q^{12+} and eNPS are great ways to measure employee engagement and loyalty. What is nice about both methods is that they give a specific score. A score not only gives you a benchmark but also allows for goal setting. For example, let's say your eNPS was 40. That is your baseline. Knowing the higher the score, the better the engagement and loyalty, you may set a goal of improving that score to 50 by year's end by using new strategies. If you have hit 50 by year's end, it means what you are doing is working. If not, you can reassess and modify your strategies to get there. Aside from the valuable metrics these methods provide, there is the benefit of employees simply appreciating that you care enough even to survey them.

Gathering Employee Feedback

In addition to formal methods of assessing employee engagement and loyalty, other ways of acquiring employee feedback can benefit organizations. These methods include having an open-door policy; surveys; start, stop, and continue exercises; and casual conversations. Soliciting employee feedback offers two benefits: improving performance and enhancing the overall work environment. Note that leaders and managers are frequently not in the trenches, so they don't have the same lens as employees. This other view can be beneficial in uncovering issues that would otherwise go unnoticed. Similar to eNPS and the Gallup Q^{12+}, these methods demonstrate that you care by giving employees a voice and listening to what they have to say.

A simple method for acquiring employee feedback is to have an open-door policy. An *open-door policy* refers to creating an environment where employees have easy and safe access to managers and leaders and where they can be open and honestly ask questions, offer suggestions, and air complaints and issues. The goal of an open-door policy is to encourage and invite employees to share. To make this effective, it has to be a part of your organization's culture. In addition, it has to be promoted and conveyed to the team regularly. This method of acquiring feedback is ongoing and builds trust with employees.

Surveys are another way to gather data and information from employees. Surveys can be general or targeted. A general survey is a great way to get overarching feedback and input. It can measure employee satisfaction, alignment with goals, and the like. Targeted surveys are designed to get more detailed information about specific aspects of an organization. Targeted surveys can reflect team members' feelings about their benefits package, new hire post-onboarding processes (as mentioned in chapter 5), or meeting effectiveness. Another type of survey that has become increasingly popular is known as a *pulse-point survey*. These concise surveys tend to be sent out frequently to see how an employee feels about something at a specific moment. Regardless of the type of survey you are sending out, it is essential to follow best practices when creating the survey. Survey creation is a topic that is an entire book itself. Briefly, you need to consider factors such as the objective, how long the survey should be, how to structure questions correctly, what platform you will use, and whether it is anonymous or not. Surveys can be a precious means of gathering employee feedback, but only if they are appropriately designed and executed—and if action is taken using the results.

Determining the appropriate frequency of surveys is a crucial consideration in the process of gathering employee feedback. While surveys are valuable tools, be mindful of the potential for survey fatigue. Excessive surveys may lead to decreased participation or the provision of unhelpful feedback. Establishing guidelines for survey frequency is advisable to strike the right balance. Factors such as the nature of the survey, its objective, and the organization's culture should be considered. Regular pulse-point surveys, for instance, provide timely insights but should be carefully managed to prevent overwhelming employees. Striking a balance between obtaining valuable feedback and avoiding survey fatigue is key to maintaining active and meaningful employee participation in the feedback process.

A final way to gather employee feedback is through casual conversations. Casual conversations are similar to an open-door policy, with the significant difference being employees initiate open-door feedback while casual conversations are initiated by management and leadership. This could also fit into the employee evaluations category.

Casual conversations happen in the moment. In practice, this would involve a manager pulling a team member aside and asking, "How are things going today?" It is a straightforward conversation that can lead to some great feedback and improve the relationship with team members. There are many instances where an employee may have an issue but is hesitant to share, for whatever reason. When a manager initiates the opportunity for sharing, it makes an employee more comfortable and more open. Since casual conversations are just that, they don't take prep time and planning. Managers and leaders just need to keep them front of mind to make sure they happen.

A key to gathering effective feedback from employees is taking action with the information received. That doesn't mean always doing what the employee says. Feedback can lead to one of three options. First is to act on it. You can act if specific feedback shows something is missing or a change needs to be made. Second is to use the feedback to open further discussions. Detailed feedback leads to digging deeper and gathering more information. It opens the door to learning more to see if things need to change. Finally, specific feedback may lead to the need to explain why things are the way they are. Particular processes and operations must be done to standards, but employees don't always see or understand that. Taking action using employee feedback is a powerful tool. The most important thing to remember is not to seek feedback if you do not use one of those three approaches. Asking for feedback without taking action destroys trust and decreases engagement.

Knowing how important it is to use feedback, take a strategic approach to sharing it with your employees. The entire team must understand that feedback is an opportunity. Keep an open mind. Don't take feedback personally. Have a mindset that positive or constructive feedback is a means to improve things. Always thank your team members

Start, Stop, Continue

The start, stop, and continue exercise is an easy and straightforward way to gather employee feedback. This three-question exercise asks the following:

- What should we start doing that we are currently not doing as an organization?
- What are we currently doing that we should stop doing?
- What should we keep doing (or do more of) that we are currently doing?

Casual staff meetings are a great way to solicit feedback from employees in a comfortable way that fits the schedules of your trainers.

vgajic/E+/Getty Images

for providing feedback. If it is a formal online survey, that might be via email. If it is a casual conversation, it should happen at the end of the moment. It is always important to express thanks. In conjunction with expressing gratitude, providing a time line of when and how they will get information about the results is a good idea. Once the feedback is analyzed and summarized, it can be communicated to the team. Note, be sure to make the information meaningful and easy to understand. Based on the type of information, choose the most appropriate method to communicate it. Use the communication plan to decide which way is best. Is this information best shared in an email, a large group meeting, or a one-on-one environment? However you choose to present it, make sure to be as transparent and straightforward as possible, and be willing to discuss and answer questions.

In summary, when properly acquired and communicated, feedback is a potent tool for improving productivity, enhancing the workplace environment, and creating higher employee engagement and retention.

Rewards and Recognition

Up to this point, the methods of engaging and retaining employees have been tactical. These tactical methods include leadership, management, coaching, assessing engagement, and acquiring and using feedback. What follows is making sure that employees feel appreciated through rewards and recognition. For example, item four of the Gallup Q^{12+} says, "In the last seven days, I have received recognition or praise for doing good work" (Gallup 2023c). This statement demonstrates how vital this component is for employee engagement and retention.

The first key to appreciation is fair compensation. To be engaged, an employee must feel they are compensated fairly. Therefore, it is essential to know what typical pay is for different roles on a national and regional level and to ensure that the pay is comparable. While it is not the most fun aspect of rewards, recognition, and appreciation, you must address it.

To gauge fair pay, explore reputable industry organizations such as the Health & Fitness Association and IDEA, among other sources, to gain insights into compensation trends within the fitness and wellness sector. Organizations like these often conduct surveys and produce compensation reports for various facility roles at both national and regional levels. Always ensure due diligence in selecting sources to guarantee the credibility of the information gathered.

Rewarding and recognizing employees for doing good work is essential. Rewards and recognition boost morale, encourage good behavior, and increase engagement. They make employees feel appreciated. Rewards can come in various forms, such as raises, bonuses, gifts, and paid time off. Recognition will be covered shortly. Get creative and have fun with rewards. One key to remember is that rewards should be tied directly to specific behaviors, such as hitting sales goals and KPIs. Doing this shows the employee how important their performance is for the organization's success. The other benefit is that team members see the rewarded behavior and become motivated. Without a defined reward system, employees may feel less motivated and won't perform as well.

Recognition is another form of appreciation. It is unique and doesn't necessarily need to be tied to performance. Rewards are always recognition, but recognition doesn't always have to be a reward. Recognition is as simple as greeting an employee in the morning or saying goodbye at the end of a shift. It could be catching someone doing something good at the moment and giving them a high five. Celebrating birthdays and work anniversaries is another form of employee recognition. Doing things like this makes employees feel important. Find excuses to "recognize" employees as much as possible.

There are three things to remember regarding offering praise to employees:

1. Praise should be frequent. Frequently find moments to celebrate. The more, the better.

2. Be timely with praise. Celebrate in the moment. Don't wait because the praise won't be as relevant later as it is in the moment.

3. Be very specific about the excellent behavior and why it is vital to the organization.

There are logistics to consider when it comes to rewards and recognition. You can use personal or group emails, make announcements at meetings, tell someone in person, or post on internal communication tools such as Slack. When choosing, consider which method will have the most significant impact and how the employee prefers to receive feedback. Two great questions for a new-hire survey are "If you could have a gift card from anywhere, where would it be?" and "How do you prefer to receive feedback?" This information is a great way to personalize the reward and recognition process and maximize its impact!

Performance Evaluations

Employee evaluations are crucial for employee engagement and retention. Most organizations perform evaluations annually, although some do them more frequently. Employee evaluations are designed to assess performance, uncover areas that need more training and coaching, and provide metrics for promotions, raises, and bonuses. Comprehensive employee evaluations often include goal setting as well. Evaluations are a crucial part of the employee journey because they give a snapshot of where an employee has come from, currently is, and is headed. Note that employee evaluations should never be a surprise. Employees should receive a copy of the formal evaluation to know precisely what is expected of them. It is recommended that a new hire gets a copy of their formal evaluation form as a part of the onboarding process. Let's take a closer look at the components of an effective employee evaluation.

The foundation of the employee evaluation should be strengths-based feedback. Recall the strength star discussed earlier in this chapter. Think of strengths-based feedback as providing insight into the team member's strengths (the points of the star) and how those strengths positively affect the organization's goals. What they do is more than just a job. It serves a bigger picture. It is also important to note that evaluations should be transparent. If a team member has any significant performance issues, those should be tackled during the regular course of operations through daily coaching, casual conversations, and performance improvement plans. Waiting for formal evaluations to address significant behavioral or performance problems is a mistake. Most feedback should be familiar to the employee. Formal evaluations should be constructive and positive, for the most part. The following are components of an evaluation:

- Goals
- KPIs
- Self-reflection
- Supervisor evaluation
- Action plan
- Celebration
- Future goals

Strengths-based feedback is a theme throughout the entire employee evaluation process. However, specific components that make for a complete and adequate employee evaluation should be included.

- The evaluation should start with specific *technical information*. This information includes the employee's name, department, and role, and the date, review period, and name and title of the manager responsible for the evaluation.

- A *skill evaluation* is essential for employee evaluations. This section varies based on department but should have items that reflect how well the employee performs, the skills necessary to do their job well, and how their job serves the organization's mission. These skills are generally rated with a 5-point Likert scale and based on a rubric. For example, the five points might be outstanding, good, average, below average, and poor. Having a written example for each of those rankings is a good idea. For instance, *poor* is defined as regularly falling short of KPIs and expectations. Specificity is critical and provides clarity. The manager fills this out to give the employee some insight into their overall performance in their role.

- In addition to the skills evaluation, include a section of the evaluation that reflects on the *employee's commitment* to the mission, vision, and values of the organization. This section reminds the employee that they are not simply doing a job; they are part of a bigger purpose. It is a reminder that their performance significantly affects their teammates. Creativity is needed for this section, but strive to make it as tangible as possible. It can be graded similarly to the skill evaluation, but rather than using role-related skills, you can list behaviors that specifically support the mission, vision, and values. Since being a culture fit is one of the essential components of an engaged employee, it is vital to find ways to evaluate it.

- *Self-evaluation* is also a beneficial component of an effective employee evaluation. Self-evaluation allows the team member to share their thoughts on their performance. One of the reasons this is so beneficial is it shows the team member that they have a voice and their input is appreciated. It also allows for a healthy discussion if there are differences of opinion between the employee and the evaluator. Open-ended questions such as "Where do you feel you did well this past year?" and "Where do you feel that you fell short?" are practical for this section. This section reminds the employee that although we share how we feel about their performance, we want to know how they feel.

- *Goal setting* should always be a part of employee evaluations. Evaluations are not just about "here's how you did." They are also about preparing for the future by setting goals. As a manager conducting the evaluation, collaborating with the employee while setting goals is a great approach. When deciding on goals, the first consideration is how that goal develops the employee personally and how it helps positively affect the organization's overall mission. Once that is agreed on, ensure the goal is a SMART goal—specific, measurable, attainable, relevant, and timely. Following this, it is vital to work together to create an action plan with checkpoints to ensure the goal is achieved. Goals will be reviewed at the subsequent evaluation, and new ones will be set.

Once all aspects of the evaluation have been discussed, both the employee and the manager performing the evaluation sign and date the evaluation form to complete the process.

It is important to note that you must follow all legal and human resources guidelines. Laws and guidelines may vary based on organization and local, state or province, or federal government. Keep evaluations as objective as possible and ensure they are consistent from person to person. These practices help protect you from any potential legal issues.

An employee evaluation should be a positive experience. It should be about strengths-based feedback, constructive criticism, goal setting, and improving and preparing for the future. Using what you have learned in this chapter thus far, you can create an evaluation process that employees don't dread but look forward to having. Figure 6.1 is a sample performance review form.

Member Services Performance Review

Employee Information

Name		Date & Review Period	
Job Title		Manager	
Department			

Ratings

	1 = Fair	2 = Satisfactory	3 = Good	4 = Outstanding
Job Knowledge	☐	☐	☐	☐
Comments				
Customer Service	☐	☐	☐	☐
Comments				
Setting & Meeting Goals	☐	☐	☐	☐
Comments				
Initiative & Prospecting	☐	☐	☐	☐
Comments				
Work Quality	☐	☐	☐	☐
Comments				
Communication/Listening Skills	☐	☐	☐	☐
Comments				
Dependability	☐	☐	☐	☐
Comments				
Team Player	☐	☐	☐	☐
Comments				
Upholds Mission Statement	☐	☐	☐	☐
Comments				
Overall Rating (average rating numbers above)				

Key Activities for Upholding the Mission Statement

☐ Attends Stevenson Fitness Events	☐ Interacts with members on Facebook
☐ Consistently sends Postcards	☐ Promotes the gym and gym events on Facebook
☐ Consistently takes classes	☐ Interacts with Stevenson Fitness Facebook page
☐ Consistently works out at the gym	☐ Consistently completes Excellence Sheets
☐ Refers new members	

(continued)

FIGURE 6.1   Sample member services performance review.

Discussion & Evaluation

SELF-EVALUATION
Where did you excel this year?

Where did you fall short this year?

How would you like to see yourself grow next year?

NEXT STEPS

Verification of Review

By signing this form, you confirm that you have discussed this review in detail with your supervisor. Signing this form does not necessarily indicate that you agree with this evaluation.

Employee Signature		Date	
Manager Signature		Date	

FIGURE 6.1   Sample member services performance review. *(continued)*

Performance Improvement Plans

In contrast to formal employee evaluations, which occur once or twice a year, performance improvement plans should be used as needed on an ongoing basis. Performance improvement plans, or PIPs, are a tool to help employees who are falling short in one or more areas. It could be that they are underperforming in one of the items in the skills assessment section of the employee evaluation. When this is noticed, it is best to implement a PIP rather than wait for the subsequent review. Typically a PIP lasts 90 days, but that can vary. Think of the PIP as a specific plan designed to give the faltering employee the skills they need to improve their performance.

A PIP begins by having a transparent conversation about the particular deficiency. This is not a one-way conversation where a manager talks to an employee. Instead, it is a two-way discussion about the expectations and why they are unmet. It is essential that the result of the conversation is an agreement that the issue is real and there is a commitment to improving. Once this happens, a clear and quantifiable outcome must be agreed on. The agreed-on outcome is the goal of the PIP.

Once the outcome is determined, the focus moves to deciding what resources are needed. What is the responsibility of the employee? What resources will the manager provide? The manager is often responsible for training, coaching, and providing necessary resources, while the employee is committed to using those resources. The answers to these questions define what it takes to improve performance. It is a team effort between manager and employee to ensure that the PIP ends with the desired outcome.

Checkpoints are ideal for breaking down the desired effect into smaller parts. A 90-day PIP can be divided into 30-, 60-, and 90-day segments. The first check-in meeting happens at 30 days. The first check-in is to ensure the employee is doing everything they agreed to and that the manager is honoring their commitment to helping in the process. If everything is tracking well at the benchmark, the PIP is effective. If things are not tracking well, alterations are necessary to the PIP to ensure effectiveness. Breaking the 90 days into 30- and 60-day parts is key to an effective PIP.

A few things can happen at the end of the 90 days. If the performance problem is fixed, the PIP was effective. This scenario is ideal. But there are cases where the opposite happens, and the desired outcome has not been achieved. When that occurs, there are two choices. You can move the team member to a different role (or, as Jim Collins would phrase it, to another seat on the bus). The other option is termination. If termination is the choice, that team member will move into the offboarding process.

PIPs should be a positive experience with great benefits. It is important to note that PIPs are most effective for employees who have value to add to the organization. If an employee isn't a strong value add, chances are that is the reason they are falling short. They just don't care. In this case, there is a good chance that a PIP will not work, and perhaps the employee shouldn't be on the team. On the contrary, when an employee has a great attitude and believes in the mission, vision, and values, sometimes they just need a little more structure and assistance to get them to perform at a higher level.

Conclusion

When it comes to retaining and engaging top talent, we have explored fundamental aspects of effective management and leadership, delved into the concept of strengths-based organizations, and learned how to develop comprehensive employee communication plans. We have discussed the crucial elements of assessing and enhancing employee engagement, including strategies for gathering valuable feedback and designing systems for rewards and recognition. In addition, we have equipped ourselves with tools to conduct meaningful employee evaluations and foster professional growth through engaging strategies. Looking ahead, the importance of talent management extends beyond retention, and in the subsequent chapter, Talent Offboarding, we will delve into the necessity of planning for employee departures by exploring proactive talent offboarding strategies and succession plans.

THINK IT THROUGH

- Why is employee engagement essential for the success of a fitness facility?
- How can leaders effectively balance management and leadership responsibilities?
- What are the benefits of focusing on employees' strengths rather than their weaknesses?
- How can organizations show appreciation for their employees beyond financial rewards?
- How do performance evaluations contribute to employee engagement and development?
- How can communication plans enhance employee engagement and productivity?

KEY TERMS

communication plan

employee engagement

employee Net Promoter Score (eNPS)

Gallup Q^{12+}

key performance indicators (KPIs)

leadership

management

performance improvement plan (PIP)

strengths-based organization

7

Talent Offboarding

Upon completion of this chapter, you will be able to do the following:

- Explain the purpose of a succession plan
- List reasons an employee or contractor may separate
- Design a positive employee exit experience
- Conduct an exit interview
- Create a separation checklist
- Identify ongoing opportunities to engage a former employee

A day will come when an employee leaves an organization. Although this isn't an uncommon occurrence, we witnessed during the "great resignation" (Pendell 2022) of summer 2022 that 47 percent of U.S. employees were reported to be actively job searching. In fact, according to the *State of the Global Workplace: 2023 Report*, 71 percent of employees in the United States and Canada say it's a good time to find a new job (Gallup 2023). Organizations, including fitness facilities, would be remiss if they do not have a succession plan.

According to the Society for Human Resource Management, or SHRM, succession planning is a future-focused practice of identifying the knowledge, skills, and abilities to perform certain functions and then developing a plan to prepare multiple individuals to be able to perform those functions (SHRM 2023). Succession planning has often been confined to C-suite leadership positions; however, not planning for employee turnover at all levels can be negligent for an organization. As discussed in chapter 5, the talent acquisition process should never stop, even if actual hiring does.

Types of Separation

Many factors may motivate an employee to leave an organization. Regardless of the motivation, employee separation falls into one of two categories—employee-initiated or organization-initiated—and is driven by either positive or negative motivating factors.

Employee-Initiated Separation

Employee-initiated separation is when an employee chooses to no longer be an active member of the organization. Employees may be presented with new opportunities, including higher pay, a new challenge, or better benefits. This does not necessarily mean that their current employer is not providing them with those benefits; it could simply mean that the employee is looking for a change at a higher level in a different organization. Sometimes an employee decides to change professions completely or pursue another educational degree in a different field. Relocation is another reason an employee may leave the organization. Family issues, such as a partner's job transfer, may bring about a move, or the employee may look for a physical change of scenery to enhance their overall well-being. No matter how many retention and engagement strategies from chapter 6 you implement, you cannot prevent all employees, even the happy ones, from leaving.

Negative motivating factors can sway an employee to leave, as well. More often than not, most of these factors can be prevented or fixed; however, by the time the employee makes the decision to leave, the damage may have already been done. According to Gallup, 52 percent of exiting employees report that their exit could have been prevented (Pendell 2021). There is truth to the saying "people don't quit companies; they quit managers." A bad boss drives employees away very quickly. Remember to train your managers to embody the mindset of a coach, rather than a boss, and remove bad managers when appropriate. With a talented manager in place, it takes more than a 20 percent pay raise to entice an employee to leave; however, with a bad manager in place, additional pay may not entice an employee to stay (Gandhi and Robison 2021). Employees are looking for a manager and organization that cares for their overall well-being. An unmanageable workload, unachievable KPIs, and a toxic work environment are evident signs that an employee's well-being is not a priority or value and, as a result, is a clear path to the exit door.

Organization-Initiated Separation

Employee separation can also be initiated by the organization. Organization-initiated separation doesn't always mean that the separation is due to negative factors. An employee may be offered a promotion within the organization, perhaps even to a regional or national level. As discussed in chapter 5, a great manager continuously coaches employees and has their best interests in mind. A great manager knows and understands an employee's career goals and sets them on a path to promotion, if desired. Reassignment is another option to give an employee a new challenge if upward mobility isn't currently available or desired. It is also an excellent way to reward an employee with (potentially) additional pay and the opportunity to learn a new scope or manage another department when a vacancy becomes available. Regardless of a positive organization-initiated separation, offboarding still needs to occur in the employee's current role as they prepare to move into the new one within the organization.

Occasionally, an organization initiates an employee separation based on negative factors. These separations come in the form of a layoff or termination. A layoff occurs when an employee is either permanently or temporarily released from employment, not because of an employee's performance but because of the organization's financial stability or the economy. A temporary layoff is considered a furlough and also warrants an offboarding process, and the furloughed employee should not be expected to perform any job-related duties or work during the furlough period.

Termination is typically related directly to an employee's performance or their violation of company policy or the law. Good hiring and training practices should prevent termination from being a surprise to an employee because, as discussed all throughout part II, a good manager provides ongoing feedback and coaching opportunities to an employee. This means if an employee is being terminated due to poor performance, then the manager has had ongoing coaching conversations with that employee about their performance and their lack of progress toward meeting the goals of the performance improvement plan. Occasionally, an employee may violate company policy, perform outside the profession's scope of practice, act against certification or licensure ethics, or even break the

Employment at Will

In the United States, employment at will is determined by each state's legislature regarding employee rights. If a state recognizes employment at will, employers can terminate an employee for any or no reason unless a law states otherwise. Employers can also elect whether or not an employee may see their personnel file. On the other hand, just as an employer can discharge an employee without warning, an employee can resign without notice. Managers must be aware of the laws in their area because the offboarding process may need to happen at a moment's notice.

Termination

If termination is the reason for separation, the offboarding process needs to be deployed in a different order than when an employee resigns. It is critical for the organization to begin the access removal section prior to the termination meeting. Key fob and key card access should be revoked before the items are collected. This prevents a terminated employee, who may be disgruntled, from doing harm to financial or other important data systems by deleting files or downloading sensitive data.

law by embezzlement, fraud, or other illegal acts. If an employee performs one of those acts, immediate termination is warranted.

When conducting a termination meeting, it is best to have the meeting in a neutral location, if possible. Larger fitness facilities may have multiple locations and a corporate office; if so, schedule the meeting to take place in the corporate office. If you do not have the option to schedule the meeting at an off-site location, host it in a private setting away from members and other employees and, ideally, near an exit. It is also recommended to include a third person, perhaps another management team member, to serve as a witness during the meeting. SHRM suggests being direct and clear at the start of the meeting that this is a termination meeting (Falcone 2018). State any justifications and facts objectively and stick to the point. Although termination meetings never get easy, it is important to remember that the individual you are talking to is human and should be treated with respect, dignity, and empathy.

Once the employee understands that they are being terminated, begin the conversation about the next steps. Be clear on the specifics of the offboarding process. If severance is included in the termination package, inform the employee and provide them with documentation on how it will be distributed and other important information. Unless the employee performed illegal acts and depending on the severity of the performance

issues, ask the employee if they need help packing personal items or if they would like to say goodbye to any colleagues. Although you need to treat the individual with dignity and respect, it is also just as important to maintain the safety and security of the organization, other employees, and members. The offboarding process should have already started behind the scenes by revoking the employee's access to any technology systems, including payroll and finance, member management, facility management, and employee management. Have a plan for what to do if the employee becomes agitated or violent during the meeting. It is critical that you follow any applicable federal, state, province, or local law and organizational policy throughout the termination process.

Positive Exit Experiences

Just as a positive recruitment experience is essential for engaged employees, a positive exit experience can leave a lasting impression on a former employee and affect the future of talent acquisition. When job searching, 71 percent of employees use referrals from inside an organization (Patrick and Sundaram 2018).

Communication is key to creating a positive exit experience when an employee chooses to leave your organization. It is important to show the employee resigning that they have a voice, a sense of accomplishment, and a sense of belonging. This

Severance Packages

Severance pay can be offered to an employee whose employment is terminated. The severance package can be based on several factors, such as length of employment, performance, and the details outlined in the offer letter at the time of hire. The Fair Labor Standards Act does not require that severance pay be offered to a terminated employee in the United States (U.S. Department of Labor, n.d.).

process may include an electronic survey, listening sessions, manager or peer feedback, and an official exit meeting.

An electronic survey should be sent before the employee's last work day. This allows the employee to invest energy and effort in answering questions. Be sure to write the questions thoughtfully to obtain valuable feedback without creating survey fatigue. The electronic survey is a great place to include the eNPS, as discussed in chapter 6. It can predict the likelihood of whether the employee will recommend the organization to friends in the future.

Listening sessions are a great way to capture qualitative information regarding the employee's experience. Consider asking questions that help improve the organization and capture insight into the things that are working really well and should be continued. It's worth noting that you shouldn't wait to ask these questions until someone leaves; questions such as these should be a continuous part of the coaching process. During the listening sessions, it is critical that you convey to the employee the amount of impact they had on the organization. Be prepared to share and highlight two or three accomplishments of the employee; they should clearly show that they mattered to the team and the organization. Before throwing a going-away party for the employee, have an honest conversation about how the employee would like to be celebrated. A good manager already knows if the employee prefers public praise with pomp and circumstance or a quiet thank you without attention; however, now is a good time to validate the employee's preference before making any final decisions.

Creating brand ambassadors and a strong alumni network is essential in developing a positive exit experience. While conducting these listening sessions and manager feedback opportunities, ask the outgoing employee how they would like to stay connected with the organization. Consider asking the employee how often and through which channels they would like to be communicated with and on what topics. If possible, obtain the employee's future mailing address so you can continue sending them invitations, holiday cards, and celebration opportunities. Continuing the relationship after

A positive exit experience includes a listening session in which the leaving employee shares insights that will help you build a better organization.

the employee is no longer an employee helps carry a positive brand image and a message about the company and the experience. This relationship makes fundraising or philanthropic outreach efforts less transactional later.

The last step in the offboarding process should be the final exit interview. The final exit interview should be primarily transactional if the listening sessions and other portions of the offboarding process have been completed appropriately. The final exit interview is when the employee turns in keys, access cards, laptops, or other job-related hardware. If the employee has an office on-site, this is also the time for the manager to assist with any last-minute item cleanup and ensure the employee hasn't left any personal belongings behind. See the sidebar Sample Offboarding Checklist for a sample employee offboarding checklist.

A positive exit experience means a former employee will be three times more likely to refer the employer to others (Gallup 2018). An employee is 85 percent more likely to have a positive exit if they experience these three things in their last three months of employment (Wigert and Agrawal 2019):

1. A manager has discussed job satisfaction and career development with the employee.
2. The employee had an honest conversation with someone about potentially leaving.
3. There is nothing the manager could have done to prevent the employee from leaving.

Simply put, cultivating a positive exit experience begins well before resignation.

Conclusion

Once you have built a rock star team and mapped out your employee journey, it is time to shift your focus to the physical environment in which your team members are working and to the programs and services they will be delivering. In the next chapter, you will learn the fundamentals of building, outfitting, and operating a brick and mortar fitness facility.

THINK IT THROUGH

- What are some of the effects of the "great resignation"?
- What are the different types of separation?
- Why is succession planning important?
- What is employment at will?
- What are critical questions to ask during an exit interview?
- What should be included in an offboarding checklist?

KEY TERMS

employment at will
exit interview
great resignation
offboarding checklist
separation
severance package
Society for Human Resource Management
succession plan

Sample Offboarding Checklist

Administrative

Complete the following paperwork:

- Collect the official letter of resignation.
- Prepare offboarding paperwork pertaining to pay and benefits.
- Obtain new mailing address, if employee is relocating.
- Process any outstanding reimbursements or expenses.
- Reconcile final company credit card statement.
- Complete any required nondisclosure agreements.

Collect the following assets:

- Laptop
- Company cell phone
- Organizational credit card
- Keys and key fobs
- Company ID cards and parking passes
- Name tags, business cards, and company-issued uniforms

Remove access to the following:

- Software licenses
- Any websites, company directories, and organizational charts
- Listserv, communication channels, and document storage platforms
- Any membership management, asset management, financial management, and employee management software

Knowledge Transfer

- Redirect emails and calls.
- Share policy, procedures, and guidelines of the supervised area with a manager or the interim employee who will be taking over the duties.
- Identify and share the structure and location of electronic and physical document storage plans.
- Update the status of ongoing projects or pipelines.
- Review recently completed and outstanding tasks.

Relationship Nurturing

- Connect internal and external stakeholders with new liaison.
- Share announcement of departure in consultation with outgoing employee.
- Plan events and gifts of appreciation.
- Deploy exit survey.
- Schedule listening sessions and official exit interview.
- Create a plan of action to continue the relationship.
- Add to alumni network database and email listservs.
- Analyze data collected during the exit process.

Products: Delivering World-Class Programs, Services, and Facilities

8

Brick and Mortar Facilities

Upon completion of this chapter, you will be able to do the following:

- Explain basic facility design principles
- Identify phases of the design process
- Interpret industry standards and guidelines
- Define and interpret the Americans with Disabilities Act of 1990
- Construct a standard operating procedure
- Create a facility opening and closing checklist

The number of online or virtual fitness businesses has grown over the last few years, and even more have continued to open since the COVID-19 pandemic. Although the number of health clubs in the United States dropped by almost 10,000 between 2019 and 2022, corresponding with the pandemic (IHRSA 2024), the fitness industry is expected to continue to bounce back with a predicted growth of 172 percent by 2028 (Smith 2023). As the growth of the fitness industry continues, understanding the basics of brick and mortar fitness facilities is compulsory for an effective fitness facility manager. As staffing models of fitness facilities have evolved, fitness facility managers' roles have too. In addition to recruiting and retaining members and employees, fitness facility managers need to become expert project managers so they can manage and grow the structural facilities, maintain and plan for equipment replacement, and remodel and expand to meet the ever-changing needs of members and evolving industry trends.

Types of Fitness Facilities

Fitness facilities come in various sizes, shapes, and structural configurations. Most fall into one of two categories: unattached or attached. Unattached fitness facilities are stand-alone buildings where the primary function is to serve as a fitness facility. Stand-alone fitness facilities are often considered midmarket, premium, premium-plus, or luxury clubs. Most nonprofits such as YMCAs, JCCs, community centers, and university and military facilities are built as stand-alone brick and mortar facilities. These stand-alone buildings may be anywhere from 20,000 square feet to more than 200,000 square feet, such as the massive 240,000-square-foot Auburn University Recreation and Wellness Center, which opened in 2013 (HOK 2024).

Attached fitness facilities, on the other hand, are housed within a structure that includes other businesses or tenants that serve other purposes than engaging in fitness. They come in various shapes and sizes and may be classed as A, B, or C properties by commercial real estate investors (Feldman Equities, n.d.). Class A properties are often the newest and most luxurious structures, with higher-end finishes and sometimes a dedicated brand and lifestyle. An example of a fitness facility in a class A property would be a lifestyle community or neighborhood built with a live, work, shop, and play purpose. Regarding leasing, a class A property costs the most per square foot compared to class B and class C properties. Class B properties are considered more practical in design. Most class B properties have basic amenities and functions. A class B property often was previously operated as a class A property, but the need for more renovation coupled with newer structures being built has changed its distinction. Class B properties lease at a lower price per square foot than class A and do not require as long of a lease. Class C properties are the lowest cost but require the most capital investment. Class C properties are typically more than 30 years old, lack updated infrastructure, and may have a lengthy deferred maintenance list. A fitness facility cannot operate in a class C property until renovations and investments shift the class to a B.

Many fitness facilities in attached locations are found in a strip mall format, often configured in a straight line or "U" or "L" shaped format. The physical location may have another business on either side of the fitness facility, or it may be located as an anchor, where only one side is attached to another business. Anchor locations typically come at a higher cost per square foot than the alternative, sandwiched option. High volume, low price, budget, and economy clubs are often located in strip mall settings. At the same time, higher-end boutique studios are also found in strip malls or, in urban environments, the popular mixed-use building where storefronts are located on the ground floor and residences are placed above them. Corporate and residential fitness centers are also located in office and residential buildings and are considered attached and class A properties, given that an on-site fitness facility is a recruitment tool for employers and a selling point for housing communities.

Building and Expanding Fitness Facilities

Fitness center owners and managers can grow their businesses in many ways. One of those ways is changing the built environment through renovating or expanding existing facilities or by opening an additional or satellite location. Construction projects are exciting, and it is expensive to build facilities. Including the fitness facility manager in the process is worthwhile, and therefore, a good fitness facility manager should know basic facility design principles.

A common term in the construction of new facilities is *design-build*. This occurs when one contract or entity manages the design and construction of a new facility. *Design-bid-build* occurs when the process includes requests for proposals, or bids, from the design process to the building process. Private, commercial, and for-profit businesses can implement the design-build strategy, while most nonprofit, community, university, or government-related facilities have to bid out projects.

Whether a project is design-build or design-bid-build, the design process occurs first. The first step of the multistage design process is to hire a licensed architect and enter into an agreement such as those provided by the American Institute of Architects (Tharrett 2017).

Programming Phase

The programming stage is an opportunity for the fitness facility's internal team to come together and answer the question, "What would it look like if we were wildly successful?" The team members should be prepared to conduct an internal review and discuss what is working well, what programs should be sunset or discontinued, what programs can grow, and what new initiatives or programs could be explored and offered with proper and adequate facilities. As mentioned in chapter 3, a SWOT analysis would be appropriate to conduct during this stage. Gather perspectives from key stakeholders, such as current fitness facility members and community partners. Update the market analysis of the area, and review industry trends and projections. Gathering information in the programming stage can be accomplished through surveys, focus groups, and structured and unstructured interview sessions. Ideally, the internal team should visit other inspirational facilities and newly constructed fitness centers to gain insight and ideas. For example, when a new recreation and well-being center is built on a college campus, it's common for the staff to travel to its peer institutions and to some of the architectural firm's recently completed projects before completing this stage. The architectural firm should request from you a preliminary overview of the programs, services, and personnel, along with any foreseeable growth plans, before beginning the schematic-design phase.

Schematic-Design Phase

The schematic-design stage pairs the programmatic wants and needs of the fitness facility and intersects them with the architect's fieldwork and expertise. The architect analyzes existing spaces and performs field measures if the project includes a renovation, expansion, second location, or new build. Behind the scenes, the firm interacts with local, state, and regulatory authorities to ensure proper zoning permissions and building permits are initiated (Tharrett 2017). This stage yields deliverables such as spreadsheets and charts with programmatic square foot allocations and a basic floor plan.

Design-Development Stage

Following the presentation of the schematic-design stage, the architect gathers feedback on the plans from the fitness facility's team to begin the design-development stage (Tharrett 2017). During the design-development stage, the architect uses the compiled feedback to change the first set of deliverables and creates a more concrete plan. The architect also meets with various engineers and contractors to gain insight into the project's structural, electrical, plumbing, and mechanical aspects. The management team's role in this stage is critical since the documents provided by the firm will include specific details about the project. You and your team should review these reports to ensure that the details meet the needs of your requested goals and objectives. A total cost for the project will be provided at the end of this stage. Any changes made to the plan should be done early on because change orders can be costly once the project begins.

Construction-Document Stage

The construction-document stage follows the design-development stage and provides the final documentation to begin the project. This includes securing permits required for the project. Similar to the schematic-design stage, the management team needs to stay closely involved with the architectural firm so that all the plans are accurate and represent the needs and desires of the group (Tharrett 2017). The final portion of this stage is to identify a selection of general contractors to be candidates for the bidding process.

Construction-Administration Stage

The final stage of the design process is the construction-administration stage. This includes the 30- to 45-day window of the bidding process and the selection of a general contractor to lead the project. The stage continues throughout the construction process until the project is completed and a final punch list is approved (Tharrett 2017). The final punch list includes all items related to the construction project that must be completed before the keys and ownership are turned over from the general contractor to the operator. The actual construction costs per square foot can vary based on market, inflation, and location. Although a team of trained professionals is overseeing the project from start to finish, the management team must stay closely involved throughout the process. Being knowledgeable and involved increases the likelihood of smoother project completion and transition when the management team takes ownership of the building. A best practice is to obtain all warranty information and documentation from the installation and have a system for management to access the materials quickly when needed.

Standards and Guidelines for Designing Fitness Facilities

In the United States, no set board or governing body dictates how a fitness facility is operated or structured. Depending on the location and what services are provided, permits and requirements are set forth by local, state, or federal laws. When a fitness facility includes an aquatic facility, for example, there are additional requirements, but this textbook does not cover aquatic facility management.

Standards and guidelines, however, do exist for fitness facilities. The American College of Sports Medicine publishes standards and guidelines in the textbook *ACSM's Health/Fitness Facility Standards and Guidelines* (2019). Standards refer to performance-based criteria and minimums to provide a safe exercise environment (ACSM 2019). Often, these standards are derived from local, state, or federal laws and regulations to protect the public. However, guidelines typically do not coincide with specific laws or regulations. They are best practices set forth by industry subject matter experts to enhance the fitness facility's member experience.

Standards

Various standards apply to a fitness facility's design, construction, and basic operation. One of the core standards is set forth by the Americans with Disabilities Act, known as ADA. Compliance with the Americans with Disabilities Act of 1990 is overseen by the Civil Rights Division of the U.S. Department of Justice. Beyond the United States, the United Nations' Convention on the Rights of Persons with Disabilities is an international treaty to promote and protect accessibility. Places such as Canada, Australia, and the European Union have their own equivalents to the ADA.

When constructing, renovating, or expanding a fitness facility, the design should include door widths with a minimum of 36 in. (91 cm) and have a ramp for any elevation change more than 0.5 in. (1.3 cm). Accessibility is essential when designing spaces, including allowing ample space for members in wheelchairs to navigate the facility and access membership desks, water fountains, light switches, and lockers while seated. In addition to navigation, fitness equipment should be spaced so that a minimum of 30 in. × 48 in. (76 cm × 122 cm) space is clear next to each equipment item to allow for safe entry and exit. Signs related to hazards and emergencies, such as exit signs, must be viewable by all members and guests and placed so that those with limited vision can still recognize exit pathways and hazards. It is important to note that these standards are a minimum and specific to human occupants.

Some fitness, maintenance, and operational equipment will not fit through a single-door frame or be within the size or weight required for a passenger elevator. Therefore, at least one freight elevator should be included when building a multi-level fitness facility. Installing or replacing fitness equipment without using a freight elevator can require technicians or staff to carry equipment up and down staircases, which increases the risk of injury to individuals and damage to equipment or the facility.

Fitness facilities must comply with all local, state, and federal building codes. The International Building Code is used or adopted in five states and some territories; however, localities may add code requirements. Be sure to check with local authorities before making any additions or renovations.

Guidelines

Space allocation and facility size may be among the most debated and controversial topics regarding fitness facility guidelines. In recent years, no industry guideline has been established for the total square feet dedicated per member in a health club; however, there are established guidelines for specific areas within a facility. For large, complex recreation centers such as those on university campuses, by the time the doors are open, the space has already been outgrown. The National Intramural and Recreational Sports Association (NIRSA), an organization for leaders in collegiate recreation, states that campus recreation centers should be based on a minimum of 10 gross square feet per student plus 1 to 1.5 gross square feet per university employee and 5 to 7.5 gross square feet per community member (Callendar 2009).

Physical Activity Spaces

When deciding how much square footage to allocate for specific areas, consider the number of members that the facility expects to have. On average, a fitness facility should allocate 10 to 14 square feet of physical activity space per member. A manager can also assume that approximately 25 percent of the total membership number would use the facility on any given day, and 33 percent of that daily total would enter during any given two-hour period (ACSM 2019).

Areas for Cardiorespiratory Training   Each physical activity area has size recommendations unique to its purpose, type of movement performed in the space, and size and quantity of equipment. Chapter 9 will address equipment-specific

Collegiate Well-Being and Recreation Centers

NIRSA space recommendations apply to basic university recreation centers. As the trend on college campuses to combine and integrate health and well-being with recreation continues to increase, space should be adjusted and expanded to accommodate the additional needs. Recreational and well-being facilities on college campuses often now include primary and secondary prevention services plus tertiary disease prevention. Examples include integrating the student health center, counseling and psychiatric services, health education and promotion, and substance use and recovery.

considerations. Allot space for cardiorespiratory training that is equivalent to 50 percent to 75 percent of the space allocated for strength training (ACSM 2019). Areas designated for cardiorespiratory training should have solid, preferably rubber, flooring, allowing space to be converted as needed. Electrical outlets appropriate for the number of cardio machines are needed, considering some machines require dedicated circuits. If Wi-Fi Internet is not strong, hardwired ethernet ports may also be needed.

Strength Training Areas   As the popularity of strength, body weight, and functional training grows, enough space must be planned for what members want (ACSM 2024). Adding new equipment as needed is much easier and more cost-effective than having too much and needing to remove it. Generally, at least one resistance training circuit should be offered, which takes approximately 600 to 800 square feet of space. Free-weight training areas should be the primary owner of space in a fitness center, with more than two times the space allocated for cardio. Qualified manufacturers should install rubberized and dedicated flooring for strength training areas. Various floor types are commonly designed as rolled or tiled products. A common practice involves installing inlay platforms designated as drop zones for Olympic lifting. Before selecting a product, consider how often, if at all, the layout may change in the future (Tharrett 2017).

Functional training areas are one of the most popular spaces in a fitness facility. Many members simply want to come in and use open space to move in a way that meets their fitness training goals. A starting point would be to dedicate the equivalent of 50 percent or more of the square footage allocated to free weights for the functional training areas. In addition to open space, this is an excellent opportunity to install turf that can be used for sports performance training and popularly used by the weekend athlete. This space can also house an area dedicated to stretching.

Group Fitness Studios   Group fitness and multipurpose studios are a must-have in most fitness facilities. Most health clubs around the globe offer group fitness programming. Facilities may have anywhere from one group fitness studio to eight or more at larger recreation centers. Group fitness studios should be built based on member demand. They typically have a capacity of 20 to 50 square

feet per person in the room, depending on the exercise performed and if any equipment is used. Shock-absorbing hardwood floors are preferred in group fitness studios. Flooring is also an excellent opportunity to represent and celebrate the company brand by designing logos to be placed on the floor.

Creating dedicated fitness studios for group cycling, yoga, Pilates, and barre is common and ideal. Group cycling has continued to grow in popularity since Johnny G (Goldberg) introduced Spinning to the world in 1991 (Spinning 2024). Group cycling studios' capacity can be determined by allocating 20 to 50 square feet of space per rider, depending on the ambience the fitness facility is trying to cultivate and on members' preferences. Flooring for group cycling studios should be rubber or hardwood. Yoga studios should have a firm, hardwood floor and a capacity that allows each class member to have 50 to 70 square feet of space. Depending on whether a fitness facility serves a niche market, apparatuses and other equipment may be installed to offer classes focused on inversions, aerial, silk, barre, and Bikram yoga. Pilates can typically be taught in the same space as yoga unless the fitness center plans to offer Pilates classes with reformers or other apparatuses, because if so, a dedicated Pilates studio with more space is needed (Tharrett 2017).

Many people attend group fitness classes for the social and community aspect, in addition to the escape from reality that group fitness provides. However, one needs to think about the five senses to create a space ideal for movement.

- *Sight.* Maximize natural light. Adjustable lighting should be placed in each space so the instructor can create an experience through illumination. Consider installing nightclub-style lighting that can move to music, change colors, and be set to scenes. It is vital to avoid flashing lights or any other strobes that could cause seizures. Equipment storage should be installed so that participants can quickly find what they need and be spaced so that an entire class doesn't go to one area of the room to get equipment. Mirrors should be on at least one wall in most studios, preferably in a space where participants can check their form from a side profile.

- *Sound.* A quality sound system designed for fitness instruction is essential. Headset microphones are required, and the instructor should be able to create an experience with sound and have access to adjusting music and microphone volume in addition to bass and treble elements. According to the American Council on Exercise, volume should not exceed 85 decibels (Jo et al. 2023).

- *Smell.* In a world that experienced COVID, members want to smell the cleanliness while in a fitness facility. This means keeping appropriate cleaners in the studios and having a regular cleaning schedule. Instructors can also introduce essential oils into classes such as yoga; it's important to ask participants in advance if they have any allergies and always provide a way to opt in or out.

- *Feel.* Regulated air temperature is essential to the exercise experience. A member should feel comfortable in the space while exercising at various levels of exertion. The temperature in physical activity areas should be adjustable and kept at 68 to 72 degrees Fahrenheit (20 to 22 degrees Celsius). Pilates and yoga studios should be held at a higher temperature than a regular physical activity area, with 72 to 76 degrees Fahrenheit (22 to 24 degrees Celsius) for Pilates and 72 to 85 degrees Fahrenheit (22 to 29 degrees Celsius) for yoga. Hot or Bikram yoga may increase the temperature to 105 degrees Fahrenheit (40.5 degrees Celsius); however, this is not typically recommended in a general health club or fitness facility and may lead to higher risks associated with exercise (Tharrett 2017).

- *Taste.* Taste doesn't have to mean literal taste, although some instructors may provide chocolates at the end of some relaxation classes. What is meant here is that discernment should be used in the design of the space. Managers should think about color choice and participant flow in the studio, and instructors should think about selecting music in good taste.

Personal Movement Experiences Another trend gaining momentum in fitness facilities is the creation of personal movement experiences and places for relaxation and recovery. These can be accommodated in a 120-square-foot space or standard office size. Personal movement experiences allow members to access an area dedicated to themselves for an at-home workout experience while in a fitness facility. These spaces often include a studio cycling bike such as a Peloton or Echelon, a digital screen on the wall that can display asynchronous workouts such as the Lululemon Studio, a small set of adjustable dumbbells, and an exercise mat. Relaxation spaces typically include a commercial-grade massage chair, a digital screen on the wall that can display asynchronous meditation classes or sounds, and props such as a yoga mat, blocks, blanket, and bolster. These spaces can be created by retrofitting offices that are no longer used or dividing unused racquetball courts into three separate spaces with dividers or branded screens.

Service Areas

In addition to the physical activity spaces, service areas and space for child care and aquatic activities are needed if the fitness facility offers those amenities. A dedicated reception, member, and guest services area should welcome those entering a facility. Expect to dedicate approximately 400 to 2,000 square feet of space to reception, depending on the total size of the facility and the membership base. Laundry is kept in the back of the house and takes up 150 to 200 square feet. Offices are around 120 square feet each. Remember that flexible workspace should be the focus, with private spaces available for meetings or services such as health coaching or massage.

According to the Health & Fitness Association (formerly called IHRSA), when designing locker rooms, expect 10 percent or more of the membership base to have access to day-use lockers at once (Aiello 2016). This trend is expected to climb as locker room sizes get smaller to make room for more inclusive and private changing spaces. Traditionally, a fitness facility manager could account for 70 percent of the membership renting lockers for long-term use; however, that number will likely decline due to the increase in private changing areas. Private showers continue to trend in popularity, and a fitness facility should allocate one shower for every 250 to 500 members.

Any experienced fitness facility manager knows that storage space and member circulation pathways are among the most important but neglected spaces when designing a fitness facility. Ideally, a minimum of 25 percent of the total fitness facility's square footage should be dedicated to storage. Space for foot traffic should account for 10 to 15 percent of the square footage and blend structured pathways and natural circulation. Members often create natural walkways based on commonly traveled areas through the facility. Hallways and transition pieces in flooring are examples of a structured pathway; however, avoid trying to develop forced pathways through physical activity areas with designs or color changes in the flooring, because what is planned isn't always what members actually do.

Front-of-House and Back-of-House Operations

Each of the areas within a fitness facility is considered either front-of-house or back-of-house. *Front-of-house* and *back-of-house* terminology is used to differentiate the amount of exposure a member, guest, or customer has to a team member or departmental area. For example, the sales department has direct contact with members, guests, and potential members daily and would be classified as front-of-house. The maintenance department has little to no direct contact with members, guests, and potential members daily; although their work directly affects the member experience, they would be considered back-of-house. Think of it as similar to a restaurant: the servers, hosts, and bartenders are front-of-house, while the kitchen team members are back-of-house. Safety and member experience are two criteria used to determine whether an area or operation should be considered back-of-house or front-of-house.

Safety

Safety should be the primary determining factor whether or not something should be considered back-of-house. Any operation, such as laundry areas and housekeeping closets, that could expose members to dangerous chemicals or agents should be kept in a secured area. If a fitness facility has a pool, aquatic features, or saunas or spas, then the equipment rooms for those should also be in a secured location. Maintenance areas where tools and equipment are stored or where maintenance work may be performed should also be secure and off-limits to members. Access to these areas should also be restricted from team members not cleared or qualified to work with hazardous materials. It is recommended that these areas be secured with key card access so an entry log can be kept of who entered the areas and at what time. Key access should also be provided as a backup if a power outage results in inoperable door sensors. Mechanical closets and server rooms are also considered back-of-house and should not be dual-purposed as storage areas.

Member Experience

After safety precautions, the member experience should be the primary consideration when determining back-of-house versus front-of-house operation. One way of keeping the separation is to limit the amount of accessory equipment needed at an equipment checkout desk, a front-of-house service requiring a team member to manage it. Use creative and aesthetically pleasing storage to place accessories such as weight belts, bar pads, jump ropes, foam rollers, and sports balls right where the member needs them. This prevents the need to dedicate such large square footage to a welcome desk or equipment checkout area. The minimalist approach to the reception and entry area encourages a welcoming environment by creating the opportunity to apply higher-end hotel-style check-in areas in a fitness facility (figure 8.1).

Consider also the team member experience and create a space for the employees to step away from the member area (figure 8.2). Employee break rooms, offices, storage areas, and conference rooms should be kept away from the members' view; this prevents breaking the fourth wall and protects the magic of the member experience.

Housekeeping as Front-of-House

In a post-COVID-19 world, members want to see, feel, and smell "the clean." Prior to 2019, it was common for housekeeping staff to clean during late night or early morning hours when a fitness facility was not open to the public. Although it is still advantageous to do deep cleaning when no members are present, it should become an expected practice that team members visibly clean the fitness facility throughout the day. In addition, housekeeping team members may interact more with members than any other team members, so they not only can help create a positive member experience but may also be able to spot unusual behaviors that could pose a risk to the facility or other members.

FIGURE 8.1   Recreation facility entrance with hotel stations.
Elke Selzle/Photographer's Choice RF/Getty Images

FIGURE 8.2   Employee space set away from the member area.
Reza Estakhrian/The Image Bank/Getty Images

Case Study: Assessing Your New Facility

Greg Corack

A New Facility

East Central University recently added a recreational facility to a satellite campus roughly 10 minutes west of its central core. The new fitness facility, located near a local hospital and in the center of a health-focused campus, serves approximately 2,000 students and a large constituent base of health care providers. The recreation space is colocated with dining, university offices, study, and meeting rooms as part of a larger student union concept. One-third of the union's 75,000 square feet is dedicated to health and well-being, housing two multipurpose courts, two exercise studios, a 5,000-square-foot cardio deck, a 5,000-square-foot strength training zone, and locker rooms. The planning team intentionally chose everything in the building, from lighting fixtures to flooring colors, to attract a more sophisticated clientele.

Left Out From the Beginning

Fitness professionals were mostly left out of the planning process, with access to architectural designs limited until the construction phase was within 12 months of completion. Change orders allowed for the last-minute installation of coaxial and ethernet cables at an increased expense and the addition of laundry facilities adjacent to the access control desk. Although many portions of the facility were aesthetically pleasing, functionality limitations presented challenges that needed to be addressed in many facilities during the fitness equipment ordering process. Rounded exterior walls with unshaded floor-to-ceiling windows, coupled with unguarded basketball court openings, made adding some machines almost impossible. Safety issues, including unpadded brick walls near a basketball goal and the lack of emergency exit alarms, created significant headaches during the first six months of operation.

Soft Opening

During the first 90 days of operation, East Central University recreation staff made important members-first decisions. The initial equipment order was split into two purchases, one to open the facility and one six months after determining member flow and popular opinion. The hours of operation mimicked those of a traditional college campus, staying open from early morning to late evening to establish usage patterns. Wall colors and branding were intentionally left out of the facility, allowing members to provide feedback on what they wanted from the new space. Last, a second group fitness studio was purposely left open and unused to see how members used the area for personalized exercise.

Assess the Right Way

After three months of operation, the 3,000 members who accessed the facility were presented with an online survey via personalized email notification. Those receiving the survey were sent two reminders and were prompted at the access control desk with friendly nudges from staff. Incentives included gift cards to dining facilities inside the student union and free East Central University apparel. Over 700 members (23 percent) responded to the questions on their feelings about facility use and operational capacity. Questions regarding the selection of new fitness equipment, the color and branding of large walls, and the outfitting of a fitness studio were presented. Additionally, the assessment allowed popular opinion to guide operating hours.

You Asked, We Listened

Using data from the survey, administrators devised a plan to complete the facility during the next eight months and host a grand opening on the building's first anniversary. Fitness equipment,

—— (continued) ——

including half-racks with drop zones, Jacobs Ladder machines, stair climbers, various cable-guided pieces, and additional free weights were purchased based on survey data. One of the two fitness studios was turned into a functional training space with new flooring, a wall-mounted Queenax training rig, room for medicine ball throws, and open areas for personalized fitness. The multipurpose courts were outfitted with new branded wall padding to accent university athletic colors and bring an identity to the satellite facility. Walls were painted to build an aesthetically pleasing view from cardio machines.

Discussion

When opening a new facility, it is vital to think about your members and how their use of the facility affects operations. Expect growing pains during the first few weeks of operation, but facility managers must keep the member experience at the forefront. The hours that work at one location may be utterly inconvenient for the members at one five miles away. Physical layout, facility flow, and even a space's color palette vary greatly based on clientele. Something as simple as changing the music played from 5:00 a.m. to 8:00 a.m. could alter who decides to renew their membership the following year. In a university setting, the different subcultures on campus determine the success of programmatic offerings, member engagement, and the use of specific equipment. Simple assessment processes provide valuable data managers will undoubtedly use to enhance member satisfaction.

Fitness Facility Signage

One of the ways to enhance the member experience and provide a safe exercise environment is to display adequate signage throughout the facility. Remember that signage may be required by local, state, or federal law, so do your homework to ensure compliance. The American College of Sports Medicine sets five standards for signage in the textbook *ACSM's Health/Fitness Facility Standards and Guidelines*. These five standards address cautionary signage, emergency and safety signage, AED locations, ADA and OSHA signage, and specifications set by ASTM International (ACSM 2019).

In addition to required signage, a fitness facility should include wayfinding, informational, and instructional signage. Wayfinding signage should indicate locations and directions to spaces such as physical activity areas, restrooms, and locker rooms. Informational signage includes group fitness class schedules, instructional programs or other activity schedules, educational information such as heart rate monitoring, hours of operation, and team member information. If displaying team member biographies or photos on public-facing directories or signage, consider only listing the person's first name and last initial to protect the team member's privacy. Instructional signage should include

fitness facility policies, procedures, and guidelines, how to provide member feedback, and any additional operating instructions for equipment or facility features.

Signage should be placed at an appropriate height that is visible to members (remember that some members may use wheelchairs) and attached to the wall in a manner that does not create a safety hazard. Limit word use so that the instructions and directions are clear to the reader, with dedicated white space around them in the sign. Include symbols and images when appropriate. When creating signage meant to educate members and guests on policies, procedures, and guidelines, be sure to write in a manner that cues the correction or provides the direction rather than addressing the negative behavior. For example, fitness facilities often display signage carrying a sentiment of "don't do this." While technically not incorrect, this creates an environment that feels authoritative and demeaning. Keep in mind that there are many reasons a person won't engage in a health-positive behavior; a fitness facility shouldn't create more reasons by adding barriers to entry or creating an unwelcoming environment. An example of cueing the correction is "Control your lift at all times while strength training" (versus "Don't drop the weights").

Continuity of Operations Plan

Fitness facilities that are considered government-affiliated facilities, such as public universities; parks and recreation areas; community centers; and Morale, Welfare, and Recreation (military) centers, may also be required to have a *continuity of operations plan*, or COOP. A COOP is designed so that organizations can continue mission-critical operations with limited disruption during or after hazards or emergencies. The plan should be ready to put into operation within 12 hours of activation and should be able to sustain operations for 30 days.

Create signs with the member in mind. Think through the basic needs, wants, or frequently asked questions. Monitor the fitness facility website or app analytics to see which topics or areas members spend the most time searching. A member often wants to know what they can do, when they can do it, and how they can participate. Signage is an opportunity to continue brand representation, and even when it comes to policies and procedures, they should still be on brand.

Standard Operating Procedures

Standard operating procedures, or SOPs, are step-by-step instructions to guide team members in carrying out complex yet routine operations. Think of SOPs as the set of instructions that come with products such as furniture. SOPs are essential for fitness facility operations because they provide guidance so that a frequently occurring procedure, such as opening or closing a facility, is carried out in a manner that promotes baseline quality no matter who is executing the duty. SOPs are warranted and critical for any duty requiring quality assurance, safety, or security.

When writing SOPs, the focus should be on systems rather than individuals. Automation is key when creating effective SOPs. Any person in a position that meets the minimum requirements to carry out the duty should be able to do so by following the directions. An updated organizational chart should always be included in the policies, procedures, and guidelines so that the SOPs may be written to indicate positions eligible to carry out duties. For example, if payment card industry data security standards (PCI compliance training) is required for anyone selling a membership or other merchandise item at the point of sale, then any person in a position who has completed the training should

be able to follow the SOP for selling memberships when needed.

SOPs should be easy to read and understand. Use language that is universally understood and instructions that are clear, concise, and action-oriented. Complement the text with flow charts, images, measurable checklists, and short videos. SOPs are considered ancillary and complementary to team member onboarding and training and should not be treated as a replacement. If possible, create demo environments for technology-related systems such as membership management, point of sale, or building controls so that team members can train, practice, and retrain as needed. Although many templates for basic fitness facility SOPs are available online, it's best to write them in-house to promote ownership from the management team and to ensure the procedures are effective for your specific environment.

Examples of fitness facility SOPs to include are opening and closing the facility, selling a membership, giving a tour to a prospective member, onboarding a personal training client, and activating portions of the emergency action plan (EAP) (which will be covered in chapter 12). See the sidebars Standard Operating Procedures: Daily Opening Checklist and Standard Operating Procedures: Daily Closing Checklist for examples of SOPs for opening and closing a fitness facility.

Conclusion

The organizational environment, size, and corporate structure of a fitness facility affect how much autonomy and the level of decision-making power you have as a fitness facility manager at a brick and mortar facility. Regardless of the scope of your responsibilities, a basic understanding of the operation of a brick and mortar facility empowers you to be successful in your career and be able to influence facility renovations and equipment purchases.

Standard Operating Procedures: Daily Opening Checklist

Casey Gilvin

Building Infrastructure
- Turn on lighting system.
- Unlock doors/rooms for open access.
- Engage auto door-opening switch.
- Turn on fans and HVAC, or confirm the system is working.
- Confirm common utilities are functioning correctly (e.g., water, Internet, cable TV).

AV System/Digital Signage/Entertainment
- Confirm audio/video and public address system are functioning.
- Turn on digital signage (if applicable).
- Turn on entertainment systems (TVs).

Emergency and Risk Management
- Confirm emergency exits are accessible and free of obstructions.
- Confirm fire alarm pull stations are accessible and free of obstructions.
- Confirm staff communication tools (radios) are functioning.
- Confirm AED is on hand, accessible, and functioning in specific locations as part of the risk management/emergency action plan (EAP).
- Confirm first aid equipment is stocked and on hand in specific locations as part of the risk management/EAP.

Member Management and Point of Sale
- Confirm that the member management system is functioning.
- Confirm that the point of sale is functioning with adequate starting cash as part of the money management and cash handling part of the PCI compliance plan.

Common Areas

- Confirm areas and hallways are accessible and free of obstructions.

Locker Rooms

- Confirm custodial staff have stocked locker rooms with necessary items (e.g., toilet paper, soap, hand sanitizer, towels).
- Unlock day-use lockers.

Laundry

- Confirm system is functioning and ready for towel service protocols.

Fitness Areas

- Confirm cardio equipment is turned on and free of visible issues.
- Confirm weight equipment and machines are free of visible issues.
- Confirm fitness areas are free of obstructions and equipment is stored in proper locations.

Studios

- Confirm that the area is free of obstructions and that equipment is stored in proper locations.
- Confirm audio/video and light system functioning.

Courts

- Confirm that court areas are free of obstructions and visible issues.
- Confirm that backboard pads and rims are secured properly and that nets are free of damage.

Staffing

- Confirm that required minimal staff personnel are on site and in assigned positions to support facility opening.

Standard Operating Procedures: Daily Closing Checklist

Casey Gilvin

Building Infrastructure
- Turn off the lighting system.
- Lock doors/rooms for closing.
- Disengage auto door-opening switch.
- Adjust fans and HVAC (or confirm schedule) as part of the ventilation plan.
- Set alarm (verify alarm system is functioning).

AV System/Digital Signage/Entertainment
- Power down (place in sleep mode) audio/video and public address system.
- Turn off digital signage (if applicable).
- Turn off entertainment systems (TVs).

Emergency and Risk Management
- Confirm emergency exits are accessible and free of obstructions.
- Confirm fire alarms are accessible and free of obstructions.
- Check in staff communication tools (radios) and charge units.
- Confirm AED is on hand, accessible, and functioning in specific locations as part of the risk management/emergency action plan (EAP).
- Confirm first aid equipment is stocked and on hand in specific locations as part of the EAP.

Member Management and Point of Sale
- Complete the point of sale procedure for daily closeout.

Common Areas

- Confirm areas are free of obstructions and furniture is returned to designated areas.

Locker Rooms

- Confirm custodial staff have stocked locker rooms with necessary items (e.g., toilet paper, soap, hand sanitizer, towels).
- Unlock day-use lockers.

Laundry

- Transfer dirty towels in the facility for laundry service.
- Stock facility areas with clean towels for the next day service.

Fitness Areas

- Return equipment (weights, barbells, benches, accessories) to designated spaces.
- Verify fitness areas are free of obstructions and ready for the next shift.
- Restock disinfecting wipes, towels, and sprayers.

Studios

- Return equipment to designated spaces.
- Power down audio/video and lighting systems.

Courts

- Verify that courts are free of obstructions and visible issues.

Final Checks

- Sweep designated spaces for members and guests.
- Confirm all patrons are out of the building and the building is prepared for shutdown.

THINK IT THROUGH

- What is the difference between standards and guidelines?
- What are examples of ACSM standards and guidelines?
- What are the square footage recommendations by ACSM, the Health & Fitness Association, and NIRSA?
- What are the stages in the design-build process?
- What is a standard operating procedure?

KEY TERMS

ACSM

Americans with Disabilities Act

closing checklist

design-build phases

guidelines

Health & Fitness Association

NIRSA

opening checklist

property classes

standard operating procedure

standards

9

Fitness Equipment

Upon completion of this chapter, you will be able to do the following:

- Differentiate between leasing and buying equipment
- Identify common types of fitness equipment
- Explain the functionality of common types of fitness equipment
- Design an effective equipment layout based on goals
- Implement a preventative maintenance program
- Create an equipment replacement plan
- Plan and budget for furniture, fixtures, and equipment

Chapter 8 showed you everything you need to know to design your fitness facility effectively. This chapter teaches you what equipment to put in your facility. Various types of fitness equipment include cardiorespiratory equipment, selectorized machines, cable-driven and plate-loaded machines, free weights, and training accessories. In the ever-changing world of fitness facility management, staying current with the latest in fitness equipment is crucial. Facilities must carefully select the right mix of equipment to create an exceptional experience and best serve their members. Done well, this can significantly enhance the effectiveness and appeal of your facility, differentiating it from the competition.

Purchasing Versus Leasing

Before delving into the different types of equipment and their purposes, understanding the two primary methods you can use to acquire fitness equipment for your facility, buying or leasing, is essential. This critical decision affects your facility's financial position and operations. Buying fitness equipment

refers to the outright purchase and ownership of the equipment. When leasing, you agree to pay a monthly fee to use the equipment for a specified period, typically one to five years. There are pros and cons you need to consider with both approaches.

Purchasing equipment has several benefits. Purchasing provides long-term cost savings since there are no monthly leasing fees. When you own equipment, it is considered an asset that can be sold or traded in on new equipment in the future. Owning equipment also allows your facility to customize and modify the equipment as desired. However, there are some drawbacks to purchasing, as opposed to leasing. Depending on the financial situation of a facility, the upfront cost can cause a financial strain. When equipment is purchased, the maintenance and repair costs are your facility's responsibility, which can also be a financial strain. Finally, due to the accelerated rate of innovation and technology, there is a risk of the equipment becoming dated or obsolete, which requires expensive upgrades or replacement.

Just as purchasing equipment has pros and cons, so does leasing equipment. Leasing can be a much more financially viable option for facilities with a tight budget due to the lower upfront cost. Since leases are for a finite amount of time, facilities can upgrade equipment more frequently to stay current with technological advances without significant upfront costs. Many leases also include a maintenance agreement for preventative maintenance and repair throughout the contract period. Leasing offers flexibility in variety and quantity, allowing fitness facilities to quickly adapt to changing member needs and evolving fitness trends. However, leasing does have its downside. Due to the leasing fees that accumulate over time, the overall cost is higher than when purchased. Since your facility doesn't own the equipment, it has no asset or resale value. Finally, unlike owned equipment, facilities cannot customize or modify the equipment because they must adhere to the terms of the lease agreement.

Making the best decision regarding leasing or buying fitness equipment for your facility is crucial for success. When making this decision, you must consider long-term goals, financial implications, commitment length, maintenance resources, technological innovation, and expansion and growth strategies. Considering these factors and the pros and cons of purchasing and leasing helps you make an informed decision that aligns with your facility's resources and supports your strategic plan.

Types of Fitness Equipment

Whether equipment is purchased or leased, a fitness facility needs to understand the diverse needs of its members and provide various types of fitness equipment to meet those needs. You must research, acquire member feedback, and analyze trends to understand those needs. Then, by aligning this information with different equipment, your facility can create an exceptional experience that meets and exceeds members' expectations.

Cardiorespiratory Equipment

Machines and devices designed to improve members' overall cardiorespiratory health and fitness are called cardiorespiratory equipment. This type of equipment is usually located in the cardio section of a fitness facility. Members use it to engage large muscle groups to elevate the heart rate and increase endurance. Cardiorespiratory equipment provides members the opportunity to perform

aerobic exercise in a way that they prefer in a controllable and safe environment. Because of the variety and ability to control cardiorespiratory equipment variables (such as speed, resistance, and incline), members of all demographics and fitness levels can benefit from cardiorespiratory equipment. It can provide beginner exercisers with a low-impact, unintimidating way to start their fitness journey. Athletes and experienced exercisers can use this equipment to push themselves to achieve goals. Cardiorespiratory equipment also benefits members with physical limitations or those recovering from injury. Due to its broad appeal, cardiorespiratory equipment is a staple of most fitness facilities. There are several different types of cardiorespiratory equipment machines for fitness facilities.

Treadmills

The treadmill is likely to be the most common piece of fitness equipment in fitness facilities. Treadmills are stationary machines that allow users to walk, jog, or run on a moving belt. Treadmills permit users to adjust the speed and grade to customize the intensity of the workout. A treadmill's soft deck minimizes impact, making it a great alternative to running outdoors. Given the low impact and ability to control workout parameters, treadmills appeal to most members.

Elliptical Trainers

Elliptical machines also are common in most fitness facilities. An elliptical trainer is a stationary machine that simulates walking, jogging, or running motions through an oval (elliptical) movement while the arms move back and forth. This elliptical motion causes little to no impact, which makes elliptical trainers a great alternative to high-impact movements, such as running. Most ellipticals allow the user to adjust the resistance, incline, and stride length, which helps accommodate various fitness levels. Elliptical trainers are great because they offer a full-body low-impact cardiorespiratory training experience.

Stationary Bikes

Along with treadmills and ellipticals, stationary bikes are popular in fitness facilities. There are several types of stationary bikes, including upright bikes, recumbent bikes, and indoor cycling bikes. Similar to an outdoor bicycle, users can adjust the bike to fit their body type by adjusting the position of the seat and handlebars. All stationary bikes allow users to simulate outdoor cycling indoors while controlling resistance. Due to their comfortable and seated design, stationary bikes offer a convenient and safe method of cardiorespiratory exercise that most members can use.

Stair Climbers

Stair climbers, also called step mills or steppers, offer users a more challenging cardiorespiratory workout by mimicking the act of climbing stairs. The user steps up and down on a rotating set of steps, which focuses on heavily engaging the muscles in the lower body while elevating the heart rate. Since stair climbers have adjustable speeds, they tend to be used by members with a higher fitness level seeking a more challenging cardiorespiratory workout.

Adaptive Motion Trainers

An adaptive motion trainer (AMT) is a combination of an elliptical and a stair climber. On an AMT, the user can adjust the stride length, incline, and resistance level. A feature that makes the AMT unique is that it offers the user a motion that is not fixed like an elliptical or stair climber. AMTs appeal to members of various fitness levels, especially those who prefer the freedom to move outside a fixed plane of motion.

Rowing Machines

Rowing machines, also known as *ergometers*, provide a full-body workout by allowing the user to simulate the motion of rowing a boat. Users sit on a seat, grab the handles, and push and pull against resistance, which engages the upper body, lower body, and core, creating a very challenging full-body workout. On most rowers, users can adjust the resistance, which allows them to customize the intensity of the exercise. In addition to traditional ergometers, SkiErgs are another popular machine located in functional training studios and on the fitness floor. Users stand, grab the handles, and pull down against the resistance. While generally considered cardiorespiratory equipment, the rower also provides some strength training.

Other Types of Cardiorespiratory Equipment

We have covered the most common cardiorespiratory machines seen in fitness facilities. However, other less standard equipment may benefit members. Self-powered treadmills are a great example. This type of treadmill moves based on the user's power, eliminating the need for electricity and providing a more natural running experience. Another example of unconventional cardiorespiratory equipment is an upper-body ergometer. This machine produces the motion of rowing or cycling for the upper body using hand pedals, creating a cardiorespiratory workout using the upper back, shoulders, and arm muscles. Upper-body ergometers are a great addition to your equipment selection and provide an inclusive environment where members who use wheelchairs can work on cardiorespiratory endurance. Vertical climbing machines simulate scaling a wall, and devices consisting of a loop of rope that can be continuously pulled provide cardiorespiratory workouts. These and other less common types of fitness equipment add variety, offer unique workout experiences, and can attract different members seeking these activities to improve their overall cardiorespiratory health and fitness. Therefore, consider them when choosing cardiorespiratory equipment for your fitness facility.

Strength Equipment

Strength training equipment is designed to help members work on their muscular strength and endurance. Most strength training does not require

---

Additional Features of Cardiorespiratory Equipment

In addition to the features specific to the equipment mentioned, cardio machines may have other features. For example, some cardiorespiratory machines have predesigned workouts, heart rate monitoring technology, wearable device connectivity, built-in fans, safety features, and entertainment options. Such features vary with the type of equipment, brand, and model. With the constant technological innovation occurring in the fitness industry, the number of features available in cardiorespiratory fitness equipment will continue to increase, thus providing a more personalized and superior experience for your members.

a power source. The various types of strength training equipment are designed to meet the needs of a wide variety of members and can be adjusted to all body types.

Plate-Loaded Equipment

Fitness facilities generally have an area dedicated to what is known as plate-loaded fitness equipment. This strength training equipment requires members to change the weight by adding or removing weight plates. These machines typically focus on one body part and consist of a frame with handles or bars and places where weight plates can be loaded. Weight plates usually come in 2.5-, 5-, 10-, 25-, 35-, and 45-pound increments. Plate-loaded equipment is versatile and practical. This equipment allows for incremental weight adjustments, accommodating members of all fitness levels. Members can gradually add weight as they become stronger, enabling them to see progress toward their fitness goals. Another benefit of plate-loaded equipment is that you can invest in a few sets of plates and use them across multiple plate-loaded machines, which adds to cost efficiency.

Plate-loaded equipment is desirable to members such as bodybuilders, powerlifters, and people looking to build strength and mass. This type of strength training equipment gives these members the flexibility to load heavy weights and target muscles or groups of muscles. Experienced exercisers also appreciate the incremental weight adjustments and the challenge that plate-loaded machines can bring to their exercise routines.

Although possibly intimidating to a beginning exerciser, plate-loaded machines can be an excellent way to learn strength training techniques, which helps build a solid exercise foundation. Most plate-loaded machines move on a fixed path, so there is little risk for error. The ability to gradually increase weight also helps a beginner progress safely and effectively.

Plate-loaded fitness equipment can be a valuable asset to a fitness facility. Whether a member wants to do serious strength training, focus on bodybuilding, or improve overall health and fitness, plate-loaded equipment offers a way to achieve those goals.

Selectorized Equipment

Selectorized fitness equipment is a common type of strength training equipment that allows members to adjust the amount of weight they are lifting by using a selector pin inserted in a specific place in a stack of weights. This type of equipment eliminates the need to change the weight by adding or removing plates. This differs from plate-loaded equipment, which requires members to load and unload weight plates across different machines. Fitness facilities often use selectorized machines because of their convenience and versatility. A selectorized machine provides a wide range of weight options that are easy for a member to adjust. These machines have a small footprint and are usually easy for members to use. Furthermore, because of their design, selectorized equipment tends to be safer and easier for members to use than plate-loaded machines or free weights (discussed later in the chapter).

Many types of members can benefit from using selectorized equipment. Due to the ability to quickly understand how to use and adjust the weight stack, beginning exercisers stand to reap huge benefits from this type of equipment. Selectorized equipment provides a high level of support and stability, adding to the comfort of newer exercisers. Furthermore, the equipment generally targets one body part and includes diagrams and clear instructions that help members use it safely, correctly, and confidently. While intermediate and advanced exercisers may prefer other types of strength training, they still appreciate the convenience and efficiency of selectorized equipment because it allows them to isolate specific muscles. Selectorized machines are great for members looking for an easy-to-follow, controlled, and guided workout experience. Often, selectorized machines are arranged according to the body parts they are tailored to, allowing members to easily follow a circuit of these machines to perform a full-body workout.

Most fitness facilities have a wide variety of selectorized fitness equipment. Its ease of use, versatility, and safety features make it a valuable tool for members of all fitness levels, allowing them to effectively achieve their health and fitness goals.

Cable-Driven Equipment

Cable-driven fitness equipment, commonly made up of cable machines or functional trainers, consists of a pulley system with adjustable cables, handles, and attachments, allowing members to perform various exercises. This modality often uses pin-adjusted weight stacks, like in selectorized equipment, to control resistance levels. The machines offer a range of exercise options that allow for diverse and creative workouts. While plate-loaded or selectorized equipment is primarily designed for one specific purpose, one cable machine may enable members to do many different exercises. Members can perform exercises targeting specific muscles or groups of muscles simultaneously. Cable machines do not have a fixed path of motion, unlike plate-loaded and selectorized machines. The adjustable nature of this equipment allows for different angles of movement, which can mimic natural movement patterns. The machines also offer a greater range of motion than other strength training equipment. Given cable-driven equipment's freedom and flexibility, it is one of the preferred modalities for *functional training*, which is defined as exercise that mimics real-life movements. The variety offered by cable machines provides members with almost endless exercise options and possibilities.

Cable-driven equipment offers different benefits for different members. Exercise enthusiasts who value functional training, such as recreational sports enthusiasts, semiprofessional and professional athletes, and advanced exercisers, will likely be attracted to cable machines. Cable machines are particularly effective for sports-specific activities and functional training because they can be used to challenge coordination, balance, strength, and core at the same time. Beginning exercisers and those with physical limitations or injuries also often enjoy using cable machines. They want the freedom and control these machines offer and the versatility to efficiently perform full-body workouts. Due to the level of control a member has over these machines, beginner exercisers tend to feel safe and confident when using them.

Cable machines appeal to members of all fitness levels, which is why they are good to offer in your fitness facility. From an advanced member seeking to improve sports performance to a beginner looking to get functionally stronger, cable machines can provide an engaging experience.

Free Weights

Free weights include dumbbells, barbells, weight plates, and other items independent from machines and other apparatus. Free weights provide a versatile and customizable way to perform strength training exercises. Fitness facilities tend to have areas designated for free weights, including racks and benches. Out of all the types of fitness equipment, free weights provide the most freedom of movement. There are few limitations to the ways members can use free weights. Free weights are excellent for compound exercises that target muscle groups and engage stabilizing muscles.

While using free weights helps with almost any fitness goal, members need a base level of knowledge, skill, and control to use them safely, so you tend to see more savvy exercisers using them. These experienced exercisers appreciate the capabilities of free weights and take advantage of them. While beginners can exercise with free weights, they often use modalities like selectorized or cable machines to build a base level of fitness and competence before moving on to free weights. If beginning exercisers decide to use free weights, they should be encouraged to start with light weights that they can control safely. Due to the skills needed, many fitness facilities provide complimentary training sessions to guide and instruct newer exercisers interested in training with free weights. Exercising with free weights can provide members with great results but requires the highest level of competency out of all the types of fitness equipment.

Free weights are an excellent option for strength training equipment at a fitness facility. Whether used as a solo solution for strength training or in conjunction with selectorized, plate-loaded, and cable machines, they provide an effective way for members to achieve their health and fitness goals.

Fitness Accessories

In addition to the different types of fitness equipment, members can also use fitness accessories to hit their health and fitness goals. Fitness accessories are equipment and tools that can be used on their own or to enhance workouts and provide additional training options and varieties. Typical accessories include resistance bands, stability balls, medicine balls, suspension trainers, kettlebells, foam rollers, exercise mats, and more. Fitness accessories can be used for various types of training, such as cardiorespiratory workouts, strength training, flexibility and mobility exercises, and injury treatment and prevention. All members of all fitness levels can use fitness accessories if they are used safely and correctly. The versatility, variety, and ability to enhance workouts of all types make them valuable tools for fitness facilities and members.

Cost and Quantity of Equipment

The cost of fitness equipment varies significantly. Factors such as the type of equipment, brand, model, quality, and features affect the cost. Most fitness equipment manufacturers have different options, ranging from budget-friendly choices to high-end, commercial-grade models. It is essential that you only use commercial-grade equipment in your fitness facility. Commercial-grade equipment is built to withstand heavy use more frequently, while home-use equipment is built for fewer people using it infrequently. Placing noncommercial grade equipment in your facility could pose a legal risk to you and injury risk to your members. The price range for fitness equipment tends to fall into three categories:

> *Entry-level equipment*—cost-effective options for smaller fitness facilities or those with a tight budget
>
> *Midlevel equipment*—moderately priced equipment that balances features and cost
>
> *High-end equipment*—cutting-edge, top-of-the-line equipment built for heavy use, with advanced features, long-term durability, and enhanced performance

The actual cost of fitness equipment can also vary based on geographic location, availability, and market demand. You should always research and compare prices from different suppliers or retailers to better understand the equipment cost and value you are getting for all types of equipment.

In addition to cost, you must also decide on the quantity of fitness machines you need to equip your facility to serve your members properly. When determining the quantity of the different pieces of fitness equipment to have at your facility, consider factors like the size of the facility, the number of members, the types of members, the kind of experience, and the expected demand. It is common to have multiple units of popular equipment to ensure the ability to accommodate large numbers of members during peak times. Ultimately you need to base the quantity of equipment on the specific needs of your facility, your members, and your budget.

Equipment Layout

As discussed in chapter 8, ADA standards cover the appropriate placement of fitness equipment within a fitness facility. You must ensure that all your fitness equipment is placed in an arrangement compliant with ADA requirements. By doing so, your fitness facility will be equipped to accommodate individuals with disabilities and demonstrate its commitment to inclusivity and equal access. Offering fitness equipment that is accessible to all individuals is not just a legal requirement but a compassionate and inclusive approach that promotes equal opportunities for exercisers of all types and abilities to engage in physical activity and maintain their fitness goals.

Three equipment layout philosophies—the traditional health club layout, the neighborhood layout, and the boutique-style layout—guide how you place your fitness equipment throughout your facility. Selecting which layout works best for your facility depends on your goals and objectives, the buyer personas of your members, built environment factors such as the structure itself, and guidance from any board oversight or franchise guidelines. Let's examine each one.

Traditional Health Club Layout

The traditional health club layout model is the design you are most likely familiar with. All the cardio equipment is placed in one section of the facility, grouped by type and displayed in rows with banks of TVs hanging from the ceiling or a wall in front of them. Strength equipment is in another section of the fitness facility and also grouped by type, such as selectorized, plate-loaded, and free weights. The selectorized circuit is traditionally placed in order so that any member could begin their workout on the first piece of equipment and move through the entire circuit while completing a total body workout. Figure 9.1 is an example of a traditional health club equipment layout.

Neighborhood Layout

A trending and newer approach to fitness equipment layout involves creating neighborhoods of fitness equipment throughout your facility. This philosophy favors grouping smaller quantities of equipment together so that a member can stay in one section of the facility and complete their entire workout, including cardio, strength training, functional training, and stretching, without leaving the designated neighborhood. For multilevel fitness facilities, someone could complete their entire workout without moving to another floor. This has many advantages, including creating an inclusive environment for members and guests that encourages socializing and community building and doesn't require a person to be on display while

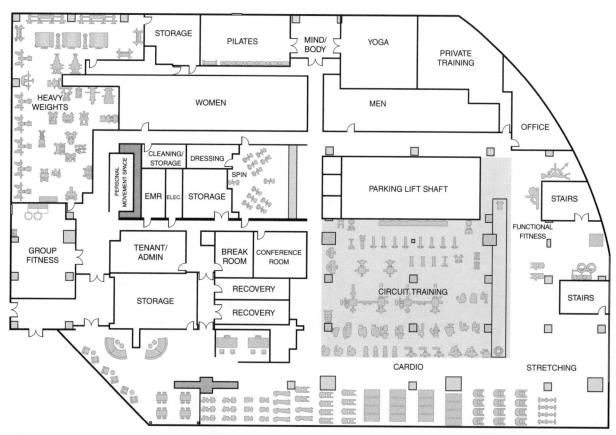

FIGURE 9.1   Health club fitness equipment layout.

working out in a large traditional open concept. Another advantage is that it allows you to diversify your equipment portfolio and brand without looking mismatched with everything in one row. You can also create better cleaning plans by cleaning one neighborhood at a time, and if needed, you can take an entire neighborhood offline without precluding a member's workout routine; they can access the equipment in another neighborhood.

Boutique Studio Layout

Boutique-style layouts are designed to fit the formula used in classes. They allow the equipment to be placed where members can move from one station to another while minimizing travel time and downtime throughout the class. The equipment layout is designed so that the coach can move from one group to another and give clear instructions to a specific group of participants without confusing other members of the workout. A classic example of this style is Orangetheory Fitness. The space is designed so that the rowers are in line behind the treadmills, and on the other end of the studio are strength stations where each member has all the equipment needed to complete the strength portion of the workout. Participants can move quickly between the treadmills and rowers during the cardio portion of the class and then transition to their strength stations when needed. An Orangetheory coach can instruct two, and sometimes three, different groups of participants in a given workout. Figure 9.2 is an example of a boutique studio layout.

Caring for Your Equipment

Caring for your fitness equipment is an essential, yet sometimes overlooked, part of fitness facility management. Routine cleaning and preventative maintenance can extend the life of your equipment, reduce equipment downtime, and create a safer environment for your members.

Routine Cleaning

Routine cleaning should be an ongoing effort throughout the day while the facility is open and operating; it is the responsibility of both members

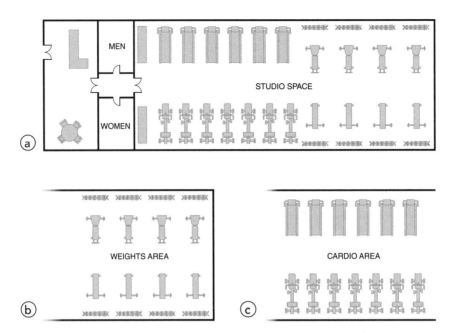

FIGURE 9.2 Boutique fitness studio layout: *(a)* total space; *(b)* weights area; *(c)* cardio area.

and staff. You should provide signage with instructions for members to wipe down their equipment after and perhaps even before use. Sanitized cleaning wipes should be placed in dispensers with waste cans by them throughout the facility and in high-traffic areas; the less distance a member has to go to obtain a cleaning wipe, the more likely the member cleans their equipment.

Fitness facility team members should also be cleaning equipment with approved cleaning agents throughout their shifts, and the cleanings should be documented as completed. When starting their shift, a team member should know what's expected of them during their shift, including what equipment and to what extent they are expected to clean.

Cleaning Schedule
Casey Gilvin

Within All Facility Areas

• Remove trash and replace liners	Daily
• Spot clean mirrors and glass	Daily
• Disinfect doors/handles/trash cans/items patrons touch	1 to 3× daily
• Dust horizontal items	Daily
• Vacuum carpets and hard floors	Daily
• Clean and disinfect hard floors	Daily
• Clean and disinfect water fountains	Daily
• Clean mirrors and glass	Biweekly

• Clean light fixtures and vertical surfaces	Monthly
• Clean HVAC vents and intake areas	Monthly
• Deep clean carpet areas via extraction	Quarterly
• Clean walls	Monthly

Member Check-In Area

• Disinfect counters/touch pads/computers/kiosks	1 to 3× daily
• Disinfect card readers/biometric readers/retina readers	1 to 3× daily

Locker Rooms

• Clean and disinfect locker locks/doors/benches	Daily
• Clean and disinfect showers/toilets/sinks and other surfaces	Daily
• Clean and disinfect the entire locker room	Weekly

Courts

• Dry mop/vacuum court floors	Daily
• Clean and disinfect court floors	Daily

Fitness Areas

• Vacuum rubber floors	Daily
• Clean and disinfect rubber floor	Daily
• Clean and disinfect fitness accessories	1 to 3× daily
• Clean and disinfect dumbbells	1 to 3× daily
• Clean and disinfect barbells	1 to 3× daily
• Clean barbell knurling with wire brush	Weekly
• Clean barbell knurling with multipurpose oil	2× monthly
• Clean and disinfect upholstery	1 to 3× daily
• Clean and disinfect selectorized and plate-loaded equipment	1 to 3× daily
• Clean and disinfect cable-driven equipment	1 to 3× daily
• Clean and disinfect free weight machines	1 to 3× daily
• Clean weight equipment frames	1 to 3× daily
• Clean and disinfect cardio machines	1 to 3× daily
• Clean treadmill belts with mild soap solution	Weekly
• Clean and disinfect indoor cycling bikes	1 to 3× daily
• Vacuum under cardio equipment	Weekly

Indoor Track

• Vacuum track surface	Daily
• Clean and disinfect track surface	Daily

Studios

• Dry mop/vacuum studio floors	Daily
• Wet mop studio floors	Daily

Preventative Maintenance

Preventative maintenance (PM) includes routine cleaning and goes a step further in the equipment care process. *ACSM's Health/Fitness Facility Standards and Guidelines* recommends you have a preventative maintenance program for your fitness equipment, including documentation of when the scheduled work was completed (ACSM 2019, p. 101). Preventative maintenance can be categorized into three levels:

> Level 1 PM includes routine cleaning and inspection. This can be performed by any team member with basic training and should be done daily.

> Level 2 PM includes more detailed inspection, including checking and tightening all screws, bolts, cables, and equipment diagnostics. This needs to be performed by a team member with required training and should be done at least weekly.

> Level 3 PM includes advanced care and maintenance, such as lubrication and internal parts cleaning. This often includes exposing internal parts or motors and should be performed only by someone trained and certified by the equipment manufacturer. Level 3 PM should be completed at monthly intervals or set schedules by the manufacturer.

While each equipment manufacturer sets forth specific guidelines for preventative maintenance, there are common practices that should be completed across all cardio equipment and all strength training equipment. Tables 9.1 and 9.2 represent common guidelines for preventative maintenance.

Creating a preventative maintenance plan doesn't have to be cumbersome or time-consuming. Most manufacturers provide recommended preventative maintenance plans and schedules for your equipment when you purchase it. Setting aside funds and personnel time to complete your regularly scheduled preventative maintenance can lengthen your equipment's life cycle and help preserve your warranty if any issues arise. You may opt to have your preventative maintenance completed by an in-house technician or contracted third party. Many manufacturers and equipment dealers can include a preventative maintenance contract as part of the purchase.

Repair

In addition to the preventative maintenance records, it's also essential to document any costs associated with maintenance or repair. Equipment issues may arise at any time and may be noticed by members and staff or during the preventative maintenance checks. You should have a clearly established method for members and staff to report equipment

TABLE 9.1   Common Preventative Maintenance Practices for Resistance Equipment

Equipment	Daily	Weekly	Monthly	As needed
Variable-resistance, selectorized resistance, and alternate resistance equipment	Clean frames with mild soap and water. Clean upholstery with mild soap and water.	Check all cables and bolts and tighten as needed. Check moving parts and adjust as needed.	Lubricate guide rods with lightweight oil.	Repair or replace pads. Replace cables if needed.
Free weight benches	Clean frames with mild soap and water. Clean upholstery with mild soap and water.	Check all cables and bolts and tighten as needed. Check moving parts and adjust as needed.		Repair or replace pads. Replace cables if needed.
Dumbbells and bars	Clean dumbbells and all bar handles (plus any free weight attachment handles) daily with an antimicrobial solution on a damp cloth or an antimicrobial wipe.	Check all screws and bolts and tighten as needed.	Use lightweight oil on cloth to remove any rust.	Repair or replace broken bars and dumbbells.

Reprinted by permission from American College of Sports Medicine (ACSM), "Health/Fitness Facility Equipment," in *ACSM's Health/Fitness Facility Standards and Guidelines*, 5th ed., edited by M.E. Sanders (Champaign, IL: Human Kinetics, 2019), 101.

TABLE 9.2 Common Preventative Maintenance Practices for Cardiorespiratory Equipment

Equipment	Daily	Weekly	Monthly	As needed
Bikes	Clean control panel with dry cloth. Clean handles with mild antibacterial soap and damp cloth. Clean seats with mild antibacterial soap and damp cloth.	Check equipment diagnostics through control panel for any potential troubles. Check all screws and bolts and tighten as needed.	Remove bike housing and clean out dust and lint that may have collected.	Refer to manufacturer's guidelines.
Elliptical trainers	Clean control panel with dry cloth. Clean handles with mild antibacterial soap and damp cloth. Clean foot pedals with damp cloth.	Check equipment diagnostics through control panel for any potential troubles. Check all screws and bolts and tighten as needed.	Remove elliptical housing and clean out dust and lint that may have collected.	Refer to manufacturer's guidelines.
Treadmills	Clean control panels with dry cloth. Clean housing with mild antibacterial soap and damp cloth.	Check equipment diagnostics through control panel for any potential troubles. Check all screws and bolts and tighten as needed.	Clean belt using a damp cloth. Check belt and deck surface and lubricate as needed and per manufacturer's specifications.	Replace belt if needed. Refer to manufacturer's guidelines.

Reprinted by permission from American College of Sports Medicine (ACSM), "Health/Fitness Facility Equipment," in *ACSM's Health/Fitness Facility Standards and Guidelines*, 5th ed., edited by M.E. Sanders (Champaign, IL: Human Kinetics, 2019), 102.

needing repair. Platforms such as Fitness Asset Manager provide QR codes for each piece of equipment, and members or staff can report an issue, which, in turn, creates a service ticket and sends it to the appropriate repair technician. *ACSM's Health/Fitness Facility Standards and Guidelines* recommends you have a system for removing broken or damaged equipment from member use until the equipment has been repaired or replaced (ACSM 2019, p. 102). If the equipment cannot be removed, then clear signs stating that the equipment is out of order should be placed on it and include an estimated repair date. As with preventative maintenance, repairs can be completed by in-house technicians or a third-party service provider. Keeping detailed records allows you to run reports on your equipment, such as the costs associated with each machine, type of equipment, and manufacturer. Once you have the actual cost to own, you can make better financial decisions when determining whether you should repair or replace a machine.

Equipment Replacement Plans

A well-thought-out equipment replacement plan is critical for any fitness facility that purchases its fitness equipment. Expect to reinvest up to

9.5 percent of annual revenue in equipment replacement and up to 15 percent every five to seven years (ACSM 2019, p. 96). Here are eight steps to developing your equipment replacement plan.

1. *Determine your budget.* You need to determine what is a reasonable amount of money you can reinvest in equipment purchases each year.

2. *Determine your true cost to own.* Use reports from your preventative maintenance and repair plan to determine what equipment costs you more than other equipment.

3. *Determine the need for replacement.* After you determine the true cost to own your equipment, you can begin to assess the need for replacement. Categorize each machine as critical (designating with a 1), moderate (2), or low (3), based on the need for replacement. Once you categorize your equipment, rank the machines. Determining your need for replacement gives you direction on where to go with your replacement.

4. *Determine the cost to replace.* Once you determine the need for replacement, you can begin to determine the replacement cost. Start gathering quotes for equipment that fall into the critical and moderate need for replacement categories. Filter

If broken equipment can't be removed, signs should be used to alert members the equipment is out of order.
400tmax/iStock/Getty Images

your costs from the most significant investment to the most minor investment. Categorize the costs as low cost (designating with a 1), moderate cost (2), and high cost (3).

5. *Create some priorities.* Now that you have ranked and categorized both the need and cost for replacement, you can begin to prioritize which equipment to replace. Add the numbers from the categories assigned for each piece of equipment. You should see numbers totaling from 2 to 6. This collective numbering system allows you to see the priority level for each machine, with 2 being a high priority and 6 being a low priority.

6. *Compare to the manufacturer's life span.* When purchasing new equipment, you should document the estimated retirement date based on the manufacturer's life span and instructions. Although this is a solid reference point, you need to consider that the volume of use, wear, and tear may decrease the

life span. You can compare the equipment life span to the priority system to make concrete decisions around replacement.

7. *Write the plan.* Writing and acting on your equipment replacement plan is the final step in setting your fitness facility up for financial and member success. Once you write your plan, you must share it with organizational colleagues and ensure it stays an organizational priority.

8. *Continuously evaluate.* An equipment replacement plan isn't a destination. It's a road map for success. You still have to make some collective decisions on what you will do. You may choose to replace multiple items that rank as a high priority, or you may choose to replace only a few items that rank as low priority. Ultimately, you have to make decisions that match your organization's mission, get you closer to your vision, and align with your goals and objectives.

Case Study: Equipment Replacement Plan

Casey Gilvin

As the fitness facility manager, you are assigned the task of developing an equipment replacement plan for your eight-year-old facility. Recently, your facility conducted a customer service survey. The results pointed to the need to update existing equipment and investigate new types of equipment consistent with the continual evolution of the fitness industry. Equipment in your facility has been regularly maintained by credentialed staff and third-party technicians, with limited instances of machine downtime. Treadmills, indoor cycling bikes, free weights, selectorized equipment, and cable-driven equipment are heavily used in your facility. Additionally, you recently visited a national fitness convention where you were exposed to a wide range of equipment brands, new technology, and options in the fitness industry. You need to develop a plan to replace equipment over time to heighten your customer experience while ensuring that new equipment is cost-effective, is durable, and meets evolving trends in the fitness industry.

Guiding Questions

- What is your yearly budget to replace equipment? Do you plan to purchase outright or through a lease program?
- Are there opportunities to trade or sell existing equipment to defray new equipment costs?
- What are your immediate priorities for replacement? What about moderate and low priority replacements?
- What pieces of equipment are more expensive than others?
- What new equipment or technology are you interested in adding to your facility?
- What pieces of equipment are used more than others?
- What feedback have you received from facility members regarding new equipment upgrades?
- With new brands and types of equipment, what warranties are available?
- Are there additional upkeep costs to consider when purchasing new brands or types of equipment?
- With new brands or types of equipment, are there new third-party service providers that service equipment?
- With adding new equipment, do you need to factor in any infrastructure needs (such as Internet, electrical outlets, or cable TV access)?
- Do you plan to adjust the layout of your facility when you execute the equipment replacement plan?
- Is there a need to adjust equipment quantities for future usage based on current use or evolution in the fitness industry?
- What installation and delivery logistics must be identified with the implementation of the replacement plan (e.g., hiring movers, making a plan to remove old equipment, acknowledging new equipment lead times)?

Debrief

You are ready to present your plan to the facility's regional manager. You have defined a course of action with a multiyear replacement plan, and you have solicited quotes, prioritized needs, and identified additional items to consider for the replacement plan. Good job!

Now comes the presentation to the regional manager. Expect follow-up questions related to the reasons for equipment selection, options and trim levels, and priority. Soon, you will be able to finalize your replacement plan. Get the checkbook ready!

(continued)

┌─ **Case Study: Equipment Replacement Plan** *(continued)* ─────────────────

Things to Consider Moving Forward

- An equipment replacement plan should be a living document and part of a yearly plan to update the facility. Always have the plan ready to go. You never know when end-of-year dollars may become available.

- Priorities may change over time with the evolution of the fitness industry. For example, elliptical or cross-trainers may not be used as much as other pieces of equipment.

- Always have an alternative course of action if your plan must be adjusted due to a wide range of issues (e.g., budget constraints, customer feedback, or space limitations).

- Keep accurate records of equipment issues and repair costs, because this will help formulate your priority list for replacement.

- Survey facility users formally and informally about equipment brands and types.

- Constantly observe equipment usage during peak times. Without pulling mileage and hours, it will become obvious what equipment is heavily used.

- Regularly attend conferences or trade shows to stay current on new technology or equipment.

- Research and investigate.

- Reach out to your peers in the industry to discuss trends and experiences with equipment. Your facility is unique, and you know the members better than anyone, but hearing about other experiences helps identify new avenues for equipment.

Conclusion

Not acting on your equipment replacement plan or not prioritizing your preventative maintenance plan can cost your facility a significant financial loss. The neglect could require you to find more money than you had initially planned if you have to replace 40, 50, or even 75 percent of the equipment in a given year because it wasn't cared for. Having a sufficient quantity, quality, and variety of fitness equipment is essential for member recruitment and retention and a basis for offering quality programs and services, as we'll discuss in the next chapter.

THINK IT THROUGH

- What are the advantages and disadvantages of leasing versus buying fitness equipment?
- Why is it important to use only commercial-grade fitness equipment?
- What are some examples of equipment layout best practices?
- How should you implement a preventative maintenance plan?
- How do you go about writing an equipment replacement plan?

KEY TERMS

commercial versus residential fitness equipment

equipment layout

equipment replacement plan

leasing versus owning

preventative maintenance

repair versus replace

types of fitness equipment

10

Member Services and Programs

Upon completion of this chapter, you will be able to do the following:

- Explain the purpose of various types of programming
- Describe the steps of a program planning process
- Identify opportunities for both in-person and online programming
- Plan and develop various types of exercise program offerings
- Assess and evaluate the organization, programs, and services

A robust selection of fitness equipment in your facility is vital for getting members in your doors. Offering world-class services and programs is critical in keeping your members active and returning. This chapter will teach you the basics of group fitness, small group and large team training, personal training, health coaching, and other services to help you be a successful fitness facility manager.

Group Fitness

Although group fitness became mainstream in the 1970s through Jacki Sorensen's introduction of aerobic dancing, followed by Richard Simmons bringing aerobics to people's living rooms, you can trace it back many years earlier. Dr. Kenneth Cooper published a book explaining the concept of aerobic fitness in 1969. However, the first actual introduction to what people now refer to as group fitness dates back to 1811 when gymnast Friedrich Ludwig Jahn opened the first fitness club, a public Turnplatz, or *turnverein*, in Germany, where male athletes trained for sport and competition.

The first question to ask yourself as a fitness facility manager is why you need to offer group fitness classes. For one, if you are operating a facility outside the low-budget club price point you learned about in chapter 4, then your membership base will expect group fitness programming. A study published by the *Journal of Osteopathic Medicine* suggests that participation in group fitness classes leads to significantly decreased stress and increased physical, mental, and emotional quality of life compared to those who exercised on their own or not at all (Yorks, Frothingham, and Schuenke 2017). Group fitness classes should be a core component of your fitness facility programming.

Certified group fitness instructors teach modern-day group fitness classes. At a minimum, all instructors should have a primary group fitness certification from an accredited organization recognized by the National Commission for Certifying Agencies (NCCA). Under certification requirements, instructors are required to participate in continuing education and recertify every two years. All NCCA-accredited certifications also require instructors to maintain certification in cardiopulmonary resuscitation, CPR, by an approved agency, such as the American Red Cross or the American Heart Association. A certificate in automated external defibrillator, or AED, is required for instructors in the United States and Canada. Each country and state has its own governing body and may have regulations around licensure and certification in the fitness industry.

The International Confederation of Registers of Exercise Professionals is a partnership and centralized professional registry among certifying bodies across the globe.

Types of Group Fitness Class Instruction

Group fitness classes come in many different modalities, including land and water; however, all group fitness classes are classified as either freestyle or prechoreographed.

Freestyle

Freestyle group fitness classes are taught by an instructor who develops their own choreography and class design and selects their own music playlist. Instructors must plan well in advance to keep the class evolving based on participant performance and feedback. Class names and descriptions should be written so that a participant knows what to expect, no matter who is teaching the class.

Prechoreographed

Prechoreographed group fitness classes are taught by an instructor who follows a scripted recipe. This recipe includes the choreography, class design, music, and compulsory cues that the instructor needs to follow to deliver the class as designed. The advantages of prechoreographed classes are the quality control of the class experience, and many branded programs are taught globally; therefore, a participant knows what to expect no matter where or when they take a class. Notably, most prechoreographed classes require instructors to hold a specialized certification or certificate and to pay licensing fees.

Delivery Methods

Selecting the delivery methods of your group fitness classes is as important as determining what types of classes you plan to offer. The COVID-19 pandemic affected people's choices of when and where they exercise, and ultimately the pandemic influenced fitness facilities to broaden how they deliver their exercise programs, including group fitness classes.

In-Person

In-person programming is the traditional and original approach to delivering group fitness

In a freestyle group fitness class, the instructor develops the routine and chooses the music, allowing the instructor to adapt the class to members' needs.

Christopher Futcher/Getty Images

classes. In this scenario, a live certified group fitness instructor is in the same studio as participants in your fitness facility, leading and instructing the experience. Feedback is delivered to the participants on the spot.

Virtual

Virtual programming is the group fitness experience where a participant can participate from anywhere with the instructor in a different location. All virtual programming occurs in two delivery methods: synchronous or asynchronous.

Synchronous   Synchronous group fitness classes happen when the instructor is actively delivering the instruction while the participants are completing the workout at the same time. You may also hear this referred to as *live streaming*. Synchronous fitness classes are classified as either a one-way broadcast or a two-way broadcast.

A one-way broadcast occurs when the instructor delivers the workout via a platform where the participants can see the instructor but not vice versa. This occurs through streaming platforms such as Facebook Live or YouTube Live. There is limited interaction with the participants. If any interaction occurs, it typically occurs through emojis or comments in a chat, if enabled.

A two-way broadcast occurs when the instructor leads the workout via a platform where the participants and the instructor can see one another. Some platforms also allow participants to see and interact with each other, while others do not. This commonly occurs through specially designed technology platforms, Zoom, or web conferencing platforms. However, interaction does occur and is encouraged. The instructor can also see the participants performing the exercise and provide feedback directly and on the spot.

Asynchronous   Asynchronous group fitness classes happen whenever the participant wants them to happen. This is commonly referred to as *on-demand*. The experience may include video, audio, text, or a combination of these. The instructor develops and records the workouts in advance and prepares all necessary instructional materials to accompany them. These experiences are often delivered in a polished style. If the instructor makes a mistake or someone unexpectedly shows up on the recording, it can be edited. Many fitness facilities partner with third parties, such as Les Mills, to offer discounted prices to virtual fitness programs and, in exchange, could receive a revenue share.

Hybrid

Hybrid group fitness classes occur when a class is delivered simultaneously both in person and virtually. Peloton is an example of a hybrid environment. The instructor is teaching a live in-person cycling class at Peloton Studios in New York City while thousands of people from around the world are taking that same class from their own homes or hotel rooms around the globe. You may have done something similar already by live streaming some of your in-person classes as you started to introduce in-person programming.

Hybrid classes can also occur by blending the live in-person experience with the virtual asynchronous experience. Les Mills+ is a classic example of this combination. Les Mills hosts live filming of programs at their Les Mills Auckland City clubs, where the instructors teach to the members on-site and to the camera. The film is later edited and released to Les Mills+ members via the app worldwide. You can further manipulate the variables here by taking the asynchronous virtual experience and scheduling it in a studio for in-person participants during low-peak times during your operating hours.

Group Fitness Demographic

One of the biggest driving factors for members to participate in group fitness classes is the community aspect and the desire to socialize and exercise in a group. Nevertheless, other factors also influence which group fitness class a member will participate in. According to the Les Mills *Global Fitness Report*, the quality of the instructor is the single largest influence on whether a person chooses to take a live class (Phillips 2021). The quality of music and the type of class follow as influential factors, along with the quality of equipment, class effectiveness, price of classes, quality of choreography, time of class, and a good sound system.

Planning a Group Fitness Timetable

Creating a group fitness class timetable (see table 10.1 for an example) to attract and engage members is an art form. It requires placing the class name and format in the ideal time block with the appropriate instructor in the correct location to attract the target audience. This process is repeated over and over until a timetable is created that works best for the members. Hiring a dedicated group

TABLE 10.1   Sample Group Fitness Schedule

MONDAY

Start	End	Location	Format
6:30 a.m.	7:30 a.m.	Mind/body studio	Morning yoga
7:00 a.m.	7:30 a.m.	Main studio	HIIT
9:00 a.m.	10:00 a.m.	Main studio	BODYPUMP (virtual)
10:00 a.m.	10:45 a.m.	Cycle studio	RPM (virtual)
11:00 a.m.	12:00 p.m.	Main studio	Step aerobics
12:00 p.m.	12:45 p.m.	Pool	Aqua fitness
12:00 p.m.	1:00 p.m.	Mind/body studio	Yoga
12:30 p.m.	1:30 p.m.	Main studio	BODYPUMP
12:30 p.m.	1:15 p.m.	Cycle studio	RPM
1:00 p.m.	2:00 p.m.	Mind/body studio	Tai chi
2:00 p.m.	2:45 p.m.	Main studio	HIIT
3:00 p.m.	3:45 p.m.	Cycle studio	The Trip (virtual)
4:00 p.m.	4:30 p.m.	Main studio	Core 30
4:30 p.m.	5:30 p.m.	Mind/body studio	Vinyasa yoga
5:00 p.m.	6:00 p.m.	Main studio	Zumba
5:30 p.m.	6:00 p.m.	Mind/body studio	Stretch 30
5:30 p.m.	6:30 p.m.	Cycle studio	RPM
6:00 p.m.	7:00 p.m.	Main studio	Kickboxing
6:30 p.m.	7:15 p.m.	Mind/body studio	Les Mills SHAPES
7:00 p.m.	7:30 p.m.	Main studio	Core 30
7:00 p.m.	7:45 p.m.	Cycle studio	Cycle 45
7:30 p.m.	9:00 p.m.	Mind/body studio	Yin yoga
8:00 p.m.	8:30 p.m.	Main studio	HIIT
9:00 p.m.	9:45 p.m.	Cycle studio	The Trip (virtual)
10:00 p.m.	11:00 p.m.	Main studio	Dance party

TUESDAY

Start	End	Location	Format
6:30 a.m.	7:15 a.m.	Mind/body studio	Morning Pilates
7:00 a.m.	7:45 a.m.	Cycle studio	Sunrise cycle
9:00 a.m.	9:45 a.m.	Main studio	Les Mills Strength Development (virtual)
10:00 a.m.	11:00 a.m.	Mind/body studio	Yoga
11:00 a.m.	12:00 p.m.	Main studio	BODYPUMP
12:00 p.m.	12:45 p.m.	Cycle studio	RPM
12:00 p.m.	12:30 p.m.	Main studio	HIIT
12:30 p.m.	1:30 p.m.	Mind/body studio	Yoga
12:30 p.m.	1:15 p.m.	Cycle studio	Cycle 45
1:00 p.m.	2:00 p.m.	Main studio	Kickboxing
2:00 p.m.	3:00 p.m.	Mind/body studio	BODYBALANCE (virtual)
3:00 p.m.	4:00 p.m.	Main studio	BODYPUMP (virtual)
4:00 p.m.	4:30 p.m.	Main studio	HIIT
4:00 p.m.	4:45 p.m.	Cycle studio	The Trip (virtual)

TUESDAY

Start	End	Location	Format
4:30 p.m.	5:00 p.m.	Main studio	Core
5:00 p.m.	6:00 p.m.	Mind/body studio	Yoga
5:00 p.m.	5:45 p.m.	Cycle studio	Cycle 45
5:30 p.m.	6:00 p.m.	Pool	Aqua fitness
5:30 p.m.	6:30 p.m.	Main studio	BODYPUMP
6:00 p.m.	7:00 p.m.	Cycle studio	RPM
6:30 p.m.	7:30 p.m.	Main studio	Zumba
7:00 p.m.	8:00 p.m.	Mind/body studio	Pilates
7:30 p.m.	8:30 p.m.	Cycle studio	Cycle 60
8:00 p.m.	9:00 p.m.	Mind/body studio	Yoga
8:30 p.m.	9:00 p.m.	Main studio	HIIT

WEDNESDAY

Start	End	Location	Format
6:30 a.m.	7:30 a.m.	Mind/body studio	Morning yoga
7:00 a.m.	7:30 a.m.	Main studio	HIIT
9:00 a.m.	10:00 a.m.	Main studio	BODYPUMP (virtual)
10:00 a.m.	10:45 a.m.	Cycle studio	RPM (virtual)
11:00 a.m.	12:00 p.m.	Main studio	Step aerobics
12:00 p.m.	12:45 p.m.	Pool	Aqua fitness
12:00 p.m.	1:00 p.m.	Mind/body studio	Yoga
12:30 p.m.	1:30 p.m.	Main studio	BODYPUMP
12:30 p.m.	1:15 p.m.	Cycle studio	RPM
1:00 p.m.	2:00 p.m.	Mind/body studio	Tai chi
2:00 p.m.	2:45 p.m.	Main studio	HIIT
3:00 p.m.	3:45 p.m.	Cycle studio	The Trip (virtual)
4:00 p.m.	4:30 p.m.	Main studio	Core 30
4:00 p.m.	5:00 p.m.	Cycle studio	Cycle 60
4:30 p.m.	5:30 p.m.	Mind/body studio	Vinyasa yoga
5:00 p.m.	6:00 p.m.	Main studio	Zumba
5:30 p.m.	6:00 p.m.	Mind/body studio	Stretch 30
5:30 p.m.	6:30 p.m.	Cycle studio	RPM
6:00 p.m.	7:00 p.m.	Main studio	Kickboxing
6:30 p.m.	7:15 p.m.	Mind/body studio	Les Mills SHAPES
7:00 p.m.	7:30 p.m.	Main studio	Core 30
7:00 p.m.	7:45 p.m.	Cycle studio	Cycle 45
7:30 p.m.	9:00 p.m.	Mind/body studio	Yin yoga
8:00 p.m.	8:30 p.m.	Main studio	HIIT
9:00 p.m.	9:45 p.m.	Cycle studio	The Trip (virtual)
10:00 p.m.	11:00 p.m.	Main studio	Dance party

(continued)

Table 10.1 Sample Group Fitness Schedule *(continued)*

THURSDAY

Start	End	Location	Format
6:30 a.m.	7:15 a.m.	Mind/body studio	Morning Pilates
7:00 a.m.	7:45 a.m.	Cycle studio	Sunrise cycle
9:00 a.m.	9:45 a.m.	Main studio	Les Mills Strength Development (virtual)
10:00 a.m.	11:00 a.m.	Mind/body studio	Yoga
11:00 a.m.	12:00 p.m.	Main studio	BODYPUMP
12:00 p.m.	12:45 p.m.	Cycle studio	RPM
12:00 p.m.	12:30 p.m.	Main studio	HIIT
12:30 p.m.	1:30 p.m.	Mind/body studio	Yoga
12:30 p.m.	1:15 p.m.	Cycle studio	Cycle 45
1:00 p.m.	2:00 p.m.	Main studio	Kickboxing
2:00 p.m.	3:00 p.m.	Mind/body studio	BODYBALANCE (virtual)
3:00 p.m.	4:00 p.m.	Main studio	BODYPUMP (virtual)
4:00 p.m.	4:30 p.m.	Main studio	HIIT
4:00 p.m.	4:45 p.m.	Cycle studio	The Trip (virtual)
4:30 p.m.	5:00 p.m.	Main studio	Core
5:00 p.m.	6:00 p.m.	Mind/body studio	Yoga
5:00 p.m.	5:45 p.m.	Cycle studio	Cycle 45
5:30 p.m.	6:00 p.m.	Pool	Aqua fitness
5:30 p.m.	6:30 p.m.	Main studio	BODYPUMP
6:00 p.m.	7:00 p.m.	Cycle studio	RPM
6:30 p.m.	7:30 p.m.	Main studio	Zumba
8:00 p.m.	9:00 p.m.	Mind/body studio	Yoga

FRIDAY

Start	End	Location	Format
6:30 a.m.	7:30 a.m.	Mind/body studio	Morning yoga
7:00 a.m.	7:30 a.m.	Main studio	HIIT
9:00 a.m.	10:00 a.m.	Main studio	BODYPUMP (virtual)
10:00 a.m.	10:45 a.m.	Cycle studio	RPM (virtual)
11:00 a.m.	12:00 p.m.	Main studio	Step aerobics
12:00 p.m.	12:45 p.m.	Pool	Aqua fitness
12:00 p.m.	1:00 p.m.	Mind/body studio	Yoga
12:30 p.m.	1:30 p.m.	Main studio	BODYPUMP
2:00 p.m.	2:45 p.m.	Main studio	HIIT
3:00 p.m.	3:45 p.m.	Cycle studio	The Trip (virtual)
4:00 p.m.	4:30 p.m.	Main studio	Core 30
4:00 p.m.	5:00 p.m.	Cycle studio	Cycle 60
4:30 p.m.	5:30 p.m.	Mind/body studio	Vinyasa yoga
5:00 p.m.	6:00 p.m.	Main studio	Zumba
5:30 p.m.	6:30 p.m.	Cycle studio	RPM (virtual)
7:00 p.m.	7:45 p.m.	Mind/body studio	Yoga

SATURDAY

Start	End	Location	Format
8:00 a.m.	9:00 a.m.	Main studio	BODYPUMP
9:00 a.m.	10:00 a.m.	Cycle studio	Sunrise cycle
11:30 a.m.	12:30 p.m.	Mind/body studio	Vinyasa yoga
12:00 p.m.	1:00 p.m.	Main studio	Zumba
2:00 p.m.	3:00 p.m.	Cycle studio	RPM
3:00 p.m.	3:45 p.m.	Mind/body studio	Barre
3:30 p.m.	4:00 p.m.	Main studio	Core 30
4:00 p.m.	5:00 p.m.	Main studio	BODYPUMP

SUNDAY

Start	End	Location	Format
8:00 a.m.	9:00 a.m.	Mind/body studio	Vinyasa yoga
12:00 p.m.	1:00 p.m.	Cycle studio	Cycle 60
12:30 p.m.	1:30 p.m.	Main studio	BODYPUMP
2:00 p.m.	2:30 p.m.	Main studio	HIIT
3:00 p.m.	4:00 p.m.	Main studio	BODYPUMP (virtual)
3:30 p.m.	4:30 p.m.	Mind/body studio	Tai chi
4:00 p.m.	5:00 p.m.	Cycle studio	RPM
5:00 p.m.	6:30 p.m.	Mind/body studio	Yin yoga
6:30 p.m.	7:30 p.m.	Main studio	Zumba

fitness manager to manage the program is ideal. As a fitness facility manager, you should know the basics of how to create a timetable. Here are some global statistics to consider when creating a timetable. High-intensity interval training is the most popular group fitness format, followed by indoor cycling, dance, stretching and mobility, core conditioning, step aerobics, strength training, and other cardio formats. Although not as popular, members still participate in Pilates, martial arts, yoga, boxing, and functional circuit training (Phillips 2021).

Selecting class names that allude to the class type and clearly describing what to expect are essential for your website, mobile app, and digital signage. As reported in Phillips (2021), 86 percent of global group fitness participants report taking a branded fitness class, one where the name and format are used in multiple types of fitness facilities around the globe. Branded formats give an immediate sense of familiarity to members. Consider adding a short video clip of the class to give members an idea of what they might do if they attend. Members should be able to easily access group fitness timetables, which should be updated as variables such as instructor, class name, or time change. List the instructor teaching the class on the timetable by first name and last initial to advertise the instructor while protecting privacy. Use electronic group fitness management systems that update the timetable when a substitute instructor is in place. If using a reservation system for group fitness, it should be easily accessible to members and provide reminders of the upcoming class. One of the most essential features of a booking system is the ability for a member to cancel or reschedule their class quickly and through their mobile app (figure 10.1).

Quality control and quality assurance are essential when developing a timetable. Members decide whether or not to take a class based on quality elements such as music, instructor, equipment, and class design. The equipment and studio should always be clean, safe, and welcoming to members. Refer to chapter 8 on characteristics of an ideal group fitness studio.

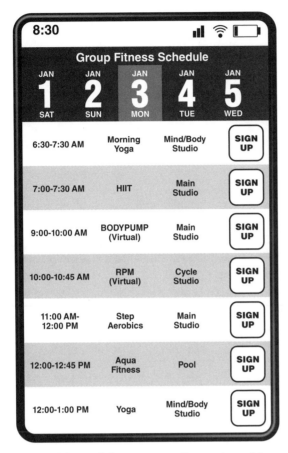

FIGURE 10.1   Mobile app group fitness timetable.

Live Group Fitness Class Experience

Once a member decides to attend a group fitness class, it is up to the group fitness instructor to deliver a world-class movement experience that encourages the participants to come back. Instructors should arrive at least 15 minutes prior to the start of class to set up the studio and create a welcoming environment. After setting up the equipment and using technology or a whiteboard to list equipment needs for participants, the instructor can greet members at the door and welcome them by name, if possible. New members should never be called out by the instructor; instead, the instructor should make a statement that if anyone needs assistance, to let them know.

At the start of the class, the instructor welcomes participants with an opening script. Here is an example of an opening script:

> Hello, my name is Steven! Welcome to BODYPUMP. BODYPUMP is the original barbell workout using high reps and low weight to strengthen your entire body. We will change our weight selection between each track, and I will give you instructions on how to do so at the time. Water fountains are located at the back of the studio. If you are new to the class, I applaud you for showing up and encourage you to participate at your own pace. If you wish to leave after the first 20 minutes, or four tracks, feel free to do so and keep adding a track each time you come back. Please pause for a moment and focus your attention on me. Before we begin, I will demonstrate a new move that we will incorporate in class today. Please stand in the set position, bend your knees, pick up the bar, and let's begin!

As mentioned in chapter 8, the studio sound system should be kept in working order with the music at or below 85 decibels. Group fitness instructors should always wear a microphone, creating an inclusive environment where all participants can listen to clear, coherent instructions.

Group fitness instructors must always start and end class at the scheduled time. Even if the previous class runs over time, it is the responsibility of the following instructor to get the group fitness

Group Fitness Is Emotional

The NeedScope model, developed by TNS (a market information provider), focuses on identifying the emotional drivers behind consumer behavior. This is particularly useful in tailoring your group fitness offerings to meet diverse member needs (Kantar, n.d.). Think about your group fitness timetable, and begin by listing which classes you think would most appeal to each of the following universal drivers: extroverted, individualistic, introverted, and affiliated. Do you have enough offerings to appeal to most of your members? By leveraging the insights from the NeedScope model, you can strategically design your group fitness timetable to cater to a broad spectrum of your members' emotional and psychological needs.

Case Study: Building a World-Class Group Fitness Schedule

Kia Williams

Core Build Studio (CBS) is a small boutique fitness studio that has been in operation for 10 years. CBS exclusively offers in-person Pilates, barre, and general yoga classes. CBS serves 253 members in a six-mile radius and has had a strong member retention rate. However, it has started experiencing a slow decline in membership renewals. It has not made a change in class offerings, services, or scheduling since the first year of its opening. Historically, the hours of operation have been 7:00 a.m. to 7:00 p.m. The most popularly attended class time blocks are early morning (7:00 a.m. to 7:45 a.m.), early afternoon (12:00 p.m. to 12:45 p.m.), and early evening (5:00 p.m. to 6:00 p.m.). CBS membership profile shows a majority (56 percent) of members who self-identify as working mothers between the ages of 32 and 45.

Two new fitness studios have opened within a 15-mile radius of CBS in the past year, and CBS members have been trying out the new studios on promotional trials. One studio is open from 7:00 a.m. to 7:00 p.m. and has yoga and personal training with a specialty focus. The other strictly offers barre and Pilates with heated and nonheated class options at select times every day and by appointment only. A former employee of CBS owns that studio. There are rumors that the managers of the newly opened studios plan to offer members of CBS discounted rates to join their studios. The owner of CBS believes it is time to innovate and revamp CBS's schedule to solidify its business presence and performance in the community and retain its members.

You are hired to build a refreshed group fitness schedule for the new year. But first you must propose a strategic plan to support all expected changes due to the schedule revamp and explain why anything remains constant.

Identify and explain any threats and risks for a schedule change.

What types of changes can maximize success for the business (time, length of time, class varieties and options, number of classes, days of the week)?

How can a schedule change affect your students and instructors?

Group fitness classes are the lifeline of gyms and clubs. When the classes occur, where the classes take place, who is leading the experience, and how easy it is to engage are vital considerations. Planning and strategizing are imperative for creating a successful group fitness schedule. Consider the following important points and factors:

- *People.* Know your employees and members very well. Know your instructors' talents, potential, needs, and strengths. Know their availability and marketability. Gauge the interest and demand of the members and potential members—how to maximize their interest, assess their needs, and give the people what they want when they want it. Familiarize yourself with your members' desires, schedules, and responsibilities to know when, how, and where they can engage and in what magnitude. Keep your people satisfied.

- *Value proposition.* Attract new customers, keep old members interested, increase engagement and average class size, and strengthen member loyalty and retention.

- *Financials.* Consider payroll budget, equipment maintenance, and other costs for providing the service.

- *Time.* Evaluate class start and end times, class length, class consistency, frequency of the class offering, the impact of seasonal change on class performance, instructor availability, members, class popularity, stacking classes, and when and how to launch a new class.

A successful group fitness schedule is fluid, flexible, and ever-evolving, and the members' lives are ever-changing. Change can be rewarding, but it will also call for behavioral change, educating, wooing, convincing, and commitment. There is value in curiosity, bravery, listening, forward-thinking, and risk-taking in building a world-class group fitness schedule.

Small Group and Large Team Training

Small group training caters to a smaller group of participants, typically 2 to 10 individuals working with a fitness professional. The format is conducive to more individualized attention, personalized modifications, and tailored programming to meet specific fitness goals and abilities because of the group's smaller size.

Conversely, large team training involves larger groups, typically exceeding 10 participants, who work out together under the guidance of one or more fitness professionals. Large group training sessions focus on high-energy workouts, building community and camaraderie, and creating a motivating environment.

Since small group and large team training classes are typically smaller than group fitness classes, they are more personalized and more focused on the individual participants' goals than group fitness. Furthermore, group fitness classes generally are included in the membership cost, while small group and large team training are usually fee-based. Both formats are valuable in promoting fitness and providing programming solutions catering to various members' preferences.

Members looking for a more personalized and targeted approach to their health and fitness are often drawn to small group training. Small group training allows for more individualized workouts, semipersonal attention, and the opportunity to achieve specific goals. Conversely, members looking for a slightly larger and more energetic group environment and team camaraderie are drawn to large team training. Large team training fosters a strong sense of community, offers a collective workout experience, and can be very attractive to members who thrive in social settings. Programs that can be used for both small group and large team training include obstacle course race (OCR) conditioning, TRX training, kettlebell circuit training, HIIT, and a six-week weight loss program. Formats can be equipment based, skill based, outcome based, or results based.

Consider the logistics of the program. How long will the program run? Six weeks? A month? Is it an ongoing program? Determining the ideal duration for small group and large team training sessions should be based on the type of workout and member preferences. Typically, sessions range from 30 to 60 minutes, allowing for an effective workout within a manageable time frame. The intensity of the session affects the duration; for example, a HIIT session is best suited to 30 minutes. For a skills-based program, such as a small group training session focused on training for an OCR, the session may need to be 60 minutes because of the number of skills to be addressed.

Since small group and large team training are generally fee-based programs, you need to decide on pricing. Consider the facility model, the target market being served, the program's length, duration, and frequency, the number of participants, the type of format, and the value offered. Your goal should be to price the program in a way that is enticing and competitive. Although there is no ideal set price, you should consider pricing your programs at least 33 percent

timetable back on schedule. After the class, group fitness instructors should give participants instructions for cleaning and storing their equipment. In addition, the instructor should provide a recap of the work performed that day and, most importantly, thank participants for attending and give them either an invitation to come back or another call to action. Group fitness instructors should also provide instructions to participants on how to provide feedback on their class experience.

Evaluating Group Fitness Classes

One of the most obvious ways group fitness participants provide feedback is by showing up. A common phrase is "members will vote with their feet." Monitoring class attendance is one of the simplest ways to determine whether or not a class is successful. The attendance of a single class on a single day cannot be used to determine long-term success, but look at the long-range data, such as the average attendance. As noted in table 10.1, there above your break-even point. Keeping all that in mind, here are three standard pricing models for small group and large team training.

Pay per program is the first standard pricing model for small group and large team training. Under this model, a member pays a one-time fee to participate. This works well for programs with a predetermined length. The second standard pricing model is a *monthly fee*. Under this model, a member is charged each month that they participate. You can make this approach attractive to members by offering a discount on the monthly fee if the member agrees to participate for a predetermined length of time, such as 3, 6, or 12 months. This works well for ongoing programs. The third standard method of pricing is known as a *drop-in fee*. The member pays for one session at a time. This method works only if there are open spots in the program, and usually, the first drop-in is complimentary because it is an opportunity for a member to try the program to decide if they want to participate regularly. This option benefits members with challenging personal schedules who cannot commit regularly. While other options exist, these are the three most common.

Generally, the best people to conduct small group and large team training sessions tend to be hybrids of personal trainers and group fitness instructors, people who exhibit the best qualities of both roles. Both types of fitness professionals are knowledgeable, good communicators, engaging, motivational, adaptable, observant, and supportive. Personal trainers generally have a slightly higher level of technical training knowledge, while group fitness instructors tend to manage and connect better with groups. Therefore, when choosing who will run your small group and large team training, you should seek out those hybrid types of fitness professionals.

Interactions throughout the session are also critical for a world-class session. It is essential to remind your fitness professional that although they oversee several people, each one of those people came for them. Encourage your fitness professional to strive for at least one sincere and focused interaction with every participant in every session. As they get to know their participants, they should try to customize that interaction for them. Some participants prefer personal verbal encouragement. Others may choose to be praised in front of the rest of the group. A high five or a smile might be effective for some. As genuine relationships are built, your fitness professional will be able to uncover the type of interaction that means the most to participants. Focused interactions make people feel like one in a million, instead of just one in a group, and enhance the program experience.

Innovation is another factor that plays a role in creating a world-class small group and large team training experience. Instructors can innovate by adding different equipment, changing choreography, or playing new music. From a scientific viewpoint, do not forget that innovating by mixing things up prevents participants from hitting plateaus, thus improving their ability to get results. Consistent innovation keeps participants returning and wanting more instead of getting bored and looking for other programs.

are peak times, shoulder times, and off-peak times throughout the group fitness timetable, so you should look at the macro-level view of attendance before making any alterations to the timetable. Cost per head (CPH) is another tool used to determine the success of a group fitness class over time. This formula looks at the number of participants in the class compared to the cost of the instructor. According to GroupEx Pro, a leading group fitness management software company, keeping CPH below $1.25 and no higher than $2.00 is ideal. Penetration rates are another tool you can use to evaluate the success of your group fitness program as a whole. Penetration rates are calculated by looking at the number of members participating in group fitness classes compared to the total number of fitness facility visits during a fixed period such as weekly, monthly, or quarterly.

Participation numbers can indicate the success of the group fitness program but do not necessarily tell the story of the program's impact. Use a net promoter score (NPS) as a method to evaluate the impact of the program and whether or not the group fitness program truly is world-class. By collecting NPS, you can compare your program to industry benchmarks as well as look at performance on an annual basis. You can also collect member testimonials by administering the survey that can be used for internal and external marketing purposes.

Working closely with your group fitness instructors is perhaps the most important way to evaluate group fitness classes and the overall program. Open and frequent communication between the management team and the instructors is critical because the instructor serves as the liaison from member to management. Group fitness instructors should be evaluated by management at least once per year. This not only shows value to the instructor but also helps with quality assurance to members and can be used to provide performance bonuses or salary increases to staff.

Personal Training

Another program most fitness facilities offer is personal training. Personal training is a one-on-one workout session delivered by a certified fitness professional, a personal trainer. While group fitness classes, small group training, and large team training focus on working with groups of different sizes, personal training caters to one or two individuals at a time. When a personal trainer works with two people, it is called *partner training*. Due to the unique focus, personal training often has a higher price point than small group training and large team training. At its core, personal training involves working with a trainer who creates and implements a personalized workout program to meet a client's health and fitness goals.

A personal trainer has a diverse knowledge base. Their expertise includes exercise physiology, exercise techniques, strength training, cardiorespiratory conditioning, flexibility and mobility, functional training, injury prevention and rehabilitation, nutrition, goal setting, behavioral change, and program design. While personal trainers may be experts only in some areas, they likely have at least a base level of knowledge in each. Some personal trainers may specialize further. They may seek additional expertise in niche areas such as sports performance, corrective exercise, pre- and postnatal fitness, or working with specific medical conditions or aging

exercisers. Regardless of the type of client, personal trainers assess their clients' fitness levels, discuss their goals, and create personalized workout plans to help them achieve them.

A personal trainer develops the skills to be a master of the craft in a few different ways. A trainer can obtain a degree in kinesiology, exercise science, sports science, nutrition, and other related fields, which provides them with the knowledge and skills to be an effective personal trainer. Others may choose to become personal trainers through certification. Accredited organizations such as the American College of Sports Medicine (ACSM), the National Academy of Sports Medicine (NASM), the American Council on Exercise (ACE), and the National Strength and Conditioning Association (NSCA) are some of the most highly regarded certification bodies in the fitness industry. These certifications require significant studying and passing grades on challenging exams. Whether they have a college degree, a certification, or both, a personal trainer who is educated and competent to work with clients safely and effectively is nonnegotiable.

While a personal trainer is responsible for training clients, you also need a personal training manager, often referred to in the health club market as the fitness director. Depending on the size and resources of a facility, this could be one of the trainers, a manager who oversees multiple departments, or, in larger facilities, a stand-alone person. The primary role of a personal training manager is to control and optimize the department. Their responsibilities are managing the personal training team, ensuring the delivery of high-quality training experiences, and overall client satisfaction and retention. The manager handles recruiting, hiring, onboarding, and performance evaluations, and provides ongoing support. They are often responsible for monitoring KPIs, client feedback, and other metrics to improve personal training programming continually. A personal training manager is a crucial role that acts as a leader, motivator, and problem-solver who drives the overall success of the personal training department.

Many great reasons exist for you to offer personal training at your fitness facility. Personal training is an excellent source of ancillary revenue. It is often the second most significant revenue stream behind memberships in traditional facilities. In addition to generating more revenue, a great personal training program increases members' ability to hit their goals, enhances member engagement, provides professional expertise, promotes injury prevention and safety, and enhances the overall member experience, thus increasing retention. By offering personalized attention, customized programs, and expert guidance, personal training contributes to your facility's overall success and reputation, differentiating it from the competition.

While all members can benefit from personal training, certain types of individuals are most likely to participate and benefit. Beginner exercisers, goal-oriented individuals, and those needing accountability and motivation are members who benefit highly from personal training. Personal training is also desirable to members with limited or busy schedules because it is one of the most efficient ways to hit their health and fitness goals. Finally, there are members with particular goals or needs that benefit from personal training. A member with a dedicated strength training goal, preparing for a sporting event or race, or someone recovering from an injury or illness falls into that category. Your facility's target market for personal training will be unique based on your location, demographics, facility type, and specific offerings. Your personal trainers need to adapt their approach and what they offer to match the needs and preferences of your unique target market.

During personal training sessions, trainers guide and instruct clients on proper exercise techniques, provide motivation and support, monitor progress, and make necessary adjustments to the workout program. They may also offer advice on general nutrition, lifestyle changes, and other factors contributing to overall health and fitness while staying within their scope of practice.

Personal training can benefit individuals of all fitness levels, from beginners to athletes. It offers a structured and individualized approach to fitness, providing accountability and guidance to help clients stay on track and achieve their desired results. Whether the goal is weight loss, muscle building, or improving athletic performance and overall fitness, personal training can provide the expertise and support needed to reach those goals efficiently and safely.

Delivery Methods for Personal Training Sessions

Like the other programming types discussed in this chapter, personal training can be delivered in person or virtually. In-person personal training involves a certified personal trainer working directly with a client, providing tailored exercise instruction, hands-on correction and modification, and support in a face-to-face setting. In-person personal training offers the highest level of engagement.

Virtual personal training, on the other hand, involves a certified personal trainer offering remote personalized guidance, instruction, and support for clients through online communication platforms. When done synchronously, this happens through live video sessions that allow the personal trainer and client to interact in real-time, which provides the opportunity for exercise demonstration, feedback, and guidance. Virtual personal training can also be done asynchronously. In this method, virtual personal training is conducted through prerecorded workout videos and personalized training plans. Communication occurs through a dedicated personal training application, messaging, or email. While it is less engaging than in-person and synchronous virtual person training because there is no real-time interaction, it allows clients to access and use the training materials at their convenience, which can appeal to certain members. When deciding whether you will offer virtual personal training at your facility, consider the client's preferences, accessibility, and technology resources. Consider also the cost and revenue potential, and ensure that it aligns with your overall strategic plan.

Conducting an Unparalleled Personal Training Session

A key to a successful personal training program is ensuring your trainers deliver unparalleled training sessions. To provide such a session, a personal trainer must focus on several crucial elements that make the session an effective, memorable, and exceptional experience. While there are differences in the delivery of the following components based on whether the session is in person or virtual, the components are needed to create a personal training experience that members desire.

First, effective communication from the get-go is essential. When a personal trainer works with someone for the first time, they should ask relevant questions, actively listen to clients, and understand their goals, preferences, and limitations. A personal trainer can then tailor the session and all future sessions to individual needs and provide personalized guidance throughout. This is referred to as the intake. While doing this, the trainer should also build trust and rapport through proper body language, asking relevant questions, and sharing appropriate personal information.

Second, a personal trainer should set goals with the client after the intake and perform appropriate assessments. This is a foundation for success. Types of assessments include body fat composition, functional movement screening, measurements, weight, and any other methods related to the client's goal. The assessment serves two primary functions. First, it provides personal trainers with reliable information to help them design the best program based on the client's fitness level, physical limitations, and goals. The data also offers a baseline that can be used to measure progress and results.

The third factor is the overall program design and the individual session design. Just like a good group fitness instructor or small group and large team training leader, preparing the session beforehand is crucial. This planning allows a personal trainer to ensure session variety and proper progression. Diverse sessions that incorporate various exercises, training methods, and equipment will consistently be engaging, challenging, and exciting. When that happens, a personal trainer can prevent boredom and physical plateaus so clients get optimal results. The trainer also must focus on strategic progression, gradually elevating the complexity and intensity as the client becomes stronger and more skilled.

During every session, the personal trainer should provide motivation, encouragement, accountability, support, and fun. A personal trainer's goal is to create a supportive and inspiring atmosphere by providing consistent positive reinforcement, celebrating milestones and achievements, and helping clients overcome mental and physical hurdles. By being a source of motivation and belief in their clients' abilities, trainers can help them stay motivated, focused, and committed to their health and fitness goals.

Finally, paying a high attention to detail is fundamental for a personal trainer. Through closely monitoring the client's exertion levels, ensuring proper form and technique, and providing real-time feedback, an excellent personal trainer is actively engaged and pays attention at every point during the session. This dedicated attention to detail creates a safe, efficient, effective, and enjoyable personal training session.

While the time spent during a training session must be a great experience, the most successful personal trainers go above and beyond. Consistent communication, check-ins, and thoughtful gestures such as handwritten thank-you notes go a long way in cultivating solid trainer–client relationships. These items demonstrate care, support, and dedication to clients. Consistent communication allows trainers to share progress, gather feedback, and stay connected outside the facility. When personal trainers prioritize these practices in conjunction with workout sessions, they create a comprehensive and personalized experience that makes a lasting positive impact on clients.

A personal trainer can deliver a great session by combining effective communication, comprehensive assessments, personalized programming, session variety, motivation, and attention to detail. When coupled with the best practices of consistent communication outside of the session and above-and-beyond gestures, an unparalleled personal training experience is genuinely created.

Personal Training Offerings

There are many ways to structure the personal training options at your fitness facility to accommodate the needs and preferences of members. The structure's first basic component is to offer one-on-one or one-on-two (partner training) options. Anything over two falls into the category of small group training. The per-session price for partner training is generally slightly higher than one-on-one since the personal trainer works with two clients simultaneously. Beyond offering these two options, it is up to you to decide how to structure personal training for members to purchase.

• *À la carte.* À la carte personal training is a pricing structure that allows clients to choose and pay for specific sessions or packages they desire based on their needs and preferences. This pricing structure offers a fixed rate for each session. The rate may vary based on the session's duration. This structure allows a client to train as needed or as desired. This can appeal to clients with challenging or irregular schedules or those with a tight budget. The challenge for a personal trainer is that this can lead to a lack of consistent training, which may hamper the client's results. The lack of predictable revenue can be challenging for a personal trainer and your facility.

• *Packages.* Structuring a personal training package means bundling a predetermined number of training sessions with a lower per-session rate than if purchased à la carte. Typical packages are 5, 10, and 20 packs, but you can offer whatever numbers make sense to you. Generally, the more sessions in the package, the lower the price per session. For example, a 10-pack of sessions might cost $800, but a 20-pack of sessions might cost $1,400. The 10-pack per-session rate is $80 per session, and the 20-pack offers a per-session rate of $70. This structure tends to reward the client for spending more at the time of purchase by lowering the per-session rate. The package structure leads to higher commitment, thus increasing the client's likelihood of achieving long-term success in attaining fitness objectives than à la carte. From a personal trainer and facility standpoint, this provides more predictable revenue, which is helpful. However, reselling the client every time a package expires is challenging.

• *Monthly (recurring).* A third structure for personal training pricing is "monthly recurring." This structure allows clients to pay a fixed monthly fee for either a certain number or unlimited training sessions over a month. This pricing structure is helpful to clients because it provides a consistent and predictable payment schedule. It also promotes regular attendance and commitment. This approach is particularly beneficial for clients with a schedule allowing consistent attendance. Monthly recurring pricing is also an excellent way for a personal trainer to nurture a long-term partnership with the client. This structure provides the best opportunity to create consistent and predictable revenue for the personal trainer and your facility. It also removes the need to resell the client because the billing is automatic until the client desires to cancel. A challenge with this structure is when a client does not use all the allocated sessions in the month. The personal trainer deals with this in one of two ways. First, they explain that the sessions have expired since the month ended. This can often frustrate clients. The second method is to "roll" the sessions into the next month. While this may make the client happier, it can be a logistical tracking nightmare for your fitness facility.

When you decide which pricing structure to use, consider the best interests of clients, trainers, and your facility. Adopting a flexible pricing structure that caters to varying needs is essential. You do not have to choose one structure. Offering a combination of à la carte pricing, package pricing, and monthly recurring options can effectively meet all parties' best interests. Once you have decided on how to structure personal training pricing, the next step is to market and sell it.

Marketing and Selling Personal Training

Now that you understand how to create and structure effective personal training programming, it is time to examine the crucial aspect of marketing and selling it. A strategic approach to creating awareness (marketing) and getting people to participate (selling) is required to have a profitable personal training program. Then, with the right tactics, you can make a compelling personal training offer that yields a steady stream of clients and increases revenue.

Highlight the Value

When marketing personal training services in a fitness facility, you need to create and employ effective strategies that attract potential clients and highlight the value your personal trainers can provide members as they attempt to achieve their health and fitness goals. There are several different tactics you can implement to market personal training effectively. As you consider what tactics to use, always keep your target market in mind. Your target market, discussed extensively in chapter 3, identifies precisely who you are marketing to. This knowledge helps guide the mediums, imagery, and copy used in your marketing. There are a variety of tactics to market personal training, and using a diverse approach to cover all facets increases the likelihood of success. Here are some personal training marketing tactics. Some need to be handled by the facility, while the personal trainer does others.

• *Highlight your personal trainers.* Finding areas in the facility, online, and on social media to showcase your personal trainers' expertise, experience, and credentials is recommended. These highlights should focus on certifications, qualifications, awards, accomplishments, personal notes, and testimonials from satisfied clients. Doing this allows members to get to know the trainers professionally and personally, which helps build trust and credibility. Highlighting your trainers adds value to the other marketing tactics. Personal trainers also need to highlight themselves. You need to encourage your personal trainers to interact and engage with members at your facility. This can be done by checking members in at the front desk, assisting in group fitness classes, or walking the workout floor and helping members. The more a personal trainer makes themselves well-known, the more likely members will be interested in their services.

• *Use traditional marketing.* Using traditional marketing methods such as flyers, postcards, and mailers can be an effective tactic for your fitness facility to market personal training. These traditional marketing pieces can be used inside the facility to market personal training to current members and outside the facility to garner interest from nonmembers. Ensuring that the imagery and copy on the marketing pieces align with your brand and trainers is essential. As part of the marketing, you must craft attractive packages or promotions that entice potential clients to engage. This offer can range from complimentary, discounted, or added value to sessions with additional perks, such as nutrition consultations or a discount at the pro shop. Traditional marketing can be an effective way of generating interest.

• *Use digital marketing.* Everything happening when highlighting personal trainers and using traditional marketing should also occur online. To maximize the impact of highlighting personal trainers and traditional marketing efforts, it is essential to replicate these strategies online by adding them to your website and using them for social media content and regular member e-newsletter communication. With the seamless integration of these marketing tactics across various digital mediums, you can effectively reach and engage more potential clients. In addition to your facility's efforts, a personal trainer should be encouraged to develop a presence on social media. Sharing workouts, client results, and testimonials helps build a strong reputation. The combination of traditional and digital marketing is a great one-two punch.

• *Create referral programs.* Create a referral program that rewards current clients for referring new clients. This program could include personal training discounts, free sessions, or special merchandise. The key is to create incentives that entice clients to spread the word. Note that independent of a formal referral program, personal trainers should be in the habit of politely and professionally asking current clients for referrals. Even with a referral incentive program, the personal trainer should thank clients for a referral. Whether it is face-to-face or a handwritten note, personal trainers should always express gratitude for referrals. Referral programs are an excellent tactic for client acquisition and are often very low cost, making them a great return on investment (ROI).

• *Host workshops and events.* A great way to generate interest in personal training is to host workshops, conduct fitness challenges, or provide other events within your facility. In addition to being a vehicle for attracting potential clients, these allow your personal trainers to establish themselves as authorities in the field while allowing attendees to experience their services firsthand. These can also be effective outside the facility, such as doing lunch-and-learns or corporate fitness classes. This is a great way to build awareness among large groups of people.

• *Network inside and outside the facility.* Building relationships with other businesses is a great way to generate interest and referrals. The key is to find businesses that are complementary, not competitive. This can be done formally through your facility, or your personal trainers can do it. Businesses such as nutritionists, chiropractors, massage therapists, and vitamin shops can be great partners because of the ability to refer back and forth. In some scenarios, it may be possible to collaborate on joint programs that benefit both parties. These types of partnerships can be win-win because they help both businesses create awareness and generate new clients.

• *Provide an exceptional training experience.* While your facility plays a part in this, much of it falls on your personal trainer. A personal trainer must provide clients with an experience that makes them want to share. Everything discussed early in this chapter regarding creating an unparalleled experience is essential, not just to keep the client happy but because other potential clients are watching. A personal trainer is always on stage. Every training session is a commercial for all the facility's members. When a personal trainer consistently demonstrates genuine care, undivided attention, and professionalism, they create that unparalleled experience everyone desires. Satisfied clients become raving fans and advocates for your personal trainers, which helps them maintain an excellent reputation and generate positive word-of-mouth marketing. All other marketing tactics mentioned are less effective if the training experience is subpar. On the contrary, if the experience is exceptional, the effect of the marketing tactics is massively amplified.

These tactics can effectively market your personal training programs when executed consistently and together. Although these tactics are geared toward marketing personal training, specifically, you will see some similar content in chapter 11, where you will learn about lead generation for new members. Consistently evaluate the ROI of your marketing efforts and adjust when necessary. Creating and implementing strategic marketing tactics is a prerequisite for generating awareness. The next step is to turn that awareness into new clients.

Make the Sale

The goal of marketing personal training is to create awareness and generate interest. Once a member expresses interest, your personal trainer's aim is to convert them into a paying client. Personal training sales are primarily made by taking prospective clients through an introductory session to demonstrate why working with a personal trainer is the best way to achieve their health and fitness goals. On completion of the introductory session, a personal trainer will attempt to sell one of the personal training options. Most people become personal trainers because they genuinely want to help people better their lives through health and fitness, not because they are excited to sell personal training packages. Therefore, providing personal trainers with the tools and training to help them feel confident when selling is foundational. Ultimately, your personal trainers need to understand that selling is simply showing a member that the trainer is the best solution to the problem the member is trying to solve. Several strategies can be used in this process to increase the likelihood that a prospective client becomes a permanent client.

Before attempting to sell personal training, a personal trainer ought to create excitement and interest during the introductory session. An effective session showcases the trainer's skills while showing that working together is the best way to achieve goals. Earlier in this chapter, you learned the basics of conducting an unparalleled personal training session, which applies to an introductory session. In addition to that, a few other things should happen during an introductory session. First, a personal trainer should use exercises that require assistance, for example, a medicine ball toss or holding a band that the prospect is using. Such

activities emphasize the need to work together. The introductory session shouldn't be too long or too challenging. It should offer enough to show value but leave the prospect wanting more. Equally important as the physical part of the workout is the way a personal trainer communicates throughout the session. The trainer should always refer to the prospect as a client when introducing them to people. There should be some education during the session, but the trainer should focus on the benefits to the prospect and what the session and activity are doing to achieve the desired goal. The session should leave the prospect energized, motivated, and wanting more.

At the end of the introductory session, it's time for your personal trainer to discuss the next steps in the client's fitness journey. This is the opportunity for the personal trainer to sell their services. Your personal trainer should sit alongside (not across from) the prospect. Sitting across from the prospective client is a negotiation. Sitting side by side is collaboration. Before pricing, a personal trainer should offer gratitude for the client's trust and praise for their performance. Next, they need to recap the session and how everything that transpired will help the prospect hit their goals. At this point, it is time to sell.

Personal trainers should recommend the most appropriate training package based on the goals, along with a plan, basic time line, and pricing. They need to remember that they are the experts. Making a recommendation is much stronger and more effective than asking someone if they would like to train. While doing so, it is essential to reinforce the benefits of having a personal trainer, such as accountability, personalized attention, and faster progress toward goals. Maintaining the energy, enthusiasm, and positivity delivered during the first impression is also crucial. By now, there are only two possibilities.

At this point, the prospect is either a new client or still a lead. Regardless of the result, a personal trainer should follow up. If the prospect says yes, reinforce that they have made a great decision and reassure them that goals will be reached. Review any necessary paperwork, policies, and procedures, and ensure the first official workout is scheduled. The process should end with a sincere thank you and excitement. It is a good idea to follow up via email, call, or text with another thank you, welcome to the program, and any other relevant information.

Conversely, if the prospect says no, your personal trainer needs to respect that the prospect is not ready to start yet. It is appropriate for your trainer to ask courteously what the hesitation to start is and politely try to overcome the objection by reinforcing the value already demonstrated. This is not a hard press to sell; it is just so the trainer can ensure that all questions or issues are answered. Finally, when a prospect does not convert to a client, a personal trainer should provide the prospect with some resources (e.g., sample exercises, basic workout templates) and schedule a follow-up to check in. This demonstrates to the prospect that the trainer is invested in their success and is here to help when ready. By continuing to support and nurture the relationship with the prospect, the trainer dramatically increases the chance of the prospect signing up when the time is right. Trainers must be aware that personal training sometimes has a long sales cycle.

While most personal training sales are made by the trainer in the process just described, personal training can be sold in other ways. Sometimes a member knows that they want training and inquires about it. You can run training specials with discounts or other compelling offers that prompt members to ask about it. A common practice is to offer a special introductory training package when someone buys a membership. This is generally a small package of sessions at a discounted rate. In all these scenarios where the member takes action, you need to have a system for pairing the member with the personal trainer you feel is the best fit based on knowledge, experience, and personality types.

Remember, selling personal training services is not just about making a sale; it's about helping individuals achieve their fitness goals and improve their lives. By effectively conveying the value you bring as a personal trainer, conducting an excellent introductory session, and recommending personal training options, your personal trainers can successfully sell your training services in a fitness facility.

With a solid understanding of personal training programming and the tactics for marketing and selling it, you and your personal trainers have the tools to create a successful and profitable personal training program in your fitness facility.

Offboarding Personal Training Clients

There comes a time when a client decides to discontinue their personal training for reasons such as financial constraints, schedule or priority changes, health issues or injuries, relocation, dissatisfaction with the personal trainer or program, or a desire to try something different. Clients could also feel they have achieved their goals and no longer need personal training. Whatever the reason, it is imperative that the client go through a well-thought-out offboarding process.

Personal training offboarding is professionally and respectfully transitioning a client out of a personal training program. This process should start with a face-to-face conversation discussing goals, progress, and any potential concerns they might have. During this confirmation, the personal trainer should review progress and celebrate accomplishments to validate the client's efforts. It is also good form to discuss the client's journey moving forward while offering advice and providing resources that will support them. If appropriate, a personal trainer can offer a final session or evaluation to answer questions and provide feedback and recommendations. The personal trainer should ensure the client has their current contact information. Finally, it is important to express gratitude for their commitment and the opportunity to work with them and ask for any feedback on the provided training. Maintain a professional relationship by staying connected through social media or periodic check-ins to offer support. The goal is to ensure they feel valued, supported, and empowered to continue their fitness journey beyond your services.

After this, your facility can send surveys to the client to gain more insight into their experience. This can be done through NPS or other customized surveys. While a personal trainer should ask for feedback during the face-to-face meeting with the client, they may not feel comfortable disclosing anything that the trainer may construe as negative. When you ask for feedback as a facility, you may get more open and honest information to help you coach the personal trainer and improve the overall personal training programming. Formally asking for feedback should be a part of your offboarding process.

Finally, it is essential that you handle all the logistical items smoothly. These items include stopping billing, issuing refunds, and completing cancellation paperwork. By addressing these logistical aspects of client offboarding, you can ensure a smooth transition while demonstrating professionalism, clarity, and transparency for your business operations.

Evaluating Personal Training Programs and Personal Trainers

Regular evaluation is crucial for the success of personal training, just as it is for other forms of programming. When conducting evaluations in personal training, three key components should be considered: the overall program, the personal training manager, and the personal trainer. Each of these elements plays a significant role in determining the effectiveness and quality of the personal training experience. When carefully assessing and optimizing these components, you can create the best personal training experience possible.

You need to consider several factors when evaluating your overall personal training program. First, regularly assessing your pricing structure helps you ensure it is competitive with other providers in the market. Second, assessing your marketing strategy's effectiveness lets you modify your approach to attract and retain clients more effectively. Third, collecting feedback through surveys such as NPS helps you understand the overall satisfaction level of clients as well as expose areas for improvement. Finally, reviewing important financial metrics is a great way to evaluate the overall financial position of your personal training program. When closely monitoring these areas, you can optimize your personal training programs to create and sustain long-term success.

To evaluate a personal training manager, you should focus on their qualifications and experience. Certifications from reputable organizations demonstrate their expertise and knowledge in the field. A competent manager should have a solid understanding of exercise science, injury prevention, and program design. They should be able to provide guidance, support, and resources to the personal trainers they oversee. A good manager effectively communicates expectations, monitors client progress, and ensures that trainers continuously develop their skills through ongoing education and training. A capable and experienced manager plays a vital role in maintaining the quality and effectiveness of the personal training services provided.

When evaluating a personal training manager's performance, you should focus on critical areas such as business results, leadership, and management skills. You should also address the ability to hit financial targets, manage expenses, and optimize profitability. A comprehensive evaluation inspects their leadership and communication skills and

knowledge to motivate and support their trainers. Their ability to manage programs, ensure seamless operations, schedule trainers, and oversee client assignments should all be addressed in evaluations. By evaluating these factors, you can gauge the personal training manager's performance and find areas for improvement.

The final area of evaluation is personal trainers themselves. When evaluating a personal trainer, there are several vital aspects to consider. To evaluate a personal trainer's performance, consider client progress and satisfaction, communication, professionalism, continuing education, and teamwork. You can also assess financial metrics such as the conversion rate of introductory sessions to paying clients, client retention rates, and the personal trainer's ability to meet sales goals. This can be done by the formal evaluation methods described in chapter 6 and by gathering client feedback.

In all the evaluations, honest communication and regular feedback are essential. Regularly discuss your progress, concerns, and satisfaction with all parties involved. This feedback loop allows for adjustments and improvements to be made, ensuring that the personal training programming and everyone involved remain effective, engaging, and aligned with your facility's goals.

Health Coaching

Health coaching adds great value to your fitness facility. A health coach's primary purpose is to cocreate a health and well-being plan for a client based on the client's personal values and goals. Although similarities do exist between health coaching and personal training, they are very different programs. A health coach works with a client well beyond fitness-related goals. A health coach can serve as a primary liaison with the allied health care continuum and can open doors related to lifestyle medicine as an offering. Many medical fitness facilities offer lifestyle medicine and health coaching as a primary service. Health coaches can accelerate the referral process both in and out of the fitness facility. Health coaching is considered an advanced certification and often requires additional education or other industry-adjacent certification, depending on the setting in which the health coach is working. Insurance is more likely to cover health coaching in the future, a supposition that correlates with the ACSM trends listed in chapter 1.

A traditional approach to member onboarding in a health club setting is to offer two complimentary personal training sessions to all new members within their first 30 days with a goal of upselling the member to a personal training package. A forward-thinking approach would be to offer all new members complimentary health coaching. The health coach could focus on understanding the member's goals and motivation and could increase the longevity of the membership, as opposed to trying to make an immediate upsell. With this being said, personal training benefits most members, so the health coach could refer the client to personal training, which would still promote behavior change and adherence.

Pricing and delivery methods for health coaching are similar to personal training and other programs offered in a fitness facility. More states in the United States are exploring insurance billing codes for health coaching, which would open more doors of opportunity for revenue generation.

Health coaching is like a dance between the coach and the client. There needs to be continuous communication and engagement between the two, and both the client and the coach need to be able to adapt and respond to the changing environment and client milestones. When this dance is done correctly, the client has higher program adherence, behavior modification, and retention levels.

Other Programming and Services

In addition to group fitness, small group and large team training, personal training, and health coaching, fitness facilities often provide other services to members. Other services include tennis, massage, nutrition, and spa services. Offering these services helps cater to members' needs and creates additional revenue streams.

Tennis and other racket sports, such as racquetball and pickleball, can be great ways to serve members. Tennis lessons, court rentals, and camps serve members who enjoy these activities while generating ancillary revenue. Experienced tennis coaches, instructors, and professionals typically conduct tennis programming at fitness facilities.

Massage therapy is a service that can be offered for an additional fee, making it a great source of ancillary revenue while helping members with relaxation and recovery. These services are delivered by a certified massage therapist or a bodywork professional trained in different massage techniques, ensuring safe and effective treatments.

Nutritional guidance, such as personalized meal plans and consultations, is a service that can be offered for a one-time fee, as a paid package, or as a subscription. This is an excellent way for your fitness facility to generate revenue while supporting the dietary goals of members. These types of services should be provided by a registered dietitian or nutritionist with the education and credentials to create personalized meal plans and offer nutritional guidance. It is important to note that each state may have different laws around nutritional guidance and meal planning.

Spa services include various treatments and beauty enhancements. These can be offered as a premium service, creating a luxurious experience for members and generating additional revenue. Spa services are delivered by aestheticians, manicurists, hair stylists, and spa technicians who provide the benefit of their expertise.

Conclusion

Given the various options for programming and services, consider factors like member demographics and preferences, target market, facility resources and expertise, revenue potential, and alignment with your mission and brand when deciding what to offer. By understanding these things, you can determine which services to provide.

Ultimately, by diversifying the offerings of your fitness facility and by choosing the most appropriate programming, you can better meet members' expectations and create viable additional revenue streams.

THINK IT THROUGH

- Why is offering group fitness a good idea for fitness facility managers?
- What are the different ways that group fitness, group training, and personal training can be delivered to members by a fitness facility?
- How can fitness facilities effectively market and sell personal training services?
- What is the role of health coaching in fitness facilities, and how does it differ from personal training?
- Other than group exercise, group training, and personal training, what additional services can you offer at your fitness facility to cater to members' needs?

KEY TERMS

group fitness
health coaching
hybrid programming
in-person programming
personal training
small group training
timetable
virtual programming

PART IV

Project Management and Profitability: Creating Systems for Success

11

Attracting and Engaging Members

Upon completion of this chapter, you will be able to do the following:

- Identify the components of a sales funnel
- Apply principles of behavior change models
- Design a positive member experience, from prospect to offboarding
- Apply sales principles
- Create a new member onboarding checklist
- Implement a consistent sales follow-up process
- Construct member incentives and engagement opportunities
- Identify causes of member separation
- Create a member offboarding checklist

Once a facility has been designed and built and staff has been hired, it's time to recruit members. Attracting and engaging members is critical. For your fitness facility to succeed, you must attract new members and retain existing members. The fitness industry is highly competitive, and your fitness facility must develop strategies to differentiate yourself from competitors and appeal to potential members.

Once you encourage a member to join, you must find ways to consistently keep them engaged and inspired so that they continue to use the facility to achieve their health and fitness goals. This chapter explores various strategies and methods you can use to attract and engage members. The importance of creating a welcoming and supportive environment that fosters community and belonging among members will be examined. Finally, best practices for when the relations between a member and facility end, which includes a comprehensive member offboarding program, will be covered.

By implementing the best practices discussed in this chapter, you will increase member satisfaction and retention, ultimately leading to long-term success and sustainability.

Sales Funnels

The first step in understanding how to attract members is understanding the sales funnel concept (figure 11.1). A sales funnel represents the customer's journey to deciding to purchase something. The journey begins when a potential customer is aware that a brand exists and carries through to turning that potential customer into a paying customer and a raving fan. Typically, a sales funnel includes five stages (OneMob 2022):

1. *Awareness.* The first stage in a sales funnel is when and where a potential customer becomes aware of your brand. At this point, the prospect has seen some of your marketing and now realizes you exist.

2. *Interest.* In the second stage, after the potential customer is aware of your brand, they show interest and want to learn more. This

interest may take them to your website, to consumer reviews, and to a visit to your facility. The goal at this stage is to improve their opinion of your brand and demonstrate why your facility is an excellent choice.

3. *Evaluation.* In the third stage, the potential customer seriously considers whether they want to do business with you. This is where they will do more in-depth research and often shop among your competitors so they are aware of their options.

4. *Engagement.* Think of the fourth stage as your sales process. This is the chance to build rapport and trust with the potential customer. It is an opportunity to uncover the problem the prospect is trying to solve and show them that your facility is the best solution. This stage is the actual sales process.

5. *Purchase.* This is the final stage of the sales funnel. It is the culmination of the effective execution of the first four stages, resulting in a new paying customer.

While stage 5 is the final stage, the journey doesn't stop there. Strategies and tactics must be in place to retain customers and build long-term relationships with them; that is, they continue to do business with you and refer your facilities to their family and friends. Some people consider this a sixth sales funnel stage and refer to it as *retention* or *loyalty.*

The goal of a sales funnel is to take potential customers on a journey of understanding a business and guiding them to a decision to purchase. A facility should use this process to improve marketing efforts, optimize sales processes, and create the best customer experience possible. If an organization understands where potential customers are in the funnel, it can customize its messaging and strategies to move them successfully to the next stage. Ultimately, the goal is to turn prospects into raving fans by building long-term relationships with them. Facilities should use sales funnels to improve their conversion rates, thus increasing revenue.

Behavior Change Models

In a process that echoes sales funnels, behavior change models shed light on how someone adopts healthy lifestyle behaviors. To understand this similarity, you should understand the transtheoretical model of behavior change, the essence of wisdom, and self-determination theory. Understanding these models' influencing behavior creates a stronger and more effective approach when converting prospects into long-term members. The sales funnel you just learned about lines up closely with the models.

Transtheoretical Model of Behavior Change

The transtheoretical model of behavior change (American Council on Exercise 2019) outlines the stages that someone goes through while considering and adopting a new behavior. This model, initially developed in the 1970s by James O. Prochaska and Carlo C. DiClemente, includes the following:

- *Precontemplation.* An individual in precontemplation has no intention of changing or adopting the behavior. Perhaps the person doesn't even know why the behavior is a good idea. An individual in precontemplation will drive by a fitness facility without even knowing it's there and without it even crossing their mind.

- *Contemplation.* An individual in contemplation thinks about potentially adopting a behavior and is curious about its benefits. The person becomes intrigued about the fitness facility as they drive past it to the office. The individual is also contemplating stopping in for a tour one day shortly.

- *Preparation.* An individual in preparation has decided to try out the new behavior. They

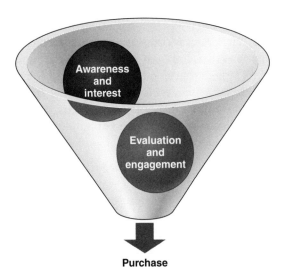

FIGURE 11.1   Sales funnel.

have decided that the pros of adopting the behavior outweigh the cons or sacrifices they must make in the decisional balance. The individual has stopped by the fitness facility and taken a tour. Perhaps the person has signed up for a free trial.

- *Action.* An individual in action is participating in the behavior regularly but has yet to make it to, say, the six-month milestone. While the individual participates in this behavior, the dropout rate can be high since the behavior is new. An example is the individual who has signed up for a fitness facility membership and consistently exercises during their first six months.

- *Maintenance.* An individual in maintenance has consistently participated in the behavior for a period of time. The individual is most likely to be a regular gym goer and is likely to refer their friends to join as well.

As a person moves through the stages of change (figure 11.2), it is not always a clean linear progression; the person can relapse at any time.

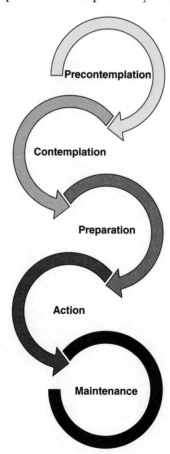

FIGURE 11.2 Stages of behavior change.

Essence of Wisdom

S.N. Goenka, a Burmese-Indian teacher of Vipassana meditation, wrote about three types of wisdom (Goenka 2010):

1. Wisdom gained from others
2. Intellectual wisdom
3. Experiential wisdom

The philosophies taught in meditation are akin to an individual going through the process of adopting a behavior. For example, if someone learns about exercise from a friend currently a member of your fitness facility, the seed has been planted. Next, the individual may begin to look into the benefits of exercise and decide whether or not participating in exercise and joining your facility is right for them. Lastly, the individual has decided to experience exercise and activates a free trial at your facility.

Self-Determination Theory

The last behavior change theory to be aware of is self-determination theory. Identified in 1985 by two psychologists, Edward L. Deci and Richard M. Ryan, self-determination theory is built on the premise that individuals have higher levels of intrinsic motivation if the following three basic needs are met (Deci and Ryan 1985):

1. *Autonomy*—the feeling of being able to control one's own decisions
2. *Competence*—the knowledge and capability to make those decisions
3. *Relatedness*—a sense of belonging and providing value to a group of people

A prospect should feel these three needs (figure 11.3) upon entering your fitness facility. If your membership team can practice applying techniques to increase an individual's competency, cultivate an environment where the individual can envision being a part of the community, and empower the individual to make decisions, the person is more likely to be consistent in their exercise behavior.

Lead Generation

Like any business in any industry, fitness facilities need a consistent funnel of potential customers to achieve and sustain success. Your potential customers have many options for their health and fitness needs, making it challenging to stand out from

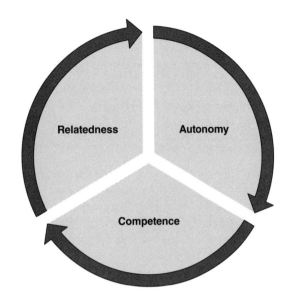

FIGURE 11.3 Basic needs in self-determination theory.

competitors. Successful facilities use diverse strategies to reach potential customers, create interest, and convert them into paying members. Effective lead generation involves diverse approaches, such as traditional content, digital, social media, and guerrilla marketing. In addition to those methods of marketing, creating strong referral programs is highly effective for lead generation. When creating marketing strategies, refer to the sales funnel steps and use them as a guideline. Regardless of the method of marketing being used, the goal should be to take a potential customer through all five stages of the funnel.

Traditional Marketing

Traditional marketing refers to print, advertising, and broadcast marketing. These methods are considered traditional because various industries have used them for years. Direct mailers, postcards, flyers, billboards, newspaper and magazine ads, and radio and television commercials are examples of this conventional marketing type. These methods are not typically interactive. Instead, an organization is reaching out to convey its message in a way that prompts a potential customer to inquire.

An advantage of traditional marketing is that it can effectively reach a large audience. A disadvantage is that it tends to be expensive and not personalized. With innovation and the advent of more modern forms of marketing, some people argue that traditional marketing is no longer effective. Even so, by implementing the appropriate strategy, many organizations still have success with traditional marketing.

Content Marketing

Content marketing builds trust and rapport with potential customers by creating and providing valuable, relevant, and consistent content. The purpose of this content is to create the desire for someone to want to do business with your brand. This content can be distributed through articles, blogs, videos, podcasts, webinars, social media posts, email newsletters, and more. Whatever the distribution channel, the content should entertain, educate, and inspire rather than simply attempting to sell. Specific examples of content for the fitness industry could be healthy recipes, fitness tips, and workouts. Whatever aligns with your brand and provides value to the audience is good content. Author and entrepreneur Gary Vaynerchuk explains content marketing in his book *Jab, Jab, Jab, Right Hook*, with the analogy that jabs are the way you provide value to customers with helpful content. The right hook is when you ask for a sale. He suggests you continually jab your potential customers with content, then after you have built a relationship and trust, uppercut them by asking them to purchase something (Vaynerchuk 2013). Content marketing can help distance a facility from its competitors, positioning it as the go-to brand authority in the market.

Digital Marketing

Digital marketing focuses on maximizing digital channels such as search engines, social media, email, websites, and mobile apps to reach potential customers. Note that there is an overlap in the different marketing methods: Content marketing and social media marketing are part of a digital strategy. Various forms of digital marketing include search engine optimization (SEO), pay-per-click (PPC) advertising, social media marketing, content marketing, email marketing, and mobile marketing. An advantage to digital marketing is that it is highly data-driven, so marketers can easily measure their effectiveness in real time. Another huge advantage of digital marketing is that it can be highly targeted. It can be used to target specific demographics and interests. A challenge with digital marketing is that it can be confusing. Most organizations hire contract experts to handle it, which is an added expense.

The importance of digital marketing can't be overstated. Fitness facilities and consumers operate in a digital age. Consumers spend a good deal of time online researching when considering purchasing a product or service. According to a 2021 global survey by Bizrate Insights, 91.3 percent of shoppers read product reviews before making a purchase, with the majority reading between one and six reviews per product. A strategic digital marketing strategy allows an organization to meet people where their eyes are, which is crucial to gaining potential customers' attention.

Social Media Marketing

Social media marketing is a form of digital marketing that warrants more discussion. It involves creating and sharing content on social media channels such as Facebook, YouTube, Instagram, and LinkedIn. Deciding which platform to use requires insight into your target market and which platform they use the most. A general example would be that a customer aged 45 years old and up may spend more time on Facebook, while people aged 18 to 24 may use Instagram more. Given that social media trends change quickly, it's crucial to keep track of the trending platforms and be willing to be flexible in the selection of platforms used to ensure effective engagement with the evolving preferences of your audience. Like the other marketing methods, the goal should be to take potential customers through the sales funnel steps. Social media marketing falls into two categories: unpaid (organic) and paid.

Organic Posts   Organic posts are nonpaid posts to engage an audience. These posts are the "jabs." Most organic posts should be jabs with the occasional hook thrown in. A good rule of thumb for organic content is 80 percent engaging content with 20 percent sales-oriented posts. One of the most significant advantages of organic posts is that they are free.

Paid Advertising   Paid advertising is another form of social media marketing. Paid advertising can be effective because it can be targeted, allowing an organization to reach a large but specific audience. It is also generally relatively low cost. There are, however, some disadvantages, such as oversaturation of ads, consumer fatigue regarding ads, and potential misspending or overspending on ineffective campaigns. Like SEO and PPC, paid advertising is often where facilities engage third-party specialists to maximize effectiveness. A combination of nonpaid and paid social media marketing can produce great results.

Influencer Marketing

Another powerful digital marketing method is influencer marketing. Influencer marketing can allow a fitness facility to reach a wider audience through trusted and respected individuals. These influencers tend to have large social media followings and are considered fitness experts by the public. By partnering with these influencers, fitness facilities can leverage their influence to promote their brand to a broader audience. While influencers are often global experts and celebrities, an effective strategy for fitness facilities is to partner with local people and members with an excellent social media presence. This strategy can be executed by providing the influential member with perks such as membership discounts or other rewards in exchange for a predetermined number of social media posts about the facility. Using these influencers can be effective because they are often more relatable than celebrities. This approach helps create community and loyalty among members while boosting brand visibility and reputation. Overall, influencer marketing, especially the local approach, is an effective and efficient way for fitness facilities to connect with their target audience, thus generating more leads.

Guerrilla Marketing

Guerilla marketing is an outside-the-box approach to marketing that uses unconventional and creative promotional strategies, generally with little or no cost. Some examples are placing lead boxes, passing out flyers at a farmer's market, or wrapping a car with your logo. (A lead box is a physical container that is strategically placed to gather people's contact information. An incentive such as a contest or raffle usually encourages people to fill out the form and drop it in the lead box.) Guerrilla marketing generates brand awareness for a low cost, which is a huge return on investment. On the other hand, guerilla marketing risks include the potential to alienate certain people, legal issues related to the use of public space, and the challenge of quantifying the effectiveness of efforts. Regardless of the pros and cons, guerrilla marketing may be a worthwhile strategy for start-ups and organizations with a limited budget.

Referral Marketing

This marketing approach encourages and incentivizes existing customers to refer new customers to the facility. Examples of referral marketing include providing guest passes, rewards programs, social events, VIP programs, and contests. Some advantages of referral marketing are the ease of implementation and cost-effectiveness. The only slight disadvantage to referral marketing is that it can be off-putting to members if done haphazardly. Therefore, all referral strategies should be designed to motivate members, not pressure them to refer. If you manage referrals correctly, you can realize massive benefits from referred customers. Annex Cloud (Miller 2023) states that referred customers are three to five times more likely to convert into paying members. Furthermore, members who come to you via referral have a 25 percent higher lifetime value, are 18 percent more loyal, are four times more likely to refer others, and have a 37 percent higher retention rate than nonreferred customers (Miller 2023). These statistics illustrate the importance of an organization having a strategic approach to generating referrals from current members.

Membership Sales

The final stage of the sales funnel is purchase. This is the point where a nurtured lead decides that they want to do business with a facility. Fitness facilities need to have a solid sales strategy in place to convert leads into paying members. Something to remember is that fitness facility membership sales are relationship based, not transactional. A transactional sale is generally a one-time sale. Someone makes a purchase, gets the product, and that is that. When a person purchases a fitness facility membership, it is only the beginning. That person may use the membership multiple times per week. The member will also be encouraged to purchase other products and services. These factors make membership sales a relationship-based process.

While a transactional sale doesn't necessarily need to be a great experience because it ends with the purchase, a membership sale does, because it is merely the beginning of what you hope to be a long-running relationship. Therefore, it is essential to create an effective system for membership sales that creates a good experience for the buyer and the seller. Creating a great sales experience keeps the buyer engaged and inspired, making it a more straightforward process for the seller.

Fitness facilities have various staffing models in place. One is the traditional structure of a sales manager overseeing the department and membership sales associates. Some models use a hybrid of front desk staff trained in sales. It can be challenging not having team members dedicated solely to sales, but it has the benefit of reducing staffing costs because roles are combined. In some facilities, a significant emphasis is put on joining via the Internet. A prospect visits a facility, is given a tour, then is directed to a kiosk to see membership options and make a purchase. Finally, some models only offer the ability to join online. Prospects can get all the relevant information and purchase immediately via an app or website. All facilities use one or a combination of these methods to convert leads into members. Regardless of the method, any staff involved in the process must be trained on the sales process for a facility to sell memberships successfully. That process, in some way, shape, or form, involves the following five steps. These five steps can vary for models that use purely online joining strategies.

1. First Impression

The goal of a first impression is to deliver a warm welcome that reinforces that it was a good decision for the prospect to inquire about joining the facility. This can be accomplished by training the staff to execute the following behaviors: Use welcoming body language, speak a luxury language, and focus 100 percent on the prospect. *Welcoming body language* in sales involves maintaining an open and confident posture, making consistent eye contact, and using gestures to enhance communication and build trust with potential clients. *Luxury language* refers to the use of sophisticated and aspirational words and phrases that evoke feelings of exclusivity and necessity, helping to create a sense of value and allure around a product or service, thereby increasing its appeal and potential for successful sales. Both body and luxury language have a strong conscious and subconscious impact on sales interactions.

With these in place, a prospect receives a focused and energetic greeting. A prospect generally asks about membership options and pricing. The staff response should be positive and reaffirming, and it needs to convey that the prospect will get answers. A reply such as "That's great, I'll be happy to get you that information" is a perfect way to make a prospect feel at ease and build rapport.

Immediately after that, the staff member should exchange names to personalize the experience and build more rapport. If the staff member doing the greeting is also making the sale, move on to step two in the sales process.

If the process involves a separate salesperson, follow these steps. First, reassure the prospect that they will be connected to someone who can answer their questions. When handing the prospect to the salesperson, a formal introduction, including an exchange of names, should occur. When conducting the introduction, using terminology such as "This is [prospect's name] and they are thinking about becoming a member" helps to plant deeper seeds regarding joining. Conclude the handoff by letting the prospect know that it was nice to meet them and that the hope is to see them in the facility again. Executed properly, prospects feel more at home and more inclined to purchase. When a first impression is a good one, it makes the rest of the sales process much easier and more effective.

2. Intake

In the health and fitness industry, selling is solving. The more a prospect's goals are understood, the better the solution can be provided. While a facility membership is an actual item that someone purchases, what they are buying is the hope of achieving health and fitness goals. To effectively sell a membership, there must be an information intake.

Before the intake, explaining the rest of the sales process to the prospect is essential. Let them know there will be an intake to learn more about them, a facility tour, and a review of membership options. When a prospect knows what lies ahead, it makes them feel more comfortable, which creates a better experience.

The intake can be digital or on paper. Typical items should include personal contact information, fitness goals, exercise history, health history, gym preferences, lifestyle habits, and other relevant information. Depending on the type of facility, these questions may vary.

The goal of gathering this information is to cultivate an understanding of what a prospect is trying to achieve regarding their health and fitness. A best practice when designing the intake is to ensure that everything asked for is relevant and that it is used in the sales process. It can be off-putting to a prospect to provide a lot of information that doesn't seem necessary. Instead, create intakes that are succinct and applicable. Use this time to actively listen, ask clarifying questions, and build rapport. Everything uncovered in the intake helps guide the next phase, the tour.

3. Tour

Each facility tour should be unique. The tour should be tailored to the individual based on everything you know up to this point. Divide the facility into areas such as the welcome desk, weight room, cardio equipment area, group fitness studios, locker rooms, pool, and courts. While tours generally explore all areas and amenities of a facility, use the information from the intake to decide which areas to start with and focus on. For example, if a prospect shows no interest in playing recreational basketball, there is no need to prioritize the basketball courts; ensure the prospect knows that these areas are available but don't spend much time on them. On the contrary, if you know that the prospect has small children, prioritize and spend time in the child care area.

In each of these areas, touch on the features but focus on the benefits. Benefits sell much more effectively than features. For example, a prospect likely won't care that the locker room is 2,000 square feet with 10 showers, four stalls, and 50 lockers; those are features. A prospect will resonate with the fact that they can come in on their lunch break, get a great workout, then conveniently use the locker room to clean up before returning to work; that is a benefit. Benefits elicit an emotional response that increases the likelihood someone will purchase. In conjunction with demonstrating the benefits, always refer the benefit back to the prospect's goal. Questions such as "Can you see how this would help you hit your health and fitness goals?" are a great way to do this. It reminds the prospect why they are there and how this is an excellent solution to their problem.

Protected Health Information

Depending on the type of facility and location, some information collected during intake may be considered protected health information and be subject to the Health Insurance Portability and Accountability Act (HIPAA). Be sure that your intake process has been reviewed by appropriate legal counsel before collecting and storing personal information, and ensure you are protecting data privacy.

Other factors make for an exciting tour as well. Introduce the prospect to other staff members and current fitness facility members. This practice helps to build trust, rapport, and comfort. The tour is also a great time to bring up relevant ancillary services, onboarding offerings, and anything that is offered that differentiates this fitness facility from the competition.

Proactively addressing potential objections to joining during the tour is also a good idea. Some of the most common objections besides cost are time, location, motivation, and the desire to shop for other options. Throughout the tour, use verbiage that conveys how convenient the site is and how easy it is to get a workout in to address time and location objections before they come up. Talk up the excellent member experience and the programming the facility provides to quash the motivation objection. Study the competition and communicate what sets the facility apart to combat the prospect's desire to shop at other locations. The more objections dealt with during the tour, the more limited objections are at the point of sale. This dramatically increases the chance of a sale. At the end of the tour, a prospect should be able to visualize what being a member would look and feel like and how they can accomplish their goals.

4. Pre-Close

The penultimate step in the membership sales process is called the *pre-close*. This step aims to uncover any remaining objections other than price. "Could you see yourself working out here? Was there anything you were looking for that you didn't see? Do you have any questions about the facility other than membership pricing?" These questions allow the salesperson to handle objections before getting to pricing. Once any remaining questions have been answered, tell the prospect that they will be shown membership options, including recommendations for which options would be best.

5. Close

Everything that has happened up to this point has led to this moment. This is the opportunity to get the prospect to become a paying member. The salesperson should express excitement at this part of the process as they show the prospect membership options and recommendations. Sitting side by side for this part of the process is best. Sitting across from a prospect feels like a negotiation, while sitting side by side feels like a partnership. Explain each option one at a time, and ask if there are any questions before moving on to the next option. After questions are answered, recommend the best membership option based on everything you've learned about the member throughout the sales process.

After the recommendation, ask for the sale. There are several ways to ask for a sale. One salesperson may say, "Let's get you signed up!" Another may ask, "Are you ready to become a member?" The specific approach is often based on the salesperson's style and skills. Regardless of the method, asking the prospect to become a member is imperative.

Hopefully, at this point, the prospect is now a paying member. Congratulate them for joining, complete all necessary paperwork, and get them started on the onboarding process. New member onboarding will be discussed in the next section.

If they decide not to join, that is okay. Spend time clarifying why they made this decision and see if the remaining objections can be addressed. While doing this, a salesperson should not be pushy. Instead, they should be helpful and encouraging while reinforcing the facility's value and why it would be a good idea for the prospect to join. If the answer is still no, the prospect should be thanked for coming in, given a fond farewell, and added to a sales follow-up protocol. Some prospects need more time before they join, so have a strategy to keep them in a sales funnel.

It's All About Relationships

Creating an effective system for membership sales is crucial to building and maintaining long-lasting relationships between fitness facilities and their members. With various sales staffing models available, all staff involved in the sales process must be trained to convert leads into paying members. Regardless of the chosen model, the process should involve the five essential steps to ensure a positive buying experience for the member and create a straightforward process for the seller. By prioritizing relationship-building over transactional sales, fitness facilities can build a loyal customer base and promote ongoing engagement with their members.

Member Onboarding

Once a prospect becomes a paying member, ensure they are properly onboarded. New-member onboarding is the process by which a new member feels welcomed and becomes familiar with the fitness facility and its services, programs, and amenities. Holding a new member's hand for the first 90 days of membership is crucial for retention, not to mention giving them a better chance of reaching their health and fitness goals.

After the prospect purchases a membership, the salesperson should thank the new member for the purchase while reinforcing that it was a good decision. This tactic makes the new member feel at home right away and helps prevent buyer's remorse. In addition to the postpurchase interaction, there should be a cadence of email, text, and phone communication welcoming the new member. As part of member engagement training, the entire staff should introduce themselves to new members. The more people that a new member meets, the more they feel welcome in this new environment.

The second part of new member onboarding is more technical. This would include a more in-depth tour of the facility, an equipment and safety orientation, a fitness assessment, and introductions to programs such as group fitness, small group training, and personal training. New member onboarding may also include resources such as apps, sample workouts, nutrition guides, and general fitness tips. To maximize the value of the membership, a member must be familiar with all that a facility has to offer and be confident to engage safely and effectively with those offerings.

A good onboarding program should leave members feeling comfortable and confident in using the facility and set them up for success in achieving their health and fitness goals. While onboarding is necessary and powerful, the journey doesn't stop there. To retain members, facilities must also create diverse ongoing engagement strategies.

Diversified Member Engagement

Member engagement is defined as the level of interaction, participation, and socialization a member has with a facility. *Interaction* refers to the overarching customer experience the fitness facility staff delivers. *Participation* refers to attending classes, using equipment, and participating in services. *Socialization* highlights the level of bonding and relationship-building a member does with other members.

A highly engaged member is more likely to be satisfied with their membership, achieve better health and fitness results, and continue their membership. Member engagement is an essential factor in the success of a fitness facility.

A highly effective type of member engagement, termed *diversified member engagement*, revolves around the idea that the more ways a member interacts, participates, and socializes in a facility, the more likely they are to continue their membership for an extended time. If a member comes to a facility for only one or two reasons, they tend to be susceptible to competitors' offers. However, when members come to a facility for many reasons, their loyalty increases tenfold. Therefore, a facility's primary goal should be to encourage diversified engagement from all members. What follows are several ways to get members engaged.

General Communication

Fitness facilities should communicate regularly with their members. Use newsletters and social media platforms to share news, events, and tips. Text messages and push notifications from apps are effective ways to communicate. Send a personalized email or make a phone call to check in with members or offer support. Using a mix of these methods, you can engage with members, keep them highly motivated, and build a strong sense of community.

Great Member Experience

Training the staff to deliver an outstanding member experience is an excellent way to engage members. A warm welcome makes a member feel like they belong and sets the tone for the member's entire day. During the visit, skills such as body language, luxury language, using names, anticipating needs, and owning questions all provide the engagement members desire during the duration of the visit. The practice of *owning questions* refers to taking control of the conversation by asking thoughtful and probing inquiries that guide the discussion and uncover valuable insights, as well as doing things for your members when possible. For example, if one of your members asks for a towel, instead of politely telling them where to get one, you would grab the towel for them.

New Member Onboarding Checklist
Marisa Hoff

Registration

Thank the member and welcome them to the facility in person. If the member has enrolled online, send a welcome email and thank them for joining.

Input all necessary member information into member management software, including the following:

- First name (initial cap)
- Last name (initial cap)
- Preferred name (initial cap)
- Referred by (member)
- Lead source
- Gender
- Pronouns
- Date of birth
- Mailing address (initial cap) including street name, city, and zip code
- Cell phone number and provider
- Name of emergency contact (capitalized)
- Phone number of emergency contact
- Relationship to emergency contact

If the member signed up online, ensure all their information is complete. Contact the member for any missing information and schedule a time for them to come into the facility to complete the process.

Take the member's photo for their account.

Explain all fees and dates of billing.

Explain the process for freezing and canceling the membership.

Have the member sign the membership agreement.

Give the member a hard copy or digital copy of their membership agreement.

Inform the member about additional services, such as nutritional guidance or spa facilities.

Discuss any discounts, special offers, or referral programs.

Demonstrate app use or sign-up protocols on the website.

Invite the member to follow the facility on social media channels.

Provide the member with information for member support and inquiries.

Sign the member up for an introductory orientation.

Ensure that the member receives a cadence of emails, texts, and calls in the first 30 days of membership to check progress and receive feedback.

Orientation

Conduct a tour of the facility, highlighting different areas and equipment.

Demonstrate all amenities.

Explain safety guidelines, rules, and codes of conduct.

Show the member where to find towels and sanitizing supplies.

Encourage the member to establish a routine.

SMILE

Stand. Stand up, smile, and bring your attention to a member or guest as they enter the fitness facility.

Make eye contact. Make eye contact with the member or guest as they approach you. (Remember, cultural differences may exist when it comes to eye contact.)

Initiate a greeting. Initiate a conversation with the member or guest with a warm greeting such as "hello," "good morning," or "good evening." Use their proper name when possible.

Listen and learn. Listen to the needs of the member or guest through active listening, including clues from verbal and nonverbal communication. Learn something unique about the member or guest.

Encourage. Encourage the member or guest with positive words as they enter and exit the fitness facility. Examples include "enjoy your workout" when they enter and "make it a great day" or "see you tomorrow" when they exit.

Bookending the experience is a fond farewell. This demonstrates that the member is valued and that the staff values the member's business and is invested in their fitness journey. Positive staff interactions throughout a member's visit create engagement that makes members want to return. The SMILE strategy, developed by author Steven Trotter, is a way for training team members to create a positive member experience.

Member Participation

Engagement improves when members participate in programming at a fitness facility. Members participating in group fitness classes, personal training, and small group training become more strongly bonded to a facility. Program participation is compelling because a member engages in the actual program, connects with the instructor, and bonds with fellow members. It is important to remember that members who participate in programming are also more likely to achieve their health and fitness goals, leading to high satisfaction and continued engagement. Given the engagement benefits of program participation, facilities must find ways to encourage it. Free trials, open houses, incentive programs, and challenges are great ways to nudge members into programs.

Special Events

Hosting events, particularly charity and social events, can effectively increase member engagement. Charity events allow members to feel part of something bigger than themselves while contributing to a good cause. Social events create an opportunity for members to connect outside of regular workouts, which assists in building a sense of community independent of exercise. These events create positive and memorable experiences for members, which lead to a level of engagement that allows them to see the fitness facility as much more than just a place where they work out. This engagement can help cultivate the feeling that the fitness facility is the "third place" for the member.

Other Ways to Engage

There are additional ways to engage members diversely that don't fall into the categories discussed. For example, many facilities use apps, wearables, reward programs, and other resources to engage members.

- *Apps.* Mobile applications provide information, track progress, and offer interactive features for members to stay engaged with the fitness facility.

Third Place

The *third place* is defined as the social environment that falls after home, referred to as the *first place*, and work, referred to as the *second place*, where a person has a sense of belonging (Oldenburg 1989).

- *Wearables.* Wearable devices such as fitness trackers and smartwatches monitor activities and provide personalized data, enhancing members' connection to their fitness journey.
- *Reward programs.* Incentive-based systems provide an opportunity for members to earn rewards, discounts, or recognition for achieving fitness goals and maintaining consistent participation.
- *Other resources.* Additional tools and platforms such as online communities, social media groups, virtual classes, and educational content diversify member engagement strategies beyond traditional methods.

All of these tactics aid you in creating various ways for members to interact with your facility.

Member engagement is a crucial factor in the success of a fitness facility and the perfect complement to a strong onboarding program. The level of interaction, participation, and socialization a member has with a facility can significantly affect their satisfaction, health, and fitness results and the likelihood of continuing their membership. Diversified member engagement, which encourages members to interact, participate, and socialize in various ways is a highly effective way to increase member loyalty and retention. By offering a range of programs, events, and services, fitness facilities can encourage diversified engagement and create a strong sense of community among members. Fostering member engagement should be a top priority for fitness facility management to ensure long-term success and satisfaction for members and the facility itself.

Case Study: Improving the Customer Experience

Kia Williams

A+ Group Fitness company acquires a personal trainer–led small group training program, Better Personal Training, and improves the net promoter score (NPS) by 108 percent.

Better Personal Training has a robust client base and provides personal training, injury recovery, and small group training sessions. Better Personal Training struggled to raise its small group training NPS score from −12 for several years. Member feedback included complaints that each personal trainer's workout was vastly different, there were differences in how the workouts were delivered, there were challenges with making reservations for the sessions, and other small group training studios' technology and exercise trackers were easier to use.

Last year A+ Group Fitness acquired the small group training component of Better Personal Training service offerings. As a result of the acquisition, A+ Group Fitness assumed all the small group training memberships and rented space from Better Personal Training to continue the program. A+ Group Fitness reviewed and evaluated Better Personal Training policies and procedures to assess areas of continuation and others to revamp or discontinue.

Prompt 1
A+ Group Fitness' proposed goal is to overhaul customer experience, increase small group training participation, and ultimately improve the NPS score. Detail and explain four key areas you believe A+ Group Fitness should prioritize to reach the goal.

Prompt 2
A+ Group Fitness knows that significant changes must occur soon to stabilize and grow the acquired program. Propose a strategic plan and time line for A+ Group Fitness to implement and follow to make this program acquisition successful.

Action Plan

After the initial evaluation, A+ Group Fitness developed a strategy to address four key areas that will make the most significant impact:

1. *Customer acquisition.* Adopt and implement a customer relationship management system. Celebrate and incentivize customers' journeys.

2. *Equipment and technology.* Update and streamline equipment and improve the technology used for the workouts.

3. *Program operation.* Develop standard operating procedures to ensure uniformity and consistency in the program delivery.

4. *Public relations and branding.* Identify marketing and branding methods that highlight, build on, and advance customers' experiences in the small group training program.

A+ Group Fitness made several immediate changes that enhanced the member experience, built brand trust, and improved member feedback. A+ Group Fitness held an open forum and dispatched a four-question survey within the first week of the acquisition announcement. By the end of the first week, a new website and social media page were launched with detailed announcements of the resolutions to the members' pain points and feedback. There were video tutorials and FAQs to help streamline all the new technologies and break down barriers to access. Member videos and written testimonials from the test groups were significant highlights for getting member buy-in and commitment to the procedure changes. Within the first 15 days of the acquisition, all coaches were trained under the new exercise program, delivering uniform and quality exercise experiences that produced brand consistency. In 30 days, A+ Group Fitness held a social gathering for the members and provided food and drinks. The members were thoroughly impressed and satisfied with the new program structure, and the average class size grew. The success of these immediate changes and flawless execution incentivized unhappy members and detractors to serve as new brand ambassadors.

Discussion Points

- Based on the example of this successful customer-centric business acquisition, explain how communication, convenience, consistency, and quick action can influence customer satisfaction and experience.

- Detail how the change in operations could worsen customer trust and loyalty.

- Explain at least one principle covered in this chapter but not listed in A+ Group Fitness's four priorities that you would adopt and use in this acquisition. Provide a thorough explanation and explain the expected results.

- Do you believe this high level of customer satisfaction is sustainable for A+ Group Fitness? Explain.

Conclusion

Customer experience describes the customer's interactions with the company and determines whether a customer will remain or leave. Positive customer experience can equate to customer loyalty, increased business revenue, and sustainability. Understanding and optimizing customer experience can improve customer satisfaction and the likelihood that a customer will recommend your company to others. Customers complain, but view your customers' complaints as an opportunity to gain their respect and deeper loyalty to your business. Acknowledgment, quick response, and action go a long way in gaining customers' respect. Companies thrive by delivering the best experiences and satisfying their customers' expectations. Customer experience appeals to customers' emotions, how they think and feel about your company, and how they would be called to action on behalf of and in support of your business.

Member Offboarding

Despite a facility's best efforts to keep members engaged and satisfied, there comes a time when a member may decide to leave the fitness facility. Certain situations also require a fitness facility to revoke a membership—although it is more commonly the member's choice to leave. In both cases, fitness facilities must have an effective and efficient member offboarding process. This crucial component of the member journey is the formal process of ending a membership. This process should be handled with sensitivity and care while simultaneously ensuring all essential protocols and procedures are followed. Specifics of a complete offboarding process will be discussed at the end of this chapter.

Although there are several reasons members cancel memberships, the reasons typically fall into one of two categories: personal and financial. Personal reasons for cancellation include physical issues such as injury or illness, schedule changes, moving, new interests or hobbies, nonuse, and dissatisfaction with the facility. Financial reasons may be things like a loss of a job, household income change, or simply a shift in financial priorities. Some of these reasons for membership cancellation are entirely out of a facility's control. For example, little can be done to prevent a member who is moving, becomes ill, or can no longer afford a membership from canceling. There are, however, things that can be done to mitigate specific cancellation reasons. When a member cancels for personal reasons such as nonuse or dissatisfaction with the facility, there is an opportunity to prevent the cancellation.

If a member has begun the cancellation process, it is essential to execute this attempt delicately and always keep the member's best interests in mind. The goal is not to force the member to maintain a membership that they genuinely don't want; it is to see if the facility can correct the issue prompting the member to want to cancel. Like selling a membership, this is simply problem-solving by engaging with the member to address their concerns. One strategy is offering support, such as one-on-one training or coaching sessions, to get them on track with their fitness goals. Another method is to partner the member with a gym buddy with whom they can attend different types of programming. The buddy could be a staff member or a gym member.

Another approach could be for the facility to offer financial incentives or discounts, such as a temporary reduction in dues or complimentary access, or a discount for paid programming or fee-based amenities. Note that while it might seem like temporary discounts would be effective for financially based cancellations, they are generally ineffective. Based on amenities and programming, facilities should get creative in their budget-conscious approaches to what they can offer members to try and prevent cancellations.

In some circumstances, a facility may decide that it is necessary to terminate someone's membership. This can occur for reasons such as failure to pay membership dues, unsafe or disruptive behavior, inappropriate engagement with other members or fitness facility staff, and violation of facility guidelines and rules. While it is the facility's right to terminate a membership, it must adhere to proper procedures, such as providing adequate notice and warning and allowing the member to address any issues (if appropriate). Following proper protocols demonstrates professionalism and fairness in how a facility deals with members. Furthermore, failing to follow appropriate protocols can open the door to potential legal or financial consequences for the facility. While this situation can be challenging, facilities should always be comfortable terminating a membership when necessary, because it helps the facility maintain a good reputation and retain its current members.

Just as a member's formal relationship with a facility begins with onboarding, it ends with a properly structured offboarding procedure. This process should allow for a smooth and professional transition from member to nonmember. While facilities approach this differently, general steps should be present in all offboarding systems.

Explain the Offboarding Process

When a member joins, a facility should explain the membership cancellation process. As part of the sign-up, the member should be told what needs to happen should they decide to cancel their membership at any point. Items such as how notice must be given, what specifically needs to occur, and the required time line should all be made clear. When a member inquires about canceling, this information should be communicated again to ensure the process is executed correctly.

This can happen in person, through email, or over the phone.

Identify the Reason for Cancellation

Understanding why the member is canceling the membership is vital for various reasons. First, it creates an opportunity to address immediate issues a member has that might prevent a cancellation. Second, it offers insight into any underlying matters a facility may have. If this member is having a bad experience, there is a chance that other members are, too. This can be considered feedback to be used to improve the overall customer journey. Note that this only applies to cancellations that the facility has control over. By acquiring and tracking reasons for cancellation, a fitness facility now has aggregated data to help improve operations.

Provide a Time Line

Provide a clear time line for the offboarding process. The information included in this time line should reflect how long the member will still have access to the facility, when any outstanding payments are due, and when any refunds (if warranted) will be issued.

Deactivate the Membership

Deactivation is the internal component of the offboarding process. At this point, the facility must ensure that facility access is deactivated and billing is stopped. This needs to happen in conjunction with the time line provided.

Ongoing Follow-Up

After the offboarding process is complete, it is good practice for the facility to follow up with the member to make sure that the process was handled to their satisfaction. This can occur in person, via email or phone, or through a more formal survey. In addition to gathering information about the offboarding process, this can be an excellent time to seek feedback on the overall experience at the facility. This helps improve your future operations and demonstrates care for the member's opinions. Finally, the member should be placed in an ongoing communication cadence and reengagement campaign. This puts them back into the sales funnel, increasing the likelihood of the member rejoining at some point and still referring others.

A comprehensive member offboarding process allows facilities to end the relationship professionally and respectfully, which helps maintain a positive reputation with the ex-member and the community. In addition, it leaves a member feeling like the door is open if and when they are ready to return.

Conclusion

Attracting and engaging members is managing the member journey. The member journey is one of the most critical aspects in determining the success of a fitness facility. By focusing on each phase of the member journey, from initial brand awareness through member offboarding, facilities

---

Member Offboarding Checklist

- Remind the member of the process for cancellation.
- Get cancellation information in writing, whether it is an email, letter, or a form at the facility.
- Make sure that the cancellation includes the member's signature.
- Record the reason for cancellation.
- Inform the member of billing information in the membership agreement.
- Let the member know the time line for the cancellation process, such as how long they will have access to the club.
- Give the member a copy of the cancellation form or send an email confirmation.
- Process the cancellation in member management software and double-check billing dates to ensure all billing occurs according to the membership agreement.
- Follow up with the member via phone call, text, or email survey to receive feedback on the facility.

can maximize lead generation, increase membership sales, improve member engagement and retention, and maintain a good reputation and positive relationships, even when members decide to leave. When everything discussed in this chapter is strategically implemented, fitness facilities can foster a customer-centric experience that delivers tremendous value and helps members reach health and fitness goals while simultaneously achieving and sustaining long-term business success.

THINK IT THROUGH

- What are the components of a sales funnel?
- What are different methods of marketing that you can use to generate leads for your fitness facility?
- Describe the stages of the sales process within a fitness facility, from the first impression to closing the sale.
- Why is diversifying member engagement important for member retention?
- What are the key components of a successful member onboarding process, and why is it important for member success?
- How can a fitness facility handle the process of member offboarding with sensitivity and efficiency?

KEY TERMS

apps and wearables
behavior change models
guerrilla marketing
lead generation
member engagement
member offboarding
member onboarding
reward programs
sales funnel

12

Emergency Preparedness and Risk Management

Upon completion of this chapter, you will be able to do the following:

- Explain basic risk management principles
- Identify types of insurance
- Identify various types of negligence
- Define the purpose of music licensing
- Identify common types of emergencies in fitness facilities
- Conduct an organizational risk assessment
- Apply and implement risk management practices
- Create an emergency action plan

An integral part of a solid member journey is providing a safe environment for your members and staff. Understanding the basics of emergency preparedness and risk management not only helps you implement systems to limit emergencies, it also helps you develop a strategic plan to respond to emergencies if and when they occur.

Risk management is a continuous process for identifying, evaluating, controlling, and managing threats to your fitness facility. Standard practices for risk management include five steps:

1. *Risk identification*—the risks that are present or have the potential to occur
2. *Risk evaluation*—the probability of the risk occurring and the severity
3. *Risk management*—the appropriate approach to manage the risk
4. *Implementation*—the plan in action
5. *Evaluation*—ongoing assessment of risks and updates to the plan

Risk Identification

The first step in risk management is to identify what risks are present or have the potential to occur. Throughout this book, you have encountered many risks associated with fitness facility management as you learned the basic standards and guidelines for management and operations of the facility. Everyday activities have associated risks; you cannot go anywhere or do anything without risk involved. Exercise and physical activity carry higher risk levels, and there are specific risks associated with exercising. Risks may include a variety of severity levels, from elevated heart rate and muscle soreness to cardiac events and even death. Risks go beyond the extent of a member entering the facility and exercising independently; additional risks can be found in instruction, supervision, facilities, equipment, and contracts and the business structure (Bryant et al. 2020).

The fitness equipment you have in your facility also poses a risk. As mentioned in chapter 9, taking care of and cleaning your fitness equipment is critical for mitigating these risks. Additional risks accompany the proper and improper use of equipment by members.

Physical Activity Readiness Questionnaire for Everyone (PAR-Q+)

The Physical Activity Readiness Questionnaire for Everyone (PAR-Q+) is a standard screening tool used to determine whether an individual can safely participate in exercise. Developed in 2011 as a revision to the original PAR-Q created in 1975, the form asks seven questions about current and past health status and medication use. These questions ask about the presence of specific chronic conditions, medications, and restrictions from health care providers regarding exercise participation.

In 2023, an additional revision was made to the PAR-Q+ to reduce barriers to exercise. If someone answers yes to one or more of the seven questions, they are directed to answer follow-up questions to further screen and determine if a physician referral is warranted.

Negligence

Supervision also comes with risks. At its simplest, your staff have people's lives in their hands daily. This power comes with responsibility and the potential for negligence. Negligence is the failure of a person to perform as a reasonable and prudent professional would perform under similar circumstances (Bryant et al. 2020). When a negligence claim is made, four elements need to be present for that claim to be substantiated:

1. The person named must have a duty to protect.
2. The person must have failed to uphold the standard of care.
3. There needs to be proof that damage or injury occurred.
4. There needs to be proof that the breach of duty caused the damage or injury.

Acts of omission and acts of commission are two examples that can lead to a negligence claim. An act of omission occurs when someone does not do something they should. For example, say you have a certified personal trainer facilitating an exercise session with a client. While the personal trainer leaves the client unattended to take a phone call, the client sustains an injury. That could be classified as an act of omission. In this case, the personal trainer should have supervised the exercise session but did not. An act of commission occurs when someone does something they should not have done. An example of an act of commission would be a personal trainer instructing a client to use an exercise machine in a manner it was not designed for and goes against the manufacturer's instructions. Because of the personal trainer's instructions, the client sustains an injury.

In some claims, a court may use comparative or contributory negligence. Comparative negligence occurs when both parties have some sort of fault in the injury. In the earlier example where the personal trainer stepped away, perhaps the client also neglected to inform the personal trainer of a recent injury that was causing pain during the execution of the exercise. Contributory negligence occurs when the plaintiff contributes to their injury. For example, contributory negligence may apply if a client was using an exercise machine in a manner it was not designed for, even after a personal trainer instructed the client on the proper use.

Another variation of negligence is gross negligence. Gross negligence is far worse than regular negligence and, when it occurs, cannot usually be protected by waivers or any other protection forms. Gross negligence typically occurs when recklessness or intentional misconduct is involved.

Risk Evaluation

The second step in the risk management process is risk evaluation. Risk evaluation is the process of taking each identified risk and determining the likelihood of its occurrence, and then analyzing the severity of the risk should it happen. Table 12.1 shows a starting point for identifying which risk management method should be used based on the frequency and severity of the risk.

Risk Management

The third step in the risk management process is to manage each specific risk. Risk should be managed using one of four methods: avoidance, transfer, reduction, or retention.

Avoidance

Avoidance is the most extreme and sometimes necessary method of approaching risk. Avoidance is simply removing or eliminating the activity and its risk altogether. If a risk has a high severity of an

Case Study: Negligence in a Health Club

Brian Greenlee

As the general manager, you receive an incident report from the fitness manager regarding an injury to a member. The incident report explains that the cable crossover piece of equipment in the northwest corner of the facility was tagged out of order due to safety concerns. One of the trainers, classified as an employee, was performing an early morning training session with a client who often used this equipment and was unhappy that it was out of order. The personal trainer took the liberty of removing the out-of-service tag and allowed the client to use the equipment. After the third repetition, a cable snapped, causing the weight stack to fall on the client's leg, causing severe injury.

- What type of negligence has taken place (e.g., act of omission, comparative negligence, contributory negligence, gross negligence)?
- Who is at fault in this situation (e.g., client, trainer, facility)?
- Does a waiver protect the facility in this type of situation?
- What should the trainer have done differently in this situation?
- What might the management do to mitigate this situation in the future?
- What if, in this situation, the trainer acknowledges that the equipment is unsafe and walks away from the client to get another piece of equipment to use? During that time, the client takes liberty and attempts to use the broken equipment and gets injured. Does that change the negligence type? Would the waiver protect the trainer and facility in this alternative scenario?

Debrief

Managers of fitness facilities must educate exercise professionals that their duty is to provide safe and effective instruction. Sometimes a team member's judgment may be tested by a member's demands or moral and ethical behavior. The manager and leader of the organization must provide guidance and support to the staff for the safety of all members, the protection of employees, and the mitigation of risk. Proper staff training should include a daily assessment of the club's surroundings. Management should train exercise professionals that they *must* consider the following before any training session:

1. Identify hazards (e.g., water, electrical, damaged equipment).
2. Note environmental concerns (e.g., heat, cold, humidity).
3. Consider space availability (e.g., size, indoor, outdoor).

After the assessment, the exercise professional can adjust the training program according to any observations they have seen.

---

injury or financial impact and has a high frequency of occurrence, then it would be best not to offer or include the activity that poses that risk.

Transfer

Transfer is when you move the risk to the responsibility of others through the use of forms and insurance policies. Transferring the risk is a commonly used method by fitness facilities and, in many locations, required by law to even own or operate a

fitness facility. One example of a transfer is when a fitness facility pays license fees to broadcast music in the facility.

Insurance

Various types of insurance help protect and mitigate some of the risks of operating a fitness facility. General liability, professional liability, and umbrella policies are common types of insurance you encounter as a fitness facility manager.

TABLE 12.1   Evaluating Risks Based on Frequency and Severity

Frequency of risk	Severity of risk	Recommended strategy	Notes
High	High	Avoidance	Eliminate the risk entirely by not offering the activity that generates the risk.
High	Low	Reduction	Implement actions to reduce the likelihood of risk occurring or lessen its severity if it does occur.
Low	High	Transfer	Transfer ownership of risk to a third party, such as insurance.
Low	Low	Retention/acceptance	Accept the risk; the cost to mitigate far outweighs the actual severity and frequency.

General liability insurance is the base insurance policy a fitness facility must have. Each fitness facility should have a minimum of one million dollars in coverage per occurrence and up to three million dollars in total coverage (Tharrett 2017). This type of policy covers most negligence and accident cases.

Professional liability insurance covers the professional competencies of licensed or certified individuals such as group fitness instructors, personal trainers, and massage therapists. This coverage not only includes injuries that could be sustained but also covers financial losses incurred due to loss of work. Fitness facilities should obtain professional liability insurance for their employees and require all independent contractors to carry their own professional liability coverage before entering into an agreement. The American Council on Exercise recommends a minimum of one million dollars in professional liability coverage. However, some facilities elect to carry more or require independent contractors to carry at least a two million dollar policy (Bryant et al. 2020).

Umbrella policies are meant to expand coverage for all other types of insurance that a fitness professional may have. The umbrella policy is intended to take over if someone's professional liability insurance does not fully cover a lawsuit or occurrence.

Additional insurance policies that a fitness facility may hold are workers' compensation insurance, which covers injuries sustained by an employee while performing job duties; property insurance that helps protect against damage done to property or the fitness facility's physical assets; business interruption insurance, which protects against revenue loss during unforeseen circumstances such as acts of God; and key person insurance, which would compensate the fitness facility in the event an employee who provides a unique or valuable service is out due to extenuating circumstances such as long-term illness or even death.

Intellectual Property and Copyright

Copyright and intellectual property violations are an often overlooked risk at a fitness facility until it's too late and fines or other legal sanctions are received. Music and sometimes broadcast television are typical added values at a fitness center. Music is often played through an in-house system, and as you learned in chapter 10, music is a critical piece of a world-class group fitness experience. Many fitness facilities also play broadcast television overhead, wall-mounted, or on cardio equipment consoles. The American Society of Composers, Authors, and Publishers (ASCAP) and Broadcast Music, Inc (BMI) are two organizations in the United States that issue licenses for fitness facilities to use music, along with the Society of European Stage Authors and Composers (SESAC). It is imperative that a fitness facility obtain these licenses, or heavy fines may be placed on the business. If you receive a phone call or voicemail from one of these agencies, it is to your advantage to take it seriously.

Forms

Forms are another standard method for a fitness facility to transfer risks. Frequently used forms are agreements to participate and informed consents, waivers, and contracts. Agreements to participate and informed consent are used when a new member joins a fitness facility or purchases an additional service such as personal training. These forms clearly state the inherent risks and benefits associated with participating in the activity or program.

Photography Release

Including a photography release clause in the waiver is a good idea when someone signs up as a member. You want to use photography for marketing purposes and to showcase your world-class fitness facility. Insert a clause into the waiver that notifies members that while participating as a member of the fitness facility, they may be photographed, and they will not receive any compensation if the photo is used for marketing purposes. If you plan a staged marketing photo shoot, an additional photography release should be available for participating members. Always follow local, state, and federal laws regarding photography use and consult with your legal counsel.

When presenting an agreement to participate or informed consent to an individual, best practice is that you explain the form to them, give them time to read the form, and allow them to ask any questions. By signing the form, individuals acknowledge that they understand the associated risks and benefits and agree to participate in the activity. This agreement does not necessarily waive their right to litigation if the individual sustains an injury or loss. A waiver will traditionally include some of the same information provided in an agreement to participate and informed consent. However, the key difference is that the waiver consists of a clause that waives the individual's right to seek damages due to injury caused by inherent risks or ordinary negligence (Bryant et al. 2020). You must note that waivers, including group waivers, may be regulated at the state level.

Contracts are binding agreements between two parties that are enforceable by law. They are used by fitness facilities with the primary purpose of transferring risks associated with finances. Commonly used contracts are those signed at the initial joining of a new member and when additional services are purchased, such as personal training. The contract lays out the payment parameters, including how, when, and where payment will be made and what services will be exchanged for the payment. Personal training contracts may also include session cancellation policies and communication parameters between the personal trainer and the client. For a contract to be valid, there should be an offer, acceptance, and consideration.

Risk Reduction

Risk reduction is an approach to managing risks by reducing or altering part of the activity, ultimately resulting in lower risks. Risk reduction can also be achieved by using industry standards and guidelines on fitness facility operation, general supervision, and recordkeeping.

Facility Operations

One of the ways to reduce risk is by maintaining a safe and clean exercise environment and using appropriate signage. As you learned in chapter 8, signage is an integral part of identifying safety hazards and properly using the fitness facility, its amenities, and equipment. Cautionary, danger, and warning signage are addressed in ACSM standard 1 for health and fitness facility signage (ACSM 2019):

- *Cautionary signage* alerts members and staff of risks associated with using specific equipment and amenities or entering particular areas. Cautionary signage must also include the steps to avoid the risks associated with the activity or location.

- *Danger signage* alerts members and staff of imminent hazards. Danger signage should also include the outcome, such as serious injury or death if the area or activity isn't avoided. As with cautionary signage, danger signage must include steps to prevent the risk.

- *Warning signage* alerts members and staff that a potential hazard may be present. Similar to danger signage, warning signage should also include that potential injury or death may occur and include the steps to avoid the risk.

ACSM standard 2 for health and fitness facility signage addresses the emergency and safety signs for fire and related emergencies as required by federal, state, or local codes. Emergency exit signage should be clear and include the location of all emergency exits and directions. Emergency phones and fire extinguishers should also have signage with instructions for use. Facility occupancy and certificate of occupancy signage should be visible, displaying the number of people allowed in the facility at one time according to local building codes. Some agencies also require displaying occupancy load signage for each room, studio, or area.

As you learned in detail in chapter 9, having clean and safe operational fitness equipment is compulsory for reducing risk. Most notably, any equipment available to use should be in working condition. If equipment needs to be repaired or replaced, it should be removed from the floor when possible and, at minimum, include an out-of-order sign.

Automated external defibrillators (AEDs) and first aid kits should be available throughout the fitness facility. AEDs are portable devices used to restore normal heart rhythms in individuals experiencing cardiac arrest or other cardiac events. They are used as an early intervention during an emergency until emergency medical services (EMS) can arrive. It is best practice for every fitness facility to have a minimum of one AED on-site. Some states require all health clubs and fitness facilities within their state lines to have them. Each fitness facility should also post signage for AEDs and first aid kit

Fitness facilities should post signs indicating where the AED is located.

locations, including directions on how to access them (ACSM 2019).

General Supervision

Providing oversight and supervision of exercise programs is essential to risk reduction. Supervision begins when a new member has completed the intake forms and is ready to start their exercise journey in your facility. Best practice is to offer every new member an orientation to the facility, including basic fitness equipment instructions. This is an excellent opportunity to involve your certified personal trainers and health coaches to be part of the process and potentially enroll the new member in a personal training program. Knowledgeable and trained staff must be the ones providing general supervision, and any specialized positions, such as group fitness instructors, personal trainers, and health coaches, must have an appropriate certification approved by the NCCA. All certifications have a scope of practice, and your certified team members must stay within their scope and refer members to health care professionals when needed.

Although there is no industry ratio on the number of staff to the number of members, ACSM recommends a minimum of one fitness professional who is trained in cardiopulmonary resuscitation (CPR) and the administration of an AED be on duty at all times while the fitness facility is open. Consider your fitness facility's goals and objectives, the types of services you offer, and your member demographics to determine your supervision model. You should also note that some states regulate the use of AEDs in unstaffed facilities.

To further reduce risks, you should perform a criminal background check on all employees and contractors and post clear policies on unlawful harassment and discrimination in the workplace as directed by the Equal Employment Opportunity Commission (EEOC).

Recordkeeping

While operating and managing a fitness facility, you will collect paperwork, forms, and records. These documents include the forms for member onboarding, health-related documents, contracts, incident or accident reports, and more. As discussed in chapter 11, many of these documents may contain protected health information and be subject to the Health Insurance Portability and Accountability Act (HIPAA) or Family Educational Rights and

Privacy Act. Any electronic or printed documents containing this information, including information on employees, should be stored in a secured and, if necessary, encrypted location. You should also check with your local and federal laws in addition to company policy on the length of record retention and guidelines for storing and, when appropriate, destroying data.

Retention

The last method and approach to managing risk is retaining it. It goes without saying that the benefits of exercise and physical activity and the risks of *not* participating in exercise far outweigh the risks associated with exercise and physical activity. As noted in table 12.1, risks classified as low or medium in severity with infrequent or seldom occurrences can be retained.

Implementation of Risk Plans

Once you have established your risk management plan, you need to implement it within the organization. You can take much of what you have learned thus far in the textbook and apply it to your plan. Managing a fitness facility according to standards, guidelines, and best practices is the first step in implementing your risk management plan.

You can group your implementation strategies into two categories: the facility and the training and development of staff. You should maintain a safe environment with clean and operational equipment and amenities. Refer to chapter 9 for guidelines related to fitness equipment. As a recap, you should include the following on your walls:

- Inherent risks associated with exercise in physical activity areas of your facility
- Clocks in physical activity areas along with target heart rate (THR) zones or rating of perceived exertion (RPE) charts
- Caution, danger, and warning signage that follows local, state, and federal law and industry standards and guidelines
- Emergency exit signage, including the directions to those exits; you should not post your emergency exits and gathering spots online, though, because this could open the opportunity for violence to be targeted at people gathered into groups in an open space
- Location of emergency phones and fire extinguishers with instructions for use
- Occupancy loads and certificate of occupancy
- Location of AEDs and first aid kits
- ADA guidelines and OSHA requirements

All team members should be trained on the risk management and emergency action plan (EAP) and evaluated on it regularly. You can never overtrain someone in risk management and emergency planning topics. Training should occur during onboarding, followed by continuous upskilling and retraining throughout employment.

Responding to Emergencies

ACSM standard 1 for emergency planning and policies states that you should have written emergency response policies, procedures, and guidelines. The purpose of the EAP is to ensure that staff can respond to basic first aid situations and emergencies in an appropriate and timely manner (ACSM 2019).

Various types of emergencies can occur in a fitness facility. However, most fall into one of the following four categories: fire, medical, violence, or structural.

- *Fire-related emergencies* pose a significant risk and are not typical. When responding to a fire-related emergency, evacuate the building as quickly and safely as possible. This response is activated by an initial alert, such as sounding an alarm and making an announcement over the public address (PA) system. Your policy's next steps should be enacted, with employees knowing their duties during the emergency and working to make sure each assigned area is clear. If you operate a large fitness facility, consider creating zones within the facility so you can assign specific employees to designated zones when responding to emergencies. You'll need to know who should be where during an evacuation and how to assist with exiting for members or employees who use a wheelchair or scooter for mobility. Exit paths should be clearly marked, and you should encourage all members and staff to congregate in groups only once outside in the designated meeting spots. Your policy should also indicate if, depending on the size and severity of the fire, and which specific employees should respond with a fire extinguisher. Your plan should include any critical systems that need to be shut down or secured before evacuating. You should communicate with your local fire department on routes and plans in the event of a fire-related emergency.

Case Study: Emergency Preparedness

Brian Greenlee

As the general manager, you and your management team are reviewing the current emergency preparedness plan in preparation for employee training events. During this review, you and your team want to ensure staff is trained to respond to various emergencies, including fire, medical, violence, or structural.

In a situation of a fire within the facility, what should you and your team be considering when reviewing the emergency preparedness plan?

- What key elements should the action plan include?
- How do you ensure that members can evacuate safely and efficiently?
- Does your facility have signage and fire extinguishers in place?
- How does the situation differ if the fire is within the building versus happening outside, such as a wildfire or a fire in an adjacent building?

In a situation of a medical nature, what should you and your team be considering when reviewing the emergency preparedness plan?

- What should be the initial steps when a medical emergency arises?
- How often should your equipment be checked (e.g., AED, first aid kits)?
- How do you ensure proper training of staff?
- What should be included in your documentation and follow-up?
- Why should you debrief staff?

In a situation of an act of violence within or outside the facility, what should you and your team be considering when reviewing the emergency preparedness plan?

- What should be the initial steps when an act of violence arises?
- How would your plan change in situations such as member altercations, member and staff altercations, or active shooters?
- How do you ensure proper training of staff?
- What should be included in your documentation and follow-up?
- Why should you debrief the team?

In a situation in which there is a structural emergency, what should you and your team be considering when reviewing the emergency preparedness plan?

- What should be the initial steps when a structural emergency arises?
- What outside factors would you need to consider (e.g., fire, weather, earthquake)?
- What is your evacuation process?
- How do you check for staff and member safety?
- How do you ensure proper training of staff?
- What should be included in your documentation and follow-up?
- Why should you debrief staff?

Debrief

As the general manager of a facility, how you train and prepare your staff for various emergency responses is vital. Reviewing your current action plans and conducting periodic training is prudent in mitigating risk and liability. General managers should have daily, weekly, and monthly protocols to check the structural integrity of the building, electrical and plumbing lines, fitness equipment, signage, medical supplies, and security.

CPR, First Aid, and AED

This chapter will not go into detail about responding to emergencies that require first aid, CPR, and the administration of an AED. You and your employees should obtain CPR, AED, and first aid certifications from an approved organization. Ensure the training has a live skill check component, and renew the certification following the organization's guidelines and requirements.

• *Medical emergencies* are the most common emergency encountered while managing a fitness facility. Medical-related emergencies range in severity from a basic first aid response to life-threatening injuries that require advanced EMS response. Your EAP should indicate what type of initial alert activates the EAP for medical emergencies. Consider using a radio system with verbal codes so that employees can communicate with each other while on duty. Consider using earpiece attachments with the radios to increase the likelihood of clear communication and to provide employee and member privacy. Your plan should also indicate who will respond to the emergency and when escalation is needed, such as activating EMS. No matter the severity, proper documentation afterward on an accident or incident report is imperative when responding to a medical emergency. If the individual refuses treatment or transport, then that should be documented on the report as well. Accident reports should follow the same records retention and privacy requirements as other forms. Your plan should also indicate whether or not follow-up with the person who sustained an injury is part of practice, including the parameters and documentation of the follow-up.

• *Violence* is an unfortunate risk and potential emergency that must also be addressed. Violence can occur in fitness facilities, the same as it can occur in any other place. Violence may occur with various people conducting harm, including a member, staff, or someone outside of the facility. IHRSA (now named the Health & Fitness Association) published a briefing paper called *How to Prepare for an Active Shooter Situation at Your Gym.* Additional resources for training for active shooter situations can be reviewed by watching "Run. Hide. Fight." The video, produced by Ready Houston, is available online.

• *Structural emergencies* occur when parts of the physical structure of your fitness facility begin to fail. These can be caused by chronic deterioration over time or by an acute event, such as a natural disaster. Depending on your location, you may be more susceptible to hurricanes, snow, tornadoes, or earthquakes than other fitness facilities. Although the likelihood of structural failure may be low, you should still have a plan, including the activation and follow-through steps of the emergency response. You should look at your local, state, and national resources and guides to prepare your EAP.

After an Emergency

Following any emergency, you should conduct a debrief with the involved parties. No matter the severity, responding to an emergency can be traumatic for an individual. Consider providing in-house support or resources from a third party, such as an employee assistance program, to guide debriefing conversations and provide ongoing mental health and well-being support.

Your plan should also include the steps for the fitness facility to resume business operations. Depending on the severity of an emergency, you may have a stepped or gradual process to resuming operations, with your mission-critical operations starting first. Included in this activation should be related SOPs and the COOP if necessary.

Code Adam

If your facility provides child care or any youth program, your EAP should include a section outlining the response and plan if a child were to go missing. Code Adam is a program of the National Center for Missing and Exploited Children that details the actions that should be taken.

Case Study: Biannual Safety Audit

TJ Hill

A colleague's recreation center recently responded to an emergency in their fitness center. After reading about their response, you started to think about how your fitness facility and fitness staff would respond to an emergency in your weight room. At your next staff meeting, you bring up your organization's emergency action plan and ask team members to show you how to set up and use an AED. To your dismay, you realize your team is not meeting your expectations regarding their knowledge and practice of your EAP and their AED skills. Since you had not previously held biannual safety audits, you decide to begin programming a full-staff safety audit every six months to practice the activation of your EAP and physically test each individual on their AED skills and other lifesaving skills. You begin creating your first safety audit for your staff and facility.

Guiding Questions

- What is the length and setting for your safety audit?
- How many staff members will be present at this biannual audit?
- What hands-on skills will be practiced?
- How will you physically practice activating an EAP?
- What are your response time goals?
- How will you record and track individuals' knowledge and performance?
- Will you assess staff further between biannual audits?
- How will you implement another biannual safety audit after six months?

Using the scenario and guiding questions, create a plan for biannual safety audits for your fitness center.

Action

Based on your outline, you are ready to host your first biannual safety audit. Your day, time, and location are selected, and almost all your team members are available and excited to take their risk management practices forward. You have a structured time plan and rotation to get all your staff members through physical practice and hands-on AED skills. Good job!

Three team members who said they would be at the audit training do not show up. With those already known to be unavailable and the three no-shows, you have seven employees who did not attend the biannual safety audit.

With your biannual safety audit plan in place, how will you manage the knowledge and practice of these staff members to be consistent with the staff that attended the training?

Things to consider moving forward:

1. Tracking and recording safety audits and training is an essential part of managing liability and increasing performance. How will you record and track your teams' key performance indicators regarding their knowledge of and ability to implement your EAP? Can you compare future biannual safety audit results with previous safety audits?

2. How will you use mock emergencies and actual data to support the *why* behind hosting biannual safety audits? What internal and external resources can provide you with data and experiences from others?

3. How will you program future audits to be fresh and exciting for the involved team members and keep audits from becoming a simple checkbox?

4. Is there support or purpose to hold hands-on safety audits more regularly than six months for your fitness center? Is there room for improvement in safety skill offerings?

As a prudent professional and risk manager, you must lead, host, and manage biannual safety audits at least twice per year, including skill checks with AEDs. By working through the details in this case study, you should feel confident in preparing and offering a safety audit at least every six months for your fitness center to test your fitness staff's emergency preparedness and response times.

Ongoing Evaluation

Your risk management plan and EAP should be reviewed regularly and updated continually. This evaluation process is essential for a quality plan that helps you avoid, reduce, transfer, and retain risks appropriately for your fitness facility. The evaluation should also include quality control measures such as making sure first aid kits, AEDs, fire extinguishers, and other items needed during an EAP activation are stocked appropriately, in good condition, and in working order.

Safety audits expand beyond the physical kits themselves. You should conduct regular audits on your staff, and ACSM recommends you physically practice the activation of your EAP with your team at least twice per year. Skill checks with AEDs should also be practiced every six months with a goal of a three-minute response time to get an AED to an individual who is in need. Although safety is everyone's responsibility, it is vital that you identify one team member who is responsible for the fitness facility's emergency response plan; for fitness facilities that include an aquatic center, the responsibility often falls under the aquatic director's job duty.

Conclusion

Emergency preparedness and risk management are foundational for a safe fitness facility that promotes a world-class member experience. It is your responsibility to prepare for as many possible emergencies as possible, mitigate risks appropriately, and respond promptly as a reasonable and prudent professional would in the unlikely event of a disaster.

THINK IT THROUGH

- What are the five steps in risk management?
- What are the four methods used to manage each risk?
- What are common types of negligence that can happen in a fitness facility?
- What forms should be included in new member onboarding to transfer risk?
- What are best practices when responding to emergencies?
- What should you do following an emergency?

KEY TERMS

CPR/AED
emergency action plan (EAP)
informed consent
insurance
liability
negligence
PAR-Q+
risk management
waiver

13

Business Strategy and Marketing

Upon completion of this chapter, you will be able to do the following:

- Differentiate between effectiveness and efficiency
- Identify various forms of technology used in fitness facility management
- Understand the components of a comprehensive marketing plan
- Create a strategic plan
- Write goals and objectives
- Formulate a plan for the future

At this point, you have the foundation for fitness facility management. It starts with creating an organizational mission, vision, and values. This gives your organization an identity, and once that identity has been established, your organization can uncover the target market to be served. With these two items in place, your organization can focus on how it will operate to serve its target market. These operational practices require a deep understanding of all financial aspects of an organization, such as funding, revenue sources, expenses, and interpreting financial statements. An organizational mission can only be accomplished and an organization can only operate effectively with a rock star team. That team comes to fruition through strategic recruiting, hiring, onboarding practices, and ongoing efforts to create a positive employee journey that promotes engagement and retention. The final piece of the infrastructure involves effective facility design, with the right equipment and amenities combined with attractive offerings and programming. When well-thought-out and executed, this foundation allows your organization to attract and retain members and keep them engaged. This formula for fitness facility management is almost complete. The last piece of the puzzle lies in the topic of this chapter, which is business strategy and marketing. As you delve into this chapter, you'll find that it serves as a crucial bridge, helping you fine-tune and integrate the knowledge gained from previous chapters. By understanding the principles of business strategy and marketing, you'll enhance your ability to strategically position your fitness facility and optimize its performance based on the comprehensive groundwork established thus far.

In this chapter we explore such topics as effectiveness and efficiency and how eliminating, automating, and delegating tasks can enhance these qualities. We examine the use of technologies such as member management software, customer relationship management tools, staff management systems, website and social media, and mobile apps and their role in fitness facility operations. We explain how overarching marketing plans are critical for promoting and growing fitness facilities and strategic growth plans aligning with the facility's vision, mission, and values. By the end of this chapter, every aspect of fitness facility management will have been revealed, providing you with the knowledge and tools necessary to take your fitness facility to the next level and succeed in a highly competitive industry.

Effectiveness and Efficiency

Management consultant Peter Drucker said, "Efficiency is doing things right. Effectiveness is doing the right things" (Martins 2022). Fitness facilities need to be effective and efficient in all aspects of operations. These concepts help you optimize time, effort, and cost resources. While they are related, fitness facility managers must understand their differences.

Effectiveness is doing only what's needed to yield the desired outcome. Conversely, *efficiency* relates to how well the task or process is executed regarding the time spent, effort needed, and cost. In other words, effectiveness assesses whether the right things are being done, while efficiency considers how well they are done. When fitness facility managers strike a balance between effectiveness and efficiency, they can achieve desired outcomes in a way that maximizes resources and minimizes waste. This balance improves the member experience, employee journey, marketing efforts, and overall business strategy, giving your fitness facility a competitive advantage. Three keys to maximizing effectiveness and efficiency are elimination, automation, and delegation.

Elimination refers to removing all unnecessary or redundant tasks or processes that do not add value or enhance operations. For example, you may eliminate paper-based records and convert them to a digital system to streamline the process while reducing the chance of errors. Reducing the number of nonessential services or amenities that are not used by members is another example of elimination. For instance, if your fitness facility has racquetball courts that are rarely used, you may consider converting them into small group training areas, pickleball courts, or other amenities that better meet the wants and needs of members. By uncovering and eliminating any unnecessary or redundant task, process, or space, your fitness facility can optimize its operations, enhance its services, and better meet the expectations of its members, leading to increased member satisfaction and, ultimately, higher retention.

Automation involves using technology to perform tasks and processes automatically. Doing so reduces human error and the need for manual labor. For example, you can implement scheduling software to schedule personal trainers and group fitness classes, saving time and money while improving accuracy.

Another example of automation is an access control system to allow members entry to the facility using a digital membership card or facial recognition biometric scan. This can reduce the staff needed to check members in manually. Automating a task like this also frees up your and your staff's time to focus on tasks such as member engagement, providing a lot more overall benefit to the facility. Finding tasks and processes to automate can significantly improve effectiveness and efficiency in your facility by decreasing the need for labor, lowering expenses, reducing errors, and creating a more frictionless member experience.

Delegation is assigning tasks to appropriate team members capable of doing them. This maximizes productivity and frees up your and your staff's time for more critical tasks. Assigning cleaning tasks to a maintenance team member instead of the fitness team, for example, allows the fitness team to focus on providing unparalleled customer service to members. In another example, you could delegate the task of taking inventory in the pro shop to a front desk attendant to free up your time for managing and coaching team members. Mastering the art of delegation allows team members to make the best use of time, thus enhancing overall operations. Delegation is the last step in the process, and you should not be delegating a task that should have been eliminated or automated.

Technology in Fitness Facilities

One of the best ways your fitness facility can become effective and efficient is by using technological solutions. Tech solutions can streamline tasks such as scheduling, booking fitness programming, and processing membership payments, which can increase revenue and reduce operating costs. Using mobile apps or a website to book classes, access workouts, and track progress enhances the member experience. Many tech solutions provide valuable data, such as facility and class attendance, equipment usage, and other metrics that can help streamline facility operations. These are just a few examples of how technology allows you to eliminate, automate, and delegate tasks and processes to improve effectiveness and efficiency at your fitness facility.

Fitness facilities use a wide range of technology for a variety of reasons. We now turn to some of the most common technological solutions and how to use them in your operations.

Member Management Software (MMS)

Member management software (MMS) manages and organizes member information and activity and provides access control. It allows you to streamline many tasks from a centralized location. Of all the technology used to run a fitness facility, MMS is the cornerstone; it is the primary tool for you to manage day-to-day operations.

MMS is an essential fitness facility technology for many reasons; some benefit the member, and others help the facility. From a member perspective, MMS enhances the experience by simplifying the process of signing up for a membership, booking into programming, and accessing the facility. While features vary from provider to provider, many also allow personalized communication with members through reminders, promotions, and general facility updates. All of these MMS features add to member satisfaction and retention.

MMS also provides a lot of value for your facility. It helps you automate many administrative tasks, freeing up your and staff members' time for more work with more impact, such as engaging with members and improving the overall experience. Reports generated from MMS provide crucial data on membership trends, attendance, revenue, and more, allowing for data-driven decision-making. MMS can also have a positive impact on revenue by allowing members to purchase, upgrade, and renew memberships at the click of a button.

Member management software is critical for fitness facilities because it improves the member experience and allows you to run your facility more effectively, efficiently, and profitably.

Customer Relationship Management (CRM)

Customer relationship management (CRM) is another essential tool you should use to run your fitness facility. CRM software is primarily used to manage and analyze interactions with prospects and members. It can help you and your staff better understand prospects' and members' needs, preferences, behaviors, and engagement, which allows for more effective marketing, sales, and overall improved experience. By providing insight into prospect and member behavior, you can create personalized communication and marketing efforts to increase sales.

CRM software is a great tool that allows you and your staff to manage leads. This is one of the most important features of CRM software. According to Finances Online research, using a CRM improves sales by 87 percent, increases customer satisfaction by 74 percent, and improves overall business process efficiency by 73 percent (Gilbert 2023). This data demonstrates just how important it is to use some sort of CRM to manage leads. Effective lead management facilitates better tracking, follow-up, and your ability to delegate tasks to team members. All that leads to a higher conversion rate of prospects to paying members.

In addition to lead management, CRM software is also an excellent vehicle for you to track sales. CRM features can track sales KPIs such as the number of leads generated, appointment show rates, conversion rates, revenue per member, and more. This data allows you to identify areas of improvement to optimize the sales process.

Even though CRM is generally considered a marketing and sales solution for the facility, it also benefits prospects and members. CRM software often includes easy and quick access to data points such as member information, interactions, and complaints. This information lets you understand members better and consistently improve the overall member experience. You can provide a better customer journey through personalized communication, robust engagement, and better relationships, all made possible by CRM software's data. As a result, members and prospects stand to benefit directly from CRM systems.

While there may be some slight overlap between MMS and CRM, they are two different technological solutions that offer you two distinct purposes. MMS primarily focuses on day-to-day operations, and CRM focuses on enhancing prospect and member relationships to generate more revenue through marketing and sales. There may be some crossover between the two solutions, including integration between the platforms, but they differ. When you use both strategically, they can dramatically increase the effectiveness and efficiency of your fitness facility.

Website

Any organization in any industry needs to have a website. According to Visual Objects, 76 percent of consumers look at an online presence before physically visiting a business, and nearly half of consumers (45 percent) are likely to visit a company's physical location after finding a robust online presence on a local search page (Jordan 2021). This reinforces just how important it is for your fitness facility to have a strong web presence. In the health and fitness industry, your website is the online representation of your fitness facility and typically contains information about the facility itself, its services, its products, and contact details. In today's digital world, a well-designed website is crucial to the success of a fitness facility.

An effective website helps create positive business outcomes. A website is your facility's opportunity to highlight all the services, amenities, and products potential members might be looking for and show them online. Your fitness facility's website should contain pricing, group fitness class information, schedules, details about amenities, and other unique features. Often, and it is good practice to do so, a website allows members to book classes and appointments online, improving the member experience and streamlining operations. Your website is also a great place to showcase testimonials and reviews. Testimonials are practical tools that help build credibility and trust, qualities that attract potential members to a facility.

Ultimately, your website should demonstrate the strengths and unique differentiators to the target market it wishes to serve. A well-thought-out and designed website can be a substantial competitive advantage.

A strong website can also benefit the member or prospective member by providing valuable information and features that lead to a superior member experience. In addition to being a lead generation and sales tool, your facility's website should provide genuine value to people. For the benefit of members, your website should provide easy access to class schedules, facility hours, staff bios, and other news affecting members' facility use. Online booking and payment options help increase your facility's revenue and make the processes easy and convenient for your members. Websites can also provide a variety of health- and fitness-related resources such as workouts, tips, nutritional advice, recipes, and more. These resources help keep members motivated and more likely to achieve health and fitness goals.

In today's digital age, having a website is not optional: It is essential for success. Your facility should use it as a tool to generate revenue and as a way to provide a better member experience. A good website is one of the best ways a fitness facility can create a solid online presence, advertise and sell itself, build relationships and engage with customers, and showcase member satisfaction through testimonials and reviews. If done well, your website provides your facility with a substantial competitive advantage.

Social Media

One of the most significant aspects of the digital age is the use of social media. Social media websites and apps allow people to create and share content with an audience. Social media platforms are constructed to be interactive and engaging, with users able to connect and share information. According to Smart Insights, 60 percent of the world's population uses social media; the average daily usage is 2 hours and 24 minutes (Chaffey 2024).

Social media is different from a website in a key way. For the most part, websites are a one-way communication tool for the facility to share information with its members. Social media, however, allows for two-way communication and engagement between an organization and its followers. Creating two-way communication channels through social media produces a higher level of engagement, increased reach, and a better ability to build your community than a website does.

Social media is crucial for a fitness facility for a variety of reasons. As discussed in chapter 11, social media is a great way to generate leads. In addition to lead generation, social media is an excellent means to connect and engage with existing members and build stronger relationships. You can accomplish this by consistently creating and posting engaging content and encouraging members to create user-generated content. Good content varies based on the brand and the target market. You should use insight tools from your facility's social media platforms to analyze what content gets the most interaction. Whatever kinds of content get the most interaction should be replicated.

User-generated content is any form of content created by users rather than your organization. User-generated content can benefit your fitness facility because members lend an extra level of authenticity to it. Such content can be an excellent way to increase brand awareness, consumer trust, and engagement. Your facility should put strategies in place to encourage members to generate content. These strategies can be check-in challenges, contests, branded hashtags, and creating areas in the facility that encourage the taking and posting of photos.

Another benefit of social media is that it allows you to solicit and respond to feedback. Feedback is crucial for running your fitness facility, and social media is a great way to acquire it. Fitness facilities can be proactive by asking for reviews, running polls, or hosting surveys. These are all great ways to find out what members are thinking. The other way feedback occurs is organic, which means the comments, reviews, and shares where members decide to give their thoughts and opinions. Organic content is also an excellent opportunity to gather data on creating a better experience. Whether the feedback is positive or negative, you must respond. Positive feedback is easy to interact with. The person who provided it should be thanked. The input can also be shared on social media or used for testimonials. Doing this fosters a sense of community and appreciation. You must also have a process in place for negative feedback. It is best practice to respond quickly and empathetically when dealing with negative comments and complaints and to use the feedback to improve operations. Taking conversations offline is acceptable and appropriate if a situation warrants or escalates. Social media is just that: social. To use social media effectively at your fitness facility, you must be committed to engaging and responding regularly.

Similarly to a website, many of the benefits the facility receives from social media add value to the member. Social media platforms allow members to stay connected with the facility, the staff, and the other members. It is a great place to share relevant and valuable information, such as fitness tips, advice, member and staff profiles, testimonials, and more. While a website can share that information, social media allows members to engage with it and with each other, which builds community. It creates a medium for members to share feedback and be heard.

Social media is an excellent technology that you can use to genuinely improve operations, increase revenue, and strengthen member engagement and retention. However, there are challenges: frequent content creation and management, staying up-to-date, consistently engaging, understanding algorithms and trends, dealing with negative feedback, and coping with the inevitable Internet trolls. Despite these challenges, the benefits social media offers you, your facility, and your members make it a worthwhile and necessary task.

Mobile App

Today, most fitness facilities have a mobile application. A mobile app for a fitness facility is a software application designed for a smartphone or tablet that is custom-built for the fitness industry. This app offers many features that members can use to enhance and simplify the member experience. Features may include accessing the facility, booking personal training sessions, scheduling classes, setting fitness goals, tracking progress, accessing workouts, and receiving push notifications and news. Having a mobile app is essential because it encourages member engagement in a convenient and personal way. This can enhance the member experience, increase engagement, and ultimately lead to greater customer loyalty.

The features of a mobile app vary. Some apps are straightforward, offering basic features. More complex apps provide an incredible variety of features. Some companies build apps specifically for fitness centers that allow a facility to white-label the app as if it were their own. These are cost-effective solutions for smaller facilities or facilities with a limited budget. The downside is that limited features may need to be more customizable. At the other end, more extensive facilities, chains, and franchises often invest a lot of capital into highly customized and very sophisticated apps. Regardless of the model of the fitness facility, an app can be used to improve operations and enhance the member experience.

Some benefits of having an app include increased member engagement, improved communication, personalization, and marketing opportunities. An app gives members a convenient and accessible way to stay connected to the facility. Communication effectiveness improves since an app can send members notifications, updates, and reminders. In addition, most apps allow the user to input goals and preferences that aid the app in providing a more personalized experience. Mobile apps can also be a great way to market to members directly through their mobile devices. Apps can directly and positively affect revenue and retention for your facility.

Members also receive a better member experience when a fitness facility provides an app. The member benefits come from the same functionality that benefits the facility. An app allows members to book services, schedule classes, track progress, and access workouts conveniently from their mobile devices. The app lets members instantaneously access news, notes, updates, and specials. An app is a powerful tool for removing friction points from the member journey, making it the best possible experience. An app is a win-win for a fitness facility and its members.

In addition to a website and a solid social media presence, an app is another excellent tool to provide benefits for the facility and the member conveniently and quickly, and many of these apps integrate directly with your CRM and MMS.

Programming Technology

Programming technology uses software, apps, and other digital tools to create or improve nutrition, fitness, and behavior change programming. Some technology is used in the facility, other technologies are used outside, and some can blend both. For example, group fitness instructors, personal trainers, and other team members often use in-house technology at the facility to enhance the delivery of current fitness programming or for members to maximize their in-facility experience. Out-of-house programming technology, conversely, allows members to access programming and resources remotely. Combining in-house and out-of-house programming technology can be a best-of-both-worlds experience, providing a comprehensive, customizable, and personalized solution for members to approach their health and fitness goals. Simply put, the fitness facility becomes a part of the member's life, whether in the facility, at home, or on the go.

You can choose from endless types of programming technology that are vastly different and serve tremendously different purposes. Assessment tools such as scanners, apps, and wearables assess health and fitness metrics, offer feedback, and track progress. Group fitness classes can be delivered via live stream or on-demand solutions. Many facilities provide apps for nutrition, mental health, and behavior change. A great example of programming technology to increase exercise adherence is using software that tracks behaviors such as attendance, program participation, or in-facility purchases and then offers rewards and perks. With programming technology, there is so much to choose from. To make the most out of fitness programming, you must decide which to use based on which you think will have the most significant impact. When making this decision, factors to consider include the type of model, the programming and services offered, and the target market being served.

It is crucial to know how machine learning and artificial intelligence (AI) play a significant role in programming technology. Machine learning and AI have become radically more sophisticated over the last few years. Tasks that were once impossible due to the lack of resources such as human capital can now be effectively and efficiently executed with the help of machine learning and AI. This trend will continue to increase, making programming technology have an even bigger impact on fitness facilities.

The use of programming technology benefits the members as well as the facility. For members, programming technology can offer a personalized and comprehensive approach to fitness and wellness which helps them stay engaged and motivated. For the fitness facility, programming technology helps to increase member engagement, loyalty, and retention. It also streamlines tasks while providing more value to members. With high-quality programming technology and an excellent member experience, facilities can differentiate themselves, attracting and retaining members and leading to increased revenue and growth. Simultaneously, they can help members achieve their fitness goals and lead healthier, happier lives.

Team Member Management

Until this point, the focus has been on how to use technology to enhance your fitness facility in a member-centric way. However, you should also use technology to manage your staff effectively. There are many areas in staff management where technology can have an impact. Using technology for staff management allows you to operate your fitness facility more effectively and efficiently while creating a superior employee experience. Here are some ways you can use technology for staff management:

• *Human resource management.* You can use software and digital tools to simplify and streamline human resource management in your fitness facility. Often the entire employee journey can be managed from a central technology. From job postings to employee reviews, human resource management technology decreases the administrative burden on you and your team and creates a seamless employee experience.

• *Hiring.* Technology is an excellent tool for attracting candidates and improving the hiring process. Using technology such as social media, online job boards, and websites to post job openings dramatically increases the number of job seekers reached. Mobile applications make the process more user-friendly. Using video interviewing modalities as prescreening tools can save time and money. Finally, you can use applicant tracking systems to manage the hiring process and make it as efficient as possible. Using technology for the hiring process makes it a far better experience for the employer and the candidate, which leads to the formation of rock star teams.

• *Scheduling.* Scheduling software is crucial to managing employee schedules effectively and accurately and essential to avoid over- or understaffing. Scheduling software automates the scheduling process and provides real-time visibility into employee availability, making it easier to ensure the facility is always adequately staffed. It frees up your time to focus on more essential duties.

• *Timekeeping.* Timekeeping software can track employee hours and manage time-off requests. Timekeeping software minimizes human error, which provides more accurate data for processing payroll. Another helpful feature of timekeeping software is that it integrates with payroll software, making for an efficient and error-free payroll process.

• *Payroll.* You should use payroll software to automate payroll processing at your fitness facility for various reasons. You can do this internal task yourself, but it is often done through a third party and its software. The use of payroll software helps to make sure that employees are paid the right amount at the right time. Another significant benefit of using payroll software is that it allows you to comply with federal and state wage and hour laws. This is extremely important because it helps minimize the risk of any legal issues. Finally, like other staff management technology, payroll software can reduce errors and provide a more streamlined and systematic payroll process, freeing up your time to focus on different aspects of the employee experience.

Fitness facilities should use technology to enhance member experiences, and it should be used to manage staff effectively. Using technology to manage teams in human resource management, timekeeping, payroll, hiring, and scheduling allows you to streamline their processes, reduce administrative costs and time, and create a better employee experience. By doing so, you can operate your fitness facilities more effectively and efficiently, which leads to organizational effectiveness and success.

Project Management Technology

In addition to using technology to support staff management, it can also be effective in project management. Effective project management is necessary for fitness facilities to succeed financially and remain competitive in a constantly evolving industry. Using the right technology can significantly fortify the project management processes, leading to numerous benefits. These benefits include improved visibility, increased efficiency, more control, and enhanced communication and collaboration. Here are a few examples of ways that you can use technology for project management in your facilities:

• *SaaS.* Software as a service (SaaS) allows you to manage a project from a centralized platform. SaaS is a cloud-based system that team members can access instead of installing and keeping the software on their computers. The software provider hosts and manages the software, making it accessible through a web browser or app. SaaS tools offer a wide range of features, including calendars, to-do lists, communication tools, and document sharing, all with the intent of helping to facilitate collaboration in simple and effective ways.

• *Task assignment and workflow.* Technology tools can help to automate and simplify task assignments and workflow. Doing so can reduce errors, eliminate redundancies, and diminish miscommunications. Task-assigning tools use specialized software to assign tasks, set deadlines, and track project progress. Workflow management software can help teams track the status of tasks, identify roadblocks, and optimize workflows. SaaS and task and workflow technologies are not mutually exclusive. Combined, they can be an effective solution that drives results. SaaS is the delivery model of software applications, and task and workflow technologies are the specific functions and tools that can be part of the SaaS. This combination helps you achieve desirable outcomes as effectively and efficiently as possible.

• *Reporting.* Reporting tools can gather data and insight into project status, productivity levels, and other key benchmarks. This information helps uncover deficiencies, identify areas for improvement, and provide other insights. You can use this data to make more accurate decisions and communicate those decisions to key stakeholders.

• *Job specific.* Project management technology can be customized for particular roles in fitness facilities. This customization allows the technology to have the most significant impact on the position. For example, project management software can be used to oversee a facility renovation with a project board to assign tasks to the right contractors, track the budget and time line, and communicate progress to the facility owner. The social media manager of a facility can use social media management tools to schedule and publish

---

Mastering Productivity: Finding Time to Move Your Fitness Business Forward

Shannon Fable

Your role is pivotal in shaping the success of your facility. Managing the day-to-day operations is essential, but focusing on the bigger picture is equally critical. While you may understand this conceptually, putting a plan into place that ensures you are consistently oscillating between the work needed for today, tomorrow, and the future presents a challenge with which most of us struggle. Here's a quick primer on ensuring you get the right things done at the right time to optimize performance while sidestepping burnout.

Consistent Innovation Is Key

First, you must commit to the idea that consistent innovation is vital for long-term success. To stay relevant and competitive, you must embrace innovation, even if it seems intimidating. For best results, you'll need to expand your definition of innovation. It is more than dreaming up big, exciting ideas. The three types of innovation are iterate, eliminate, and generate.

Iterate
- Continuously improve your offerings based on feedback, industry trends, or identified gaps.
- Keep track of what's working, and implement ideas for enhancement.
- Continuing education can be a valuable resource for innovation.

Eliminate
- You'll need to discontinue aspects of your business that aren't yielding results.
- Regularly evaluate what's not working or providing a good return on investment.
- Streamlining your business creates space for innovation and growth.

Generate
- You'll also need to create something entirely new, not just better versions of existing products or services.
- Start experimenting with new ideas, formulate hypotheses, and put small experiments into the world.
- Be willing to adjust and adapt until you achieve a breakthrough.

posts, track insights, and monitor comments and engagement. Task management tools help a personal trainer organize the training schedule, follow the client's progress, and set reminders for check-ins and follow-ups. In all these examples, job-specific project management solutions help a fitness facility improve productivity, effectiveness, and efficiency, yielding better overall business outcomes as well as member satisfaction.

By leveraging technology tools such as SaaS platforms, task and workflow management software, reporting tools, and job-specific software, you can optimize fitness facility project management processes and stay ahead of the competition.

Deep Work: The Foundation of Innovation

To innovate, you must find time for deep work, a concept popularized by Cal Newport. This type of work is often overlooked due to its need for focused, uninterrupted time. This deep work is categorized into three vital areas: vision, strategy, and creative.

Vision

- Vision work involves brainstorming, researching, and anticipating innovation and growth needs.
- Consider moves that are necessary for your business, areas requiring attention, and potential projects.
- Vision work lays the foundation for strategic planning.

Strategy

- Strategy work is about designing a road map to realize your vision.
- Allocate time to thoroughly plan projects, identifying necessary steps, resources, and knowledge.
- Comprehensive planning makes project execution more manageable.

Creative

- Creative work involves implementing plans and strategies to realize your vision.
- Creative work includes writing, designing, creating marketing assets, and developing new processes.

Your deep work sessions should encompass all these aspects.

Designing Time

Time for deep work is often hard to come by because it can't be done in the "in-between"; that is, between meetings, urgent tasks, phone calls, or similar time-bound activities. You must commit to and set aside dedicated time to work on your business or it won't get done. Here's an overview of a method for designing your time to make it happen.

Determine the total number of hours you work each week. If your job is full-time, you may quickly write down 40 hours, but be discerning. Is that truly the number? Once you know your total number of hours, multiply by 15 percent, the minimum time you should set aside each week to do deep work. Now, divide the 15 percent into 90-minute blocks and start arranging your schedule to fit these blocks of deep work into your schedule.

Of course, there's nothing magical about determining how much time you should spend focused on deep work, but it's a start. Once you get in the habit of designing your time, you'll need to simultaneously ensure you have a system to keep track of your issues (problems in your business that need to be solved) and projects that could solve your issues (iterate, eliminate, generate). From there, planning time to prioritize, break down, and put plans into action is the final step in mastering productivity, which is essential for your business's growth and success.

Facility Management Technology

A final way technology plays a vital role in fitness facility management is in actual facility management. With strategic implementation, facility management can significantly improve effectiveness and efficiency. Facility management technology is generally divided into two categories: facility operations and equipment operations.

Cleaning, energy management, and security all fall into the category of facility operations. For example, building automation systems, a facility management technology, helps control heating, cooling, and lighting systems to manage energy usage and reduce costs. Security is another area that can be enhanced through technology. Access control systems and biometric identification can regulate facility access, reducing the risk of theft, vandalism, and other security breaches. This technology also provides real-time activity tracking, enabling facilities to know who uses the facility and when. You can use technology solutions to help with facility operations.

In addition to facility operations, technology plays a part in equipment operations. You can use technology to monitor equipment, track equipment usage, ensure optimal performance, and reduce the risk of unexpected breakdowns, which minimizes downtime and saves money from costly repairs. An example of technology that assists in this is computerized maintenance management systems (CMMS). Using data collected manually or from sensors built into equipment, you can use CMMS to create maintenance schedules, set inspection reminders, and assign specific maintenance tasks. Just like facility operations, equipment operations can be significantly enhanced using technology.

These facility management technology solutions aid in reducing costs, improving efficiency, and reinforcing the overall quality of the facility and its equipment. When you invest in and use this type of technology, the facility runs better, which improves the member experience, creating a competitive advantage in the industry.

Omnichannel Versus Multichannel

As you have learned, technology plays a huge role in fitness facility management. From managing members and prospects to overseeing staff to enhancing programming experiences to running the facility effectively, there is not an area of fitness facility management that technology doesn't touch and can't improve. With that being the case, a final item for you to consider is multichannel and omnichannel approaches to the implementation of technology solutions.

Multichannel methods involve giving customers multiple ways to interact with the facility. These operate independently and can be in person or via phone, email, or social media. Thus, the member experience varies.

Omnichannel approaches are geared to create a seamless and consistent experience for members across all channels. This approach aims to institute a consistent, personalized experience independent of the medium or touchpoint a member chooses to engage with. When implementing an omnichannel strategy, a fitness facility must integrate all channels and contact points into a cohesive system that enables customers to move seamlessly between channels.

An omnichannel approach is generally preferred over a multichannel strategy. Multichannel approaches risk being disjointed, which can lead to member frustration, confusion, and dissatisfaction. On the other hand, omnichannel approaches provide members with a seamless and personalized experience when executed correctly. This allows you to increase satisfaction and loyalty while improving operational efficiency and effectiveness. For example, if the member management system has tagged a member as an avid runner, then this member will receive notifications about new small group and large team training programs related to running. These and special events such as road races may appear first and at the top of any notification lists. This approach is similar to how targeted advertisements work in e-commerce.

Marketing Plans

A marketing plan is an indispensable tool for you to use in your fitness facility because it provides a comprehensive strategy for promoting all the products and services a facility offers. Lead generation was discussed in depth in chapter 11. Think of a marketing plan as a vehicle for you to take those lead-generation methods and other promotional tactics and put them into a long-term strategic plan. A well-designed plan serves as a strategic road map to guide you and your facility in reaching its target market, achieving its marketing objectives, and ultimately increasing revenue. When you create a clear and concise marketing plan, your fitness facility can remain relevant to its target market and stay competitive.

A comprehensive marketing plan includes a business summary, business initiatives, target market, market strategy, and budget. These elements are critical in helping fitness facilities achieve their marketing goals.

Business Summary

The business summary component of a marketing plan offers an overview of the facility and its history, vision, mission, values, and current position in the market. It should also include any achievements or challenges. The business summary should provide an understanding of the facility to anyone who reads it, including employees, owners, and potential investors. The business summary is critical because it sets the tone for the rest of the plan and helps define the overall goals and objectives.

Business Initiatives

Specific actions and strategies for achieving marketing goals and objectives are outlined in the business initiatives section of a marketing plan. This section examines opportunities and challenges in conjunction with a plan to address them. The plan should include goals, a time line, and a budget. Initiatives often include advertising campaigns, new product or service launches, public relations efforts, and more. All initiatives should be based on the wants and needs of the target market and the competition in the marketplace. Clearly defined business initiatives create a high level of alignment and focus.

Target Market

The target market aspect of a marketing plan revolves around identifying the specific people the marketing efforts are designed to reach. Chapter 3 covered the process of how to define the target market. When constructing a marketing plan, it is vital that you use the techniques from chapter 3 to ensure a completely clear understanding of the intended target audience. A marketing plan's target market component is crucial for ensuring the marketing efforts resonate with a facility's ideal customer, thus achieving the desired results.

Market Strategy

A specific plan of how you intend to reach and engage your target market is called a *market strategy*. This component is the concrete plan for reaching your target market and identifying what marketing channels to use. Examples of marketing channels were discussed in chapter 11 in the section titled Lead Generation. To decide which media will produce the best results, research your target market's behaviors and determine which channels resonate most. In addition to discovering the most effective channels, a successful market strategy involves developing relatable branding and messaging that speaks to the target market's wants and needs. The market strategy is the actionable component of a marketing plan. Figures 13.1, 13.2, and 13.3 show examples of market strategy charts for a special event, membership sales, and personal training.

Budget

The last element in a marketing plan is the budget. The budget describes the financial resources needed to execute the marketing plan. The budget is broken down based on the objectives and the cost associated with each objective. Costs include items such as advertising, promotions, research, and staffing. The budget must be realistic and align with the overarching financial goals of a facility. By including a budget component in a marketing plan, you can adequately allocate resources to maximize the ROI of all the initiatives to best contribute to the facility's overall success.

A marketing plan is crucial to the success of your fitness facility. It allows your facility to take lead-generation, promotional, and advertising tactics and incorporate them into a long-term actionable plan. Your fitness facility can effectively reach its target market with messaging that engages and relates, thus increasing revenue and long-term success.

stevenson FITNESS

memo:

Specifications for 12th Annual Raise the Roof Powerlifting Competition

Date: November 1

Description: Features squat, bench, and deadlift disciplines

Target audience: Rec center members, community members, and the local powerlifting community

Registration period: August 1 to October 21

Call to action: Visit our website for details and to register

Location: Fitness floor

Tactics	Assignee	Start date	Deadline for completion	Implementation date	Complete?	Specs, follow-up dates, or notes
Update website	Director of marketing	July 1	July 31	August 1	False	Webpages that need to be updated include X, X, and X.
Design visuals for print, digital, and social media	Graphic designer	July 1	July 31	August 1	False	Build a design checklist that includes A-frame posters, 8.5 x 11 inch print ads, and social media graphics for X.
Update app	Outreach intern	July 1	July 31	August 1	False	Contact app developers with the necessary information and call to action of X.
Schedule social media campaign	Outreach intern	July 15	August 15	August 16 to October 21	False	Campaign should include promotions that begin two weeks prior to event date and use user-generated content.
Schedule email marketing campaign	Director of marketing	July 15	August 15	August 16 to October 21	False	Craft the type that will go out to our members using their email addresses from our CRM.
Assign photographer or videographer	Outreach intern	August 1	September 1	November 1	False	Contract media team to be on-site to collect content throughout the event.
Schedule community outreach campaign	Director of marketing	August 1	September 1	November 1	False	Coordinate with local media outlets to pitch the event for advertising and coverage.

FIGURE 13.1   Sample marketing strategy for a special event: 12th Annual Raise the Roof Powerlifting Competition.

⚕ 🏋 🧘 🤸
stevenson
F I T N E S S

memo:

Specifications for Membership Drive

Date: January 1 to 31

Description: Join our vibrant fitness community and embark on a journey of wellness like no other. With our diverse range of membership options, including access to state-of-the-art facilities, unlimited group fitness classes, top-notch equipment, and exclusive amenities, we have the perfect fit for every health enthusiast. Whether you're a beginner seeking guidance or a seasoned athlete looking for a new challenge, our gym is the ultimate destination to transform your body, boost your energy, and achieve your fitness goals. Don't wait any longer—take the first step toward a healthier, happier you by becoming a valued member of our dynamic fitness family.

Target audience: External (community members)

Registration period: January 1 to 31

Call to action: Visit our website, download our app, or stop by in person to purchase a membership

Location: Recreation center

Tactics	Assignee	Start date	Deadline for completion	Implementation date	Complete?	Specs, follow-up dates, or notes
Assign photographer or videographer	Outreach intern	August 1	October 1	December 1	False	Conduct a media shoot that supports the visual needs for this campaign.
Design visuals for print, digital, and social media	Graphic designer	November 1	December 15	January 1	False	Build a design checklist that includes A-frame posters, 8.5 x 11 print ads, and social media graphics.
Schedule social media campaign	Outreach intern	November 1	December 15	January 1	False	Campaign should include promotions that run for the duration of the membership drive.
Update website	Director of marketing	December 1	December 30	January 1	False	Webpages that need to be updated include X, X, and X.
Schedule email marketing campaign	Director of marketing	November 1	December 15	January 1	False	Use CRM to identify former members, one-time guests, and other potential members and include them in an email campaign.
Update app	Outreach intern	December 1	December 30	January 1	False	Contact app developers with the necessary information and call to action.
Schedule community outreach campaign	Director of marketing	December 1	December 30	January 1	False	Coordinate with local media outlets to pitch the event for advertising and coverage.

FIGURE 13.2 Sample marketing strategy for membership sales: Membership drive campaign to recruit and sell memberships.

stevenson
F I T N E S S

memo:

Specifications for Personal Training Upselling

Date: Ongoing

Description: Unlock the full potential of your fitness journey with our exclusive personal training packages, meticulously tailored to your unique goals and needs. Elevate your workouts, maximize results, and unleash your inner strength with the expert guidance and personalized support of our highly skilled trainers. Upgrade your membership today and experience the transformative power of one-on-one coaching that will take your fitness game to new heights.

Target audience: Internal (existing members)

Registration period: Ongoing

Call to action: Visit our website for details and to register

Location: Personal training studio

Tactics	Assignee	Start date	Deadline for completion	Implementation date	Complete?	Specs, follow-up dates, or notes
Update website	Director of marketing	July 15	August 1	August 1	False	Audit webpage to ensure the information remains current.
Design visuals for print, digital, and social media	Graphic designer	July 15	August 1	August 15	False	Build a design checklist that includes trifold brochures, 8.5 x 11 print ads, and digital graphics for email headers.
Update app	Outreach intern	July 15	August 1	August 15	False	Schedule a recurring app push notification that reminds users of personal training services.
Schedule social media campaign	Outreach intern	July 15	August 1	August 15	False	Collect client testimonials to share via an ongoing social media campaign.
Schedule email marketing campaign	Director of marketing	July 15	August 1	August 15	False	Build a campaign that will go out to our members two months from membership activation date and continues biannually.

FIGURE 13.3 Sample marketing strategy for personal training: Upselling members to purchase personal training packages.

Strategic Plans

Creating and using a strategic plan is essential for managing a fitness facility. A strategic plan comprehensively outlines a fitness facility's vision, mission, and values. If you lack a well-thought-out strategic plan, you may go through the motions without the desired results, due to a lack of clear purpose and direction. Conversely, an effective strategic plan empowers you and your facility to set priorities, properly allocate resources, and create an action plan to achieve your goals. A complete strategic plan assists you in defining areas of focus and combining them with an actionable plan to achieve your goals.

Both macro- and micro-level categories are essential for a complete strategic plan. *Macro-level* refers to high-level areas of focus, while *micro-level* addresses

Questions to Consider During the Strategic Marketing Process

Will Trent

Target Audience

How would my target audience want to receive information? Far too often, we sell our audience on something because we think it's important to them rather than asking them what they need and how we can better serve them. It's easy for marketing strategy to fall into this trap, too, where we advertise without asking our audience specifically how they want to co-communicate with us.

Media

Do I have high-quality imagery or graphics to support this campaign? To lead a successful digital campaign, understand that content is critical and must represent what you are advertising to your audience. A strong media team and a robust media asset library should be at the forefront of priorities to support your current and future marketing campaigns.

Automation

What can I automate within my marketing planning process to more effectively assign and organize my tactics? Automate the marketing request process to ensure colleagues provide you with the necessary information to build a successful campaign.

Delegation

What do I, as the marketing planner, need to do before delegating tactics to others? Create a common call to action, and ensure that those resources are solidified. For example, if your call to action is "visit our website to register," you, as the marketing planner, should ensure that the website is up-to-date so your team can follow suit with their duties of creating tactics that send your audience there.

Elimination

What tactics can I eliminate because I cannot assess their effectiveness? "If you're not assessin', you're guessin'," as the saying goes. Seek to understand the effectiveness of your tactics and rely on that data to shape future advertising decisions. Track QR codes on print ads, audit social media analytics, and form focus groups from your audience to conclude what channels and tactics work best.

Social Media

Do I have any user-generated content that can support my tactics? If I show my audience that users like them have participated and enjoyed what I am advertising, they are more likely to perceive that it, too, could be for them. Testimonials are critical, and whether they are visual (through imagery) or written, they can serve as proof of attendance and satisfaction.

---

operational details. Macro-level strategic plan categories include market analysis, financial planning, and facility improvements, among others. Micro-level categories may focus on member retention, staff development, and community building. These two categories combined drive the business forward while ensuring that the individual components of the facility are running effectively.

Every strategic plan must include a clear set of goals. Goals give you and your team targets to work toward. All goals set should be SMART goals (specific, measurable, achievable, relevant,

Case Study: Formulating a Plan for the Future

Greg Corack

National Fitness Limited recently opened a new fitness facility in the suburbs of a major metropolitan area. Its owner, Craig, a longtime personal trainer, is excited to take on this new business opportunity, hoping to expand membership and scale the business to multiple locations around the city. Within the first six months of operation, National Fitness Limited attracted 75 percent of its membership goal through an extensive marketing push and special promotional rates. Craig has his eyes on rapid expansion, even touring a new space across town for a second location and the ability to add group fitness, massage, and specialized fitness training. As National Fitness Limited enjoys a tremendous period of success, Craig realizes that to gather the support necessary from his investment partners, he must develop a comprehensive three- to five-year plan with an ability to measure impact and ensure growth targets.

Developing the Plan

Twelve months after opening, National Fitness Limited is bursting at the seams, and Craig meets with his management team to develop a plan. The group starts with a brainstorming session to discuss their dream scenarios for one-year, three-year, and five-year success. The process entails a comprehensive list of possibilities, including scaled growth, franchise opportunities, and expansion to new cities. After their brainstorming session, the group narrows their list to five themes: membership growth, staffing excellence, customer service, market reach, and financial stability. These themes are the backbone of their strategic plan, and now they focus on timely objectives to scale National Fitness Limited into a successful multifacility enterprise. To ensure their goals are within the realm of possibility, they host multiple workshops with current members, business partners, and trusted colleagues in the industry. This last step is crucial because their plan for growth must be feasible to attract financing, members, and the staff they need to expand.

Targeted Growth

With a five-year strategic plan in hand, Craig meets with local investors and secures the financing necessary to open a second location near a massive new apartment complex. He chose the site based on its proximity to public transit, housing geared toward his target demographic of young professionals, and ample parking. National Fitness Limited targets membership growth at 20 percent annually for the next five years, with plans to open a third location in 24 months and a fourth location in 48 months. The conservative approach to growth allows Craig to develop staff, research locations, and upgrade facilities to meet trends in the industry. A marketing campaign is launched alongside the second facility's grand opening with membership promotions, television and social media advertisements, special events, and the hiring of a new marketing director to coordinate outreach. Craig and his investors realize growth can be achieved only through human and physical capital investment.

Measuring Impact

National Fitness Limited reaches its fourth anniversary with two thriving facilities while scouting locations for a third. The marketing director realizes the company needs data to determine if it is reaching its target market, if members are satisfied, and if employees feel valued. Social media and website data are analyzed to determine traffic, reach, and engagement. A digital survey is developed for members to gather essential data about programs offered, facility quality, access, and their propensity to recommend National Fitness Limited to friends through the net promoter score (NPS) scale. Craig contracts with a third-party firm to conduct focus groups with his more than 100 team members to ensure they provide honest feedback regarding their experience. He understands employees who are treated well and valued are his best brand ambassadors.

Tell Your Story

Data gleaned from the impact assessment process is used as a new marketing campaign promoting the third National Fitness Limited location. The company is voted as one of the area's best places to work, has a world-class NPS score, and has excellent engagement, with videos created by personal trainers depicting the fun side of exercising. New graphics adorning front-facing windows tout the positive response from employees and members, and social media posts include similar messaging emphasizing testimonials from satisfied users. The director of marketing even produced a live-action local commercial using staff and members to celebrate the opening of the newest location. Craig's dream of growth is just beginning, and he knows continuing this journey is predicated on the ability to share the benefits of health and well-being with the entire city.

and time-bound). A typical goal might be increasing membership by 10 percent in a year. Another goal might be to decrease attrition by 5 percent in the next six months. Both examples pass the SMART goal test. The strategic plan is the road map, and SMART goals are the destination of that road map.

Objectives go hand in hand with goals. They are the actions and steps that must be taken to achieve the goals outlined in the strategic plan. Just like goals, objectives should be designed using the SMART methodology. For example, an objective to support the goal of increasing membership might be to start a referral program that incentivizes current members to refer friends and family. This objective could be SMART by tracking the new members joining the program over a certain period. Another example for the goal of decreasing attrition could be to institute an attendance reward program. Tracking the length of membership among members receiving awards for attending over a certain period would make this objective SMART. SMART goals plus SMART objectives equal a formula for fitness facility success.

You should evaluate your strategic plan regularly and adjust it when needed to remain relevant and effective. Evaluating a strategic plan once a year is a good rule of thumb. This frequency can vary based on the type of model, size, complexity, and other factors. Be aware that any significant changes in the organization, industry, or environment, in general, warrant the need for you to evaluate it more frequently. Strategic plans are necessary to guide an organization but are not set in stone. They should be reevaluated and adjusted to ensure they always drive a facility forward.

A strategic plan is a crucial component for effectively managing a fitness facility. When thoughtfully created, it outlines the facility's vision, mission, and values and provides a road map to achieve its goals. Trying to operate without one is like driving around without a destination. While there is movement and action, you never end up anywhere.

Conclusion

This comprehensive textbook has equipped you with a wealth of knowledge and applicable skills essential for successfully managing your fitness facility. From understanding the current landscape of the health and fitness industry to designing an organization that thrives, building a rock star team, creating and delivering top-notch programs and services, and establishing effective and efficient project management and profitability systems, you have taken a journey through all of the essential aspects of this incredible industry.

By practicing and mastering the concepts presented in this book, you'll be well-prepared to tackle the challenges of fitness facility management and achieve fantastic success. Remember this: A successful facility involves revenue and operations and, more importantly, centers around its impact on people's lives. Your role as a facility manager enables you to provide a place where individuals can embark on their health and fitness journey, positively affecting their overall health and well-being. There's nothing quite as fulfilling as knowing that your efforts contribute to creating a space that fosters physical, mental, and social transformation. As you move forward in your career in our essential industry, remember that the ripple effect of your work extends far beyond the four walls of your facility, touching countless people seeking to improve their lives through health and fitness. Embrace this responsibility with passion and dedication, and you'll find that the fulfillment derived from making a difference is immeasurable.

THINK IT THROUGH

- What is the difference between effectiveness and efficiency?
- Why is it important to use various technology solutions to successfully operate your fitness facility?
- What are the key components of a strategic plan, and why is it important to regularly evaluate and adjust it?
- What are some examples of SMART goals that your fitness facility might set to achieve membership growth or retention?
- What are the pros and cons of omnichannel and multichannel approaches to implementing technological solutions in your facility?

KEY TERMS

customer relationship management (CRM)

effectiveness

efficiency

member management software (MMS)

omnichannel versus multichannel

SMART goals

strategic plan

References

Introduction

Tharrett, S.J. 2017. *Fitness Management: A Comprehensive Resource for Developing, Leading, Managing, and Operating a Successful Health/Fitness Business in the Era of the 4th Industrial Revolution.* 4th ed. Monterey, CA: Healthy Learning.

Chapter 1

Centers for Disease Control and Prevention. 2023. "Physical Activity Helps Prevent Chronic Diseases." Infographic. Last reviewed May 8, 2023. www.cdc.gov/chronicdisease /resources/infographic/physical-activity.htm.

Elgaddal, N., E.A. Kramarow, and C. Reuben. 2022. "Physical Activity Among Adults Aged 18 and Over: United States, 2020." NCHS Data Brief No. 443. Hyattsville, MD: National Center for Health Statistics. https://dx.doi.org/10.15620/cdc:120213.

IHRSA. 2022. "New IHRSA Data Shows High, Growing COVID-Related Closure Rates for Fitness Facilities." January 28, 2022. www.ihrsa.org/about/media-center /press-releases/new-ihrsa-data-shows-high-growing -covid-related-closure-rates-for-fitness-facilities/#.

IHRSA and L.E.K. Consulting. 2022. *The 2022 IHRSA Health Club Consumer Report.* www.ihrsa.org/publications/the -2022-ihrsa-health-club-consumer-report.

Newsome, A.M., R. Reed, J. Sansone, A. Batrakoulis, C. McAvoy, and M. Parrott. 2024. "2024 ACSM Worldwide Fitness Trends: Future Directions of the Health and Fitness Industry." *ACSM's Health & Fitness Journal* 28(1):14-26. https://doi.org/10.1249/FIT.0000000000000933.

Sinclair, K., and T. Kanakri. 2021. "Physical Activity May Reduce Risk of Poor COVID-19 Outcomes." Kaiser Permanente. https://about.kaiserpermanente.org /our-story/health-research/news/physical-activity-may -reduce-risk-of-poor-covid-19-outcomes.

Thompson, W.R. 2023. "Worldwide Survey of Fitness Trends for 2023." *ACSM's Health & Fitness Journal* 27(1): 9-18. https://doi.org/10.1249/FIT.0000000000000834.

Tipping, E. 2023. "Our 2023 Report on the State of the Managed Recreation Industry." Rec Management. https://recmanagement.com/articles/153713/our-2023-report-state-managed-recreation-industry.

Waters, J. 2022. "Supply Chain Issues Not Over Yet." *Supply Chain Management Review.* www.scmr.com/article /supply_chain_issues_not_over_yet.

Chapter 2

Business Model Analyst. 2023. "Tesla Mission and Vision Statement." May 22, 2023. https://businessmodelanalyst .com/tesla-mission-and-vision-statement/.

Centers for Disease Control and Prevention (CDC). 2018. "Gaining Consensus Among Stakeholders Through the Nominal Group Technique." www.cdc.gov/healthyyouth /evaluation/pdf/brief7.pdf.

Collins, J. 2000. "Aligning Action and Values." www.jimcollins .com/article_topics/articles/aligning-action.html.

Collins, J. 2001. "Vision Framework." www.jimcollins.com /tools/vision-framework.pdf.

Collins, J., and J.I. Porras. 2011. *Built to Last: Successful Habits of Visionary Companies.* New York: HarperCollins.

Commons Club. n.d. "Mission and Vision Statement." www .thecommonsclub.com/living-a-healthy-life/mission -and-vision-statement. Retrieved January 28, 2024.

Cotter, A. 2023. "Cultivating Corporate Culture: The Role of Company Values." www.workvivo.com/blog/company -values/. Workvivo by Zoom.

East Carolina University. n.d. "Mission, Vision, and Goals." Campus Recreation & Wellness. https://crw .ecu.edu/about-us/our-story/mission-vision-and-goals/. Retrieved January 28, 2024.

Gill, R. 2022. "Vision and Mission Statements, Are They Still Relevant in 2022?" LinkedIn. www.linkedin.com/pulse /vision-mission-statements-still-relevant-2022-russell -gill/?trk=articles_directory.

LinkedIn. 2023. "About LinkedIn." https://about.linkedin .com/.

McKinsey & Company. 2023. "Patagonia Shows How Turning a Profit Doesn't Have to Cost the Earth." McKinsey.com. April 20, 2023. www.mckinsey.com/ industries/agriculture/our-insights/patagonia-shows-how-turning-a-profit-doesnt-have-to-cost-the-earth.

Orangetheory Fitness. n.d. "Our Mission, Vision and Values." www.orangetheory.com/en-us/our-commitment.

Panmore Institute. 2023. "Walt Disney's Mission Statement and Vision Statement (An Analysis)." September 20, 2023. https://panmore.com/walt-disney-company -mission-statement-vision-statement-analysis.

Sinek, S. 2009. *Start With Why.* New York: Portfolio.

Tsang, S. 2020. "Best Mission Statements: 12 Examples You Need to See." Fond company website. www.fond.co/blog /best-mission-statements/.

Virgin Active. n.d. Virgin Active Corporate Website. www .virginactive.com/index.html.

Walt Disney. 2023. "About the Walt Disney Company." https://thewaltdisneycompany.com/about/.

Chapter 3

Hayes, A. 2023. "Barriers to Entry: Understanding What Limits Competition." www.investopedia.com/terms/b /barrierstoentry.asp.

Qualtrics XM. 2023. "How to Create a Buyer Persona." www.qualtrics.com/experience-management/product /create-buyer-persona.

Shopify. 2022. "What Is a Focus Group? Definition and Guide." www.shopify.com/blog/what-is-a-focus -group.

U.S. Small Business Administration. 2023. "Market Research and Competitive Analysis." February 1, 2024. www.sba.gov/business-guide/plan-your-business /market-research-competitive-analysis.

Chapter 4

Accounting Tools. 2023. "Activity-Based Budgeting Definition." www.accountingtools.com/articles/activity -based-budgeting.html.

Aguilar, O., and F. Shaikh. 2023. "Zero-Based Budgeting." Deloitte. www2.deloitte.com/us/en/pages/operations /articles/zero-based-budgeting.html.

Chase for Business. 2023. "Nine Reasons Why You Need a Business Plan." www.chase.com/business/knowledge -center/start/reasons-for-business-plan.

JCC Association of North America. 2023. "History." https:// jcca.org/about-us/history/.

Medical Fitness Association. 2023. "About Us." www .medicalfitness.org/about-us.

QuickBooks. 2022. "Cash vs. Accrual Accounting: What's Best for Your Small Business?" https://quickbooks .intuit.com/accounting/cash-vs-accrual-accounting -whats-best-small-business/.

Schmidt, J. 2023a. "Incremental Budgeting." Corporate Finance Institute. https://corporatefinanceinstitute .com/resources/fpa/incremental-budgeting/.

Schmidt, J. 2023b. "The Four Main Types of Budgets and Budgeting Methods." Corporate Finance Institute. https://corporatefinanceinstitute.com/resources/fpa /types-of-budgets-budgeting-methods/.

Small Business Administration. 2023. "Write Your Business Plan." www.sba.gov/business-guide/plan-your-business /write-your-business-plan.

YMCA Canada. n.d. "Quick Facts." www.ymca.ca/who-we -are/about-us/quick-facts.

YMCA of the USA. n.d. "Key Facts and Figures." www.ymca .org/who-we-are/our-reach/key-facts.

Chapter 5

Clifton, J. 2022. "The World's Workplace Is Broken—Here's How to Fix It." Gallup Workplace. www.gallup.com /workplace/393395/world-workplace-broken-fix.aspx.

Qualtrics. 2023. "What Is Employee Net Promoter Score (eNPS) and How Can It Be Used to Improve Employee Engagement?" September 17, 2023. www.qualtrics.com /blog/employee-net-promoter-score-enps-good-measure -engagement/.

Rath, T., and J. Harter. 2010. Wellbeing: The Five Essential Elements. New York: Gallup Press.

Chapter 6

Bain & Company. n.d. "The History of Net Promoter." www.netpromotersystem.com/about/history-of-net -promoter.

Buckingham, M., and C. Coffman. 2016. First, Break All the Rules: What the World's Greatest Managers Do Differently. New York: Simon & Schuster.

Collins, J. 2001. Good to Great. New York: Harper Business.

Gallup. 2023a. State of the Global Workplace: 2023 Report. Gallup. https://www.gallup.com/workplace/349484 /state-of-the-global-workplace.aspx.

Gallup. 2023b. "How to Create a Strengths-Based Company Culture." www.gallup.com/cliftonstrengths/en/290903 /how-to-create-strengths-based-company-culture.aspx.

Gallup. 2023c. "Gallup's Employee Engagement Survey: Ask the Right Questions With the Q^{12+} Survey." www .gallup.com/workplace/356063/gallup-q12-employee -engagement-survey.aspx.

Hanson, T., and B. Zacher. 2007. Who Will Do What by When?: How to Improve Performance, Accountability and Trust with Integrity. 1st ed. N.p.: Power Publications.

Stevenson, C. 2020. "Six Steps to Effective Staff Coaching." The Athletic Business Journal. www.athleticbusiness .com/operations/personnel/article/15159906/six-steps -to-effective-staff-coaching.

Tran, M. 2016. "How Much Does Employee Retention Impact Customer Satisfaction?" Medallia. www.medallia.com /blog/how-much-does-employee-retention-impact -customer-satisfaction/.

Chapter 7

Falcone, P. 2018. "How to Have the Termination Discussion." Society for Human Resource Management (SHRM). www.shrm.org/resourcesandtools/hr-topics/talent -acquisition/pages/the-termination-discussion.aspx.

Gallup. 2018. "Gallup's Perspective on Exit Programs That Retain Stars and Build Brand Ambassadors." https:// www.gallup.com/workplace/246512/exit-perspective -paper.aspx.

Gallup. 2023. State of the Global Workplace: 2023 Report. https://www.gallup.com/workplace/349484/state-of -the-global-workplace.aspx.

Gandhi, V., and J. Robison. 2021. "The 'Great Resignation' Is Really the 'Great Discontent.'" Gallup Workplace. www.gallup.com/workplace/351545/great-resignation-really-great-discontent.aspx.

Patrick, C., and D. Sundaram. 2018. "The Real Value of Getting an Exit Interview Right." www.gallup.com/workplace/236051/real-value-getting-exit-interview-right.aspx.

Pendell, R. 2021. "5 Ways Managers Stop Employee Turnover." Gallup Workplace. www.gallup.com/workplace/357104/ways-managers-stop-employee-turnover.aspx.

Pendell, R. 2022. "7 Gallup Workplace Insights: What We Learned in 2021." Gallup Workplace. www.gallup.com/workplace/358346/gallup-workplace-insights-learned-2021.aspx.

SHRM. 2023. "Engaging in Succession Planning." Society for Human Resource Management (SHRM). www.shrm.org/resourcesandtools/tools-and-samples/toolkits/pages/engaginginsuccessionplanning.aspx

U.S. Department of Labor. n.d. "Severance Pay." www.dol.gov/general/topic/wages/severancepay. Retrieved February 1, 2024.

Wigert, B., and S. Agrawal. 2019. "3 Ways to Create a Positive Exit Experience for Your Employees." Gallup. www.gallup.com/workplace/246203/ways-create-positive-exit-experience-employees.aspx.

Chapter 8

Aiello, M. 2016. "Everything You Need to Know About Health Club Locker Room Size." IHRSA. June 23, 2016. www.ihrsa.org/improve-your-club/everything-you-need-to-know-about-health-club-locker-room-size/.

American College of Sports Medicine (ACSM). 2019. ACSM's Health/Fitness Facility Standards and Guidelines, 5th ed., edited by M.E. Sanders. Champaign, IL: Human Kinetics.

American College of Sports Medicine (ACSM). 2024. "ACSM Trends 2024." www.acsm.org/education-resources/trending-topics-resources/acsm-fitness-trends.

Callendar, M. 2009. Campus Recreational Sports Facilities: Planning, Design, and Construction Guidelines, edited by G. Kassing, p. 103. Champaign, IL: Human Kinetics.

Feldman Equities. n.d. "What Is the Difference Between Class A, B, and C Properties?" www.feldmanequities.com/education/what-is-the-difference-between-class-a-b-and-c-properties/.

HOK. 2024. "Auburn University Recreation and Wellness Center." www.hok.com/projects/view/auburn-university-recreation-and-wellness-center/.

IHRSA. 2024. "2021 IHRSA Media Report: Part 2." https://www.ihrsa.org/publications/2021-ihrsa-media-report-2/.

Jo, S., C.S. Gagliardi, J. Shroeder, and D.J. Green. 2023. The Exercise Professional's Guide to Group Fitness Instruction. San Diego: American Council on Exercise.

Smith, S. 2023. "Fitness Industry Perseveres Through 2022 to Get Back on Top." International Health, Racquet and Sportsclub Association (IHRSA). January 6, 2023. www.ihrsa.org/improve-your-club/industry-news/fitness-industry-perseveres-through-2022-to-get-back-on-top/.

Spinning. 2024. "Spinning History." https://spinning.com/spinning-history/.

Tharrett, S.J. 2017. Fitness Management: A Comprehensive Resource for Developing, Leading, Managing, and Operating a Successful Health/Fitness Business in the Era of the 4th Industrial Revolution. 4th ed. Monterey, CA: Healthy Learning.

Chapter 9

American College of Sports Medicine (ACSM). 2019. ACSM's Health/Fitness Facility Standards and Guidelines, 5th ed., edited by M.E. Sanders. Champaign, IL: Human Kinetics.

Chapter 10

Kantar. n.d. "NeedScope." www.kantar.com/north-america/expertise/brand-growth/brand-purpose-and-positioning/needscope.

Phillips, J. n.d. "2021 Global Report Reveals 7 Key Trends for the New Fitness Landscape." Les Mills. www.lesmills.com/clubs-and-facilities/research-insights/fitness-trends/2021-global-report-reveals-7-key-trends-for-the-new-fitness-landscape/.

Yorks, D., C. Frothingham, and M. Schuenke. 2017. "Effects of Group Fitness Classes on Stress and Quality of Life of Medical Students." Journal of Osteopathic Medicine 117(11), e17-e25. https://doi.org/10.7556/jaoa.2017.140.

Chapter 11

American Council on Exercise. 2019. The Professional's Guide to Health and Wellness Coaching: Empower Transformation Through Lifestyle Behavior Change. San Diego: American Council on Exercise. https://doi.org/10.1016/b978-1-890720-72-8.00001-6.

Bizrate Insights. 2021. "The Impact of Customer Reviews on Purchase Decisions." Bizrate Insights. https://bizrateinsights.com/resources/the-impact-of-customer-reviews-on-purchase-decisions/.

Deci, E.L., and R.M. Ryan. 1985. Intrinsic Motivation and Self-Determination in Human Behavior. Springer-Verlag. doi:10.1007/978-1-4899-2271-7.

Goenka, S.N. 2010. "The Essence of Wisdom." Vipassana Research Institute. www.vridhamma.org/discourses/The-Essence-of-Wisdom.

Miller, G. 2023. "42 Referral Marketing Statistics That Will Make You Want to Start an RAF Program Tomorrow." Annex Cloud. August 12, 2023. www.annexcloud.com/blog/42-referral-marketing-statistics-that-will-make-you-want-to-start-a-raf-program-tomorrow/.

Oldenburg, R. 1989. The Great Good Place: Cafes, Coffee Shops, Bookstores, Bars, Hair Salons, and Other Hangouts at the Heart of a Community. New York: Paragon House.

OneMob. 2022. "5 Stages of a Successful Sales Funnel." www.linkedin.com/pulse/5-stages-successful-sales-funnel-onemob/?trk=pulse-article_more-articles_related-content-card.

Vaynerchuk, G. 2013. *Jab, Jab, Jab, Right Hook*. New York: Harper Business.

Chapter 12

American College of Sports Medicine (ACSM). 2019. *ACSM's Health/Fitness Facility Standards and Guidelines*, 5th ed., edited by M.E. Sanders. Champaign, IL: Human Kinetics.

Bryant, C.X., S. Jo, L. Dalleck, C.S. Gagliardi, D.J. and Green. 2020. *The Exercise Professional's Guide to Personal Training: A Client-Centered Approach to Inspire Active Lifestyles*. San Diego: American Council on Exercise.

Tharrett, S.J. 2017. *Fitness Management: A Comprehensive Resource for Developing, Leading, Managing, and Operating a Successful Health/Fitness Business in the Era of the 4th Industrial Revolution*. 4th ed. Monterey, CA: Healthy Learning.

Warburton, D.E.R., V.K. Jamnik, S.S.D. Bredin, and N. Gledhill. 2023. "The Physical Activity Readiness Questionnaire for Everyone (PAR-Q+) and Electronic Physical Activity Readiness Medical Examination (ePARmed-X+)." *Health & Fitness Journal of Canada* 9(1), 3-23. https://doi.org/10.14288/hfjc.v4i2.103.

Chapter 13

Chaffey, D. 2024. "Global Social Media Statistics Research Summary 2024." Smart Insights. www.smartinsights.com/social-media-marketing/social-media-strategy/new-global-social-media-research/.

Gilbert, N. 2023. "75 Basic CRM Software Statistics: 2024 Data Analysis and Market Share." Finances Online. https://financesonline.com/crm-software-statistics/.

Jordan, S. 2021. "76% of Consumers Look at Online Presence Before Physically Visiting a Business." April 20, 2021. www.prnewswire.com/news-releases/76-of-consumers-look-at-online-presence-before-physically-visiting-a-business-301272462.html.

Martins, J. 2022. "Efficiency vs. Effectiveness in Business: Your Team Needs Both." Asana. October 19, 2022. https://asana.com/resources/efficiency-vs-effectiveness-whats-the-difference.

Index

About the Authors

Steven A. Trotter, MS, is a global well-being consultant and adjunct professor. With over two decades of experience in the fitness and wellness industry, Trotter is renowned for his expertise in people management and the development of programs and facilities. He founded Globe-trotter Wellness Solutions, LLC, in 2017 after seven years of providing independent consulting services. His firm collaborates with universities; health clubs; organizations; and morale, wellness, and recreation (MWR) units to improve organizational and employee well-being and to build systems for success.

Trotter was formerly the director of well-being at a major university. During that time, he led a comprehensive, holistic well-being program that served over 35,000 individuals across three campuses and a distance education program. He managed two indoor fitness facilities and several outdoor fitness areas, totaling over 200,000 square feet. In his earlier roles as fitness director at various universities, he was instrumental in managing fitness programs and overseeing numerous facility expansion and construction projects.

Trotter is an international speaker and presenter, regularly presenting at local, state, regional, national, and international conferences on subjects such as facility management, employee engagement, organizational development, project and priority management, and strategic marketing. He is a regular contributor to *Campus Rec Magazine* and the website of American Council on Exercise (ACE). He has served as a subject matter expert for ACE since 2014 and works with the credentialing department to develop and continuously improve the four NCCA-accredited ACE certifications.

Trotter has a master of science degree in health and physical education from Virginia Tech and a bachelor of science degree in exercise science from the University of North Carolina at Charlotte. He holds the American College of Sports Medicine (ACSM) exercise physiologist certification, four certifications from ACE, and multiple specialty certifications from Les Mills. He is an American Red Cross instructor in CPR, AED, and first aid; a certified mental health first aid trainer; a Green Dot bystander intervention facilitator; and a Gallup-certified strength coach. He is also a continuing education provider with ACE, National Academy of Sports Medicine (NASM), and Athletics and Fitness Association of America (AFAA).

Chris Stevenson, BA, CSCS, is the founder of The Empower Group, a comprehensive consulting firm headquartered in Westlake Village, California. The firm specializes in delivering keynote presentations, interactive workshops, and strategic advising services to facilities worldwide. The Empower Group collaborates with facilities of varying scales and types, spanning domestic and international markets. Their core competencies encompass business planning, strategic design, fostering exceptional workplace culture, optimizing staffing strategies, enhancing marketing and sales efforts, refining member experiences, and more.

Stevenson has over 25 years of experience in the health and fitness industry, from personal training and group exercise classes to owning and operating a full-service health club. For six years, he was a faculty member at the California Health and Longevity Institute (CHLI), located at the Four Seasons in Westlake Village, California, and named one of the top 10 executive health programs in the nation by *Worth* magazine. He presented on exercise science and behavioral change and oversaw a team of exercise specialists who performed one-on-one assessments and training sessions for the executives.

Stevenson is an international speaker and has presented keynote speeches and breakout sessions in over a dozen different countries and throughout the United States. He regularly presents at fitness and business events, including those of Health & Fitness Association (formerly IHRSA), Athletic Business, IDEA, NASM Optima, and Club Industry. He has written for Club Business International (CBI), Health Club Management (HCH), Chartered Institute for the Management of Sport and Physical Activity (CIMSPA), National Academy of Sports Medicine (NASM), Club Solutions, and Club Industry, and he is a regular columnist for *Athletic Business*.

He serves on the board of directors of the Health & Fitness Association, the largest nonprofit trade association for the health and fitness industry; the owners committee of IDEA; and the events committee of the Climbing Wall Association. In those roles, he advises on strategic planning, standards, policies, values, and vision to increase the organizations' benefits to their members.

Stevenson has a bachelor of business administration degree from Baldwin Wallace University in Berea, Ohio. He holds the Certified Strength and Conditioning Specialist (CSCS) credential from the National Strength and Conditioning Association (NSCA) and is certified as a Technogym master educator.

About the Contributors

GREGORY J. CORACK, EdD, Senior Director of Recreation and Wellness at East Carolina University

Greg Corack is a recreational sports professional with 17 years of experience at multiple universities across the United States. He currently serves as the senior director of recreation and wellness at East Carolina University and was formerly an adjunct professor. His passion for recreation comes from 15 years of sports officiating experience in soccer and basketball and a commitment to lifetime physical activity. Dr. Corack regularly contributes to *Campus Rec* magazine, has served as the NIRSA Club Sports work team chair, and has presented at numerous higher education conferences. His research interests are focused on student success and sports involvement, and he remains a strong proponent of developing the next group of great team sports officials.

Education and Certifications

> EdD in Educational Leadership, Eastern Kentucky University
>
> MS in Sport Management, James Madison University
>
> BS in Sport Management, James Madison University
>
> CPR Instructor, American Red Cross
>
> Mental Health First Aid, National Council for Mental Wellbeing

SHANNON FABLE, Founder and CEO of SF Resources

Shannon Fable is a sought-after speaker, author, and thought leader in strategic innovation, implementation, and integration. Over the past 25 years, she has helped impressive brands, including ACE, Anytime Fitness, Schwinn, Power Systems, Silver Sneakers, Fit4Mom, and Bosu, as well as solopreneurs, create, clarify, and simplify their products and services to increase their impact. Fable served as chair of the ACE board of directors, cofounded and successfully sold GroupEx Pro, and is recognized as the 2013 IDEA Fitness Instructor of the Year and 2006 ACE Group Fitness Instructor of the Year. As a Book Yourself Solid licensed professional and an EOS Integrator Mastery Forum pro member, she helps companies build scalable and sustainable businesses. She currently serves as the senior director of education and digital programming for Exos.

Education and Certifications

> BA in High Honors Sociology, Minor in Communication Studies, University of Florida
>
> Executive Certificate in Innovation Strategy, Dartmouth Tuck School of Business
>
> Certified Group Fitness Instructor, American Council on Exercise
>
> Certified Personal Trainer, American Council on Exercise
>
> Certified Health Coach, American Council on Exercise
>
> Book Yourself Solid Licensed Professional

CASEY GILVIN, MS, CSCS, Co-owner of LCG Fitness & Performance, Associate Director for Facilities at University of Kentucky Department of Campus Recreation, Race Director for the Ironman Group

With more than 19 years in the fitness industry, Casey Gilvin has served in various capacities as a performance coach, personal trainer, strength and conditioning specialist, MWR fitness coordinator, and fitness director. With experience in the collegiate, military, and private fitness sectors, Casey has had vast experience in fitness, facility, and programming operations.

Education and Certifications

- MS in Kinesiology and Health Promotion, Sport Leadership, University of Kentucky
- BA in Kinesiology and Health Promotion, Exercise Science, University of Kentucky
- Certified Strength and Conditioning Specialist (CSCS), National Strength and Conditioning Association

BRIAN GREENLEE, MS, MBA, CSCS, Consultant

With over 24 years of experience in the fitness, health, and credentialing industries, Brian Greenlee has developed numerous programs to help further advance the exercise and health coach profession. He has served on several academic advisory panels and ICE and ATP credentialing committees throughout his tenure at American Council on Exercise.

Education and Certifications

- BA in Sports Management, St. Ambrose University
- MS in Kinesiology, Point Loma Nazarene University
- Masters in Business Administration, National University
- Certified Strength and Conditioning Specialist (CSCS), National Strength and Conditioning Association
- Certified Group Fitness Instructor, American Council on Exercise
- Certified Personal Trainer, American Council on Exercise
- Certified Health Coach, American Council on Exercise
- Certified Medical Exercise Specialist, American Council on Exercise

LIZ GREENLEE, MS, CSCS, Owner and Founder of The Hues of Green, LLC, Consultant to Globetrotter Wellness Solutions, LLC

Liz Greenlee has served in multiple roles in the fitness and recreation industry over the past 18 years. Having served as an associate director for recreation and wellness, assistant director of fitness and wellness, fitness coordinator, and adjunct professor, she excels at program management and leadership development with a knack for teaching. With extensive experience managing leadership teams, group fitness programs, personal training services, well-being initiatives, marketing teams, facility operations, and large-scale events, Liz now provides consultative services and speaking engagements for teams from many industries. Liz founded The Hues of Green, LLC, in 2022, along with her partner, to provide services in marketing, fitness and wellness, leadership, horticulture, and bartending. Liz is a national media consultant with Peake Media, serving multiple health and fitness industry audiences.

Education and Certifications

- MS in Public Health, Western Illinois University
- BAE in Secondary Education, Arizona State University
- Certified Strength and Conditioning Specialist (CSCS), National Strength and Conditioning Association
- Certified Group Fitness Instructor, American Council on Exercise
- Certified Personal Trainer, American Council on Exercise

TJ HILL, Assistant Director for Facilities and Aquatics at Colorado State University Campus Recreation

TJ Hill is a collegiate recreation professional with 10 years of experience in risk management, staff supervision, facility innovation, and student development. TJ is currently the assistant director for facilities and aquatics at Colorado State University Campus Recreation and a faculty member with Core Unlimited and its Connect2 Academy. TJ's expertise includes facility management, aquatic management, and student leadership to create and maintain high-level collegiate recreation facilities, programs, and services.

Education and Certifications

- Masters of Business Administration, Colorado State University
- MS in Kinesiology and Health Promotion, University of Wyoming
- MS in Environment and Natural Resources, University of Wyoming
- BS in Kinesiology and Health Promotion, University of Wyoming
- CPR for the Professional Rescuer Instructor, American Red Cross
- Certified Pool and Spa Operator

MARISA HOFF, MEd, Partner at The Empower Group

With nearly 15 years of unwavering dedication to the fitness industry, Marisa Hoff is a seasoned expert and trailblazer in fitness business consulting. Her journey commenced as the general manager of a flourishing, independent health club, where she honed her skills in management, operations, and customer service. A true visionary, she quickly became an influential figure in the industry, becoming a sought-after speaker at numerous conferences, including IHRSA, Athletic Business, and various state parks and recreation conferences. Marisa passionately shared her knowledge on these platforms, focusing on best practices and innovative strategies to elevate the fitness profession. Today, Marisa is a distinguished partner in a reputable consulting firm renowned for its versatility in assisting a broad spectrum of fitness models, from boutique studios to independent health clubs and parks and recreation facilities. With a razor-sharp focus on delivering results, she employs her extensive experience to steer facilities of diverse types toward enhanced profitability, operational efficiency, and member satisfaction. Marisa continues to inspire and guide fitness professionals with her invaluable expertise, profoundly affecting the industry's growth and success. Her journey from a dedicated health club manager to a distinguished speaker and consultant exemplifies her unwavering commitment to shaping the future of the fitness industry.

Education and Certifications

> MEd in Educational Leadership, University of California at Los Angeles
>
> BS in Psychology, University of California at Los Angeles

AVERETTE PACKARD, Territory Manager at US Fitness Products

Averette Packard has dedicated his life to fitness and sports. With nearly a decade of expertise in fitness facility design, he provides turnkey solutions worldwide. A former NCAA soccer player, Averette has been deeply entrenched in the fitness industry for over 16 years. He specializes in crafting a successful fitness space, whether indoor or outdoor, encompassing everything from flooring to equipment. His mission is to design spaces that are both functional and invigorating, tailored to the needs of their market.

Education and Certifications

> BS in Health Fitness Specialist, East Carolina University
>
> Certified Personal Trainer, American College of Sports Medicine

WILL TRENT, MS, Founder of Willy T Media, Chief Marketing Officer of Globetrotter Wellness Solutions, LLC

Will Trent is a higher education marketing professional with experience at Virginia Tech, University of North Carolina at Chapel Hill, James Madison University, and Duke University. As the assistant director of marketing for Virginia Tech recreational sports, Trent directed visual communication efforts and oversaw full-time graduate assistants and student staff. In addition to his full-time work, Trent creates contagious content for brands worldwide with his freelance media and design business, Willy T Media. He serves as the chief marketing officer for Globetrotter Wellness Solutions, LLC, and is a seasoned photographer, videographer, and social media strategist.

Education and Certifications

MS in Sport and Recreation Leadership, James Madison University

BA in Communication, Virginia Tech

KIA WILLIAMS, MBA, MS, Founder of At the Core of It All, LLC

Kia Williams is a global fitness presenter, published author, project manager, and the 2022 IDEA Fitness Instructor of the Year. Kia is the youngest and the first Black person awarded this highly acclaimed recognition. She is recognized for her ability to incorporate innovative, progressive, and critical thinking that results in enhanced business services; two decades of artistry-level public speaking and presenting experience; multicultural, diversity, and wellness engagement in global business; and leveraging transformative change and establishing organizational vision to adapt to evolving customer-facing communication and value propositions. Kia's heart dedications are for serving as the wellness chairwoman for the NAACP Fort Worth–Tarrant County chapter; founding board member of Striking + Strong hair care brand; Fit4Mom board member; and an executive board member for Jeremiah 33:6, a not-for-profit holistic health education and preventative medicine corporation. Kia has managed several fitness and wellness programs and facilities. She uses her transferable professional skills and business experience to develop talent, manage cross-functional teams, champion groundbreaking ideas, support multicultural engagement, and make various opportunities accessible, inclusive, and feasible for the masses. Kia's career mission is to support people affected by marginalization in jobs, education, health care, and lack of representation in the fitness industry. Kia has a love for all health and wellness categories. Kia is committed to helping others live a creative, sustainable, gratifying, and healthy lifestyle and work life.

Education and Certifications

Masters in Business Administration, University of Illinois

MS in Recreation and Sports Management (Concentration in Fitness Program Management), University of North Texas

Certified Group Fitness Instructor, American Council on Exercise